P9-ELS-778

"We held it ever certain that going towards the sunset we would find what we desired."—ALVAR NUÑEZ CABEZA DE VACA IN NEW MEXICO, 1535

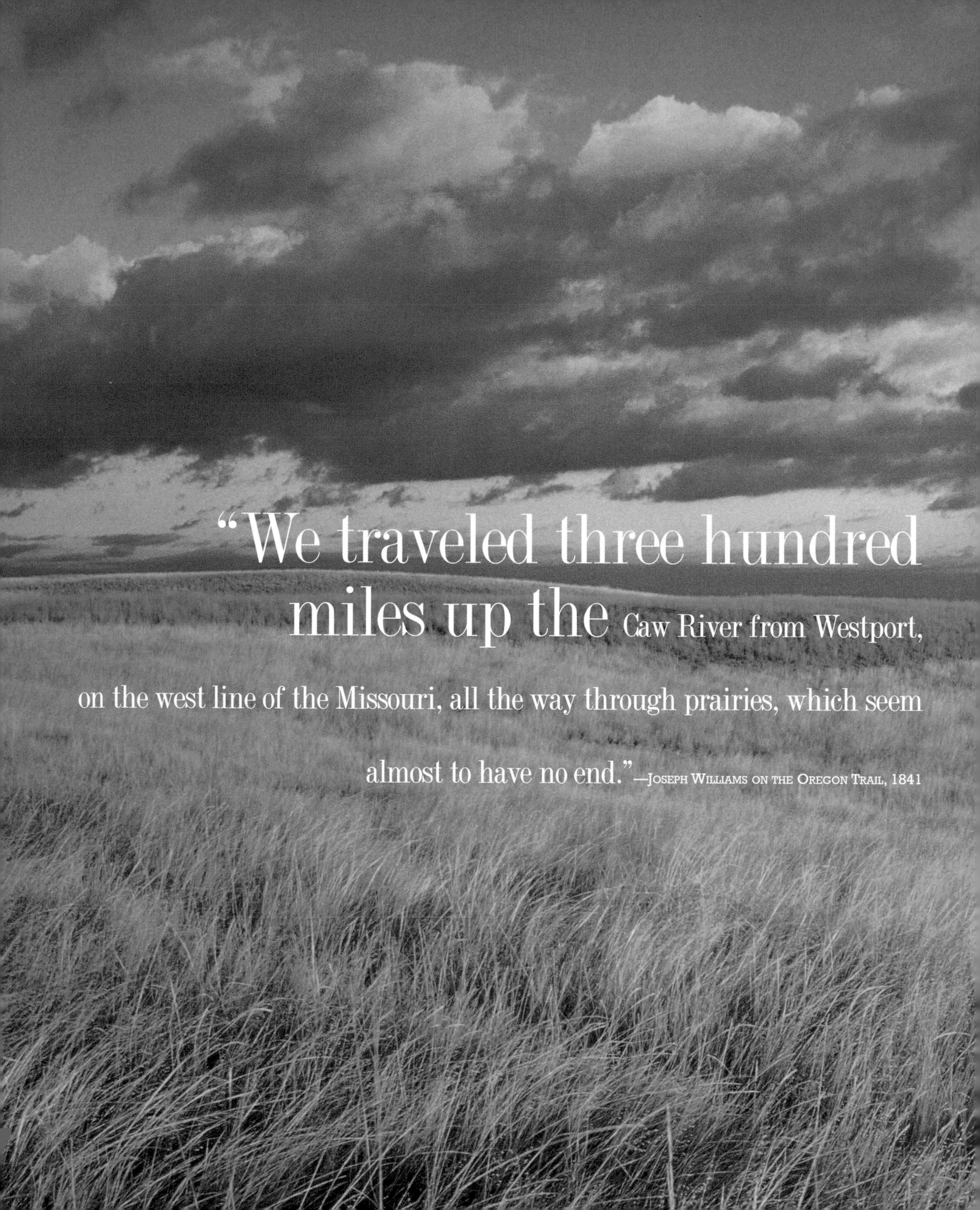
"We traveled three hundred miles up the Caw River from Westport, on the west line of the Missouri, all the way through prairies, which seem almost to have no end."—JOSEPH WILLIAMS ON THE OREGON TRAIL, 1841

WINNING THE WILD WEST

THE EPIC SAGA OF THE AMERICAN FRONTIER
1800–1899

PAGE STEGNER

FOREWORD BY LARRY McMURTRY

THE FREE PRESS
New York London Toronto Sydney Singapore

Dedication

For Lynn—wife, partner, and one who loves the West even more than I.

TEHABI BOOKS

Tehabi Books designed and produced *Winning the Wild West: The Epic Saga of the American Frontier* and has developed and published many award-winning books that are recognized for their strong literary and visual content. Tehabi works with national and international publishers, corporations, institutions, and nonprofit groups to identify, develop, and implement comprehensive publishing programs. Tehabi Books is located in San Diego, California.
www.tehabi.com

President: Chris Capen
Senior Vice President: Tom Lewis
Vice President of Operations: Sam Lewis
Design Director: Josie Delker
Editorial Director: Nancy Cash
Sales Director: Eric Pinkham
Director, Corporate Publishing: Tim Connolly
Director, Trade Relations: Marty Remmell
Editor: Terry Spohn
Contributing Editor: Jeremy Schmidt
Permissions Coordinator: Shelby Reed
Copy Editor: Lisa Wolff
Editorial Assistant: Christine Huynh
Art Directors: Debra McQuiston, Vicky Vaughn
Production Artist: Mark Santos
Proofreader: Robin Witkin
Indexer: Ken DellaPenta
Map Illustrator: Chadric Humphreys

Photography and illustration credits appear on page 398–99.

The paper used in this publication meets the minimum requirements of the American National Standard for Information Sciences—Permanence of Paper for Printed Library Materials, ANSI Z39.48-1992.

THE FREE PRESS
A Division of Simon & Schuster, Inc.
1230 Avenue of the Americas
New York, NY 10020

Printed by Dai Nippon Printing Co., Ltd., in Hong Kong.
First edition
10 9 8 7 6 5 4 3 2 1
Library of Congress Cataloging-in-Publication Data
Stegner, Page.
Winning the Wild West : the epic saga of the American frontier, 1800-1899 / Page Stegner ; foreword by Larry McMurtry.— 1st ed.
p. cm.
ISBN 0-7432-3291-7 (hc.)
1. West (U.S.)—History—19th century. 2. West (U.S.)—History—19th century—Pictorial works. 3. West (U.S.)—Discovery and exploration. 4. Frontier and pioneer life—West (U.S.) 5. United States—Territorial expansion. I. Title.

F591 .S6448 2002
978'.02—dc2l

2002070287

For information regarding special discounts for bulk purchases, please contact Simon & Schuster Special Sales: 1-800-456-6789 or business@simonandschuster.com

Contents

Among the Sierra Nevada Mountains, California, Albert Bierstadt

Foreword

The historian who sets out to encompass, as Page Stegner admirably has, the winning of the American West—or at least a century of it—in a volume of modest length has to combine the breadth of the polymath with the precision of the aphorist. He must master, at least to a workable degree, all the disciplines that Thomas Jefferson insisted his young secretary Meriwether Lewis study up on before he sent him off with his friend William Clark, toward the western ocean: botany, zoology, geology, astronomy, cartography, a bit of medicine, and a lot of this-and-that. In the case of the writer, the this-and-that has to include a good deal of political history: the struggle for Texas, for Oregon, for California. Following close upon the political history and oftentimes driving it was the commercial history.

My favorite of the many informative short essays sprinkled through this book is the one about the beaver hat, a fashion or craze so intense while it lasted that it caused the rivers, creeks, and ponds of the west to be virtually denuded of beaver by 1840. Most of us have heard of the fur trade, but how many of us know that the term "mad as a hatter" derived from the custom of brushing the stripped beaver pelts with nitrate of mercury, whose vapors had a very bad effect on the nervous systems of the hatters doing the work? Throughout this handsomely produced and ably illustrated volume Page Stegner seems able to broaden or narrow his focus just as a photographer might adjust the lens of his camera, shifting back and forth between the panorama—the story of the 1849 Gold Rush, say—and the close-up that puts the cost of all this winning in human terms, as becomes so evident with the quote from Buffalo Bird Woman of the Hidatsa tribe of the upper Missouri River:

Often in summer I rise at daybreak and steal out to the cornfields; and as I hoe the corn I sing to it, as we did when I was young. No one cares for our corn songs now. Sometimes at evening I sit, looking out at the big Missouri. The sun sets and dusk steals over the water. In the shadows I see again our Indian village with smoke curling upward from the earth lodges; and in the river's roar I hear the yells of the warriors, the laughter of the little children as of old. It is but an old woman's dream. Again I see but shadows and hear only the roar of the river; and tears come to my eyes. Our Indian way of life, I know, is gone forever.

In this narrative we travel across a great spread of land, and also across a century, from Lewis and Clark's brilliantly managed and measured expedition to John Wesley Powell's struggle, toward the end of the century, for a sane water policy for our western lands, something, in my opinion, yet to be achieved.

What I like best about this book is its sense of how severe and how equivocal the struggle to win the west was, after all. We "won" the Colorado River only to mismanage it. We "won" many millions of buffalo and very soon reduced them to ragged remnant. With the native people we did even worse, eliminating many tribes in California completely, with no more regard shown for their humanity than had they been rabbits.

"Winning" all along has been a more or less ambiguous thing; thousands of hard-working and hopeful farm families were defeated merely by aridity, as is still happening at this moment in my county in north central Texas.

My grandparents came to Texas as pioneers in the 1870s. In time they produced twelve children, most of whom migrated to the Panhandle, eventually producing nearly fifty children of their own. I have a wonderful photograph taken at the first McMurtry family reunion near Clarendon, Texas, in 1918: attending were thirty-six McMurtrys and one tree. Eighty years later—about one human lifetime—I made a speech at the opening of a new public library in Pampa, just a few miles from where the picture was taken. Only two people in the large audience had ever heard of the McMurtrys, although the uncle I was named for had fallen to his death from a grain elevator just

Sunset: California Scenery, Albert Bierstadt

three blocks from where I spoke. We came as pioneers, we worked extremely hard, for a time we prospered; then the old folks died and their children died; little by little the hard-acquired land got sold and vanished, making it a close question as to exactly what we won. Strong lives, I suppose.

I've been reading quite unsystematically about the west for about fifty years. Three times I was offered the opportunity to write the sort of history that Page Stegner has just written. In all three cases I demurred, but wistfully. Did I know enough? Could I organize it? Now I'm very glad that I demurred. Page Stegner knows enough, and he organized it.

—Larry McMurtry

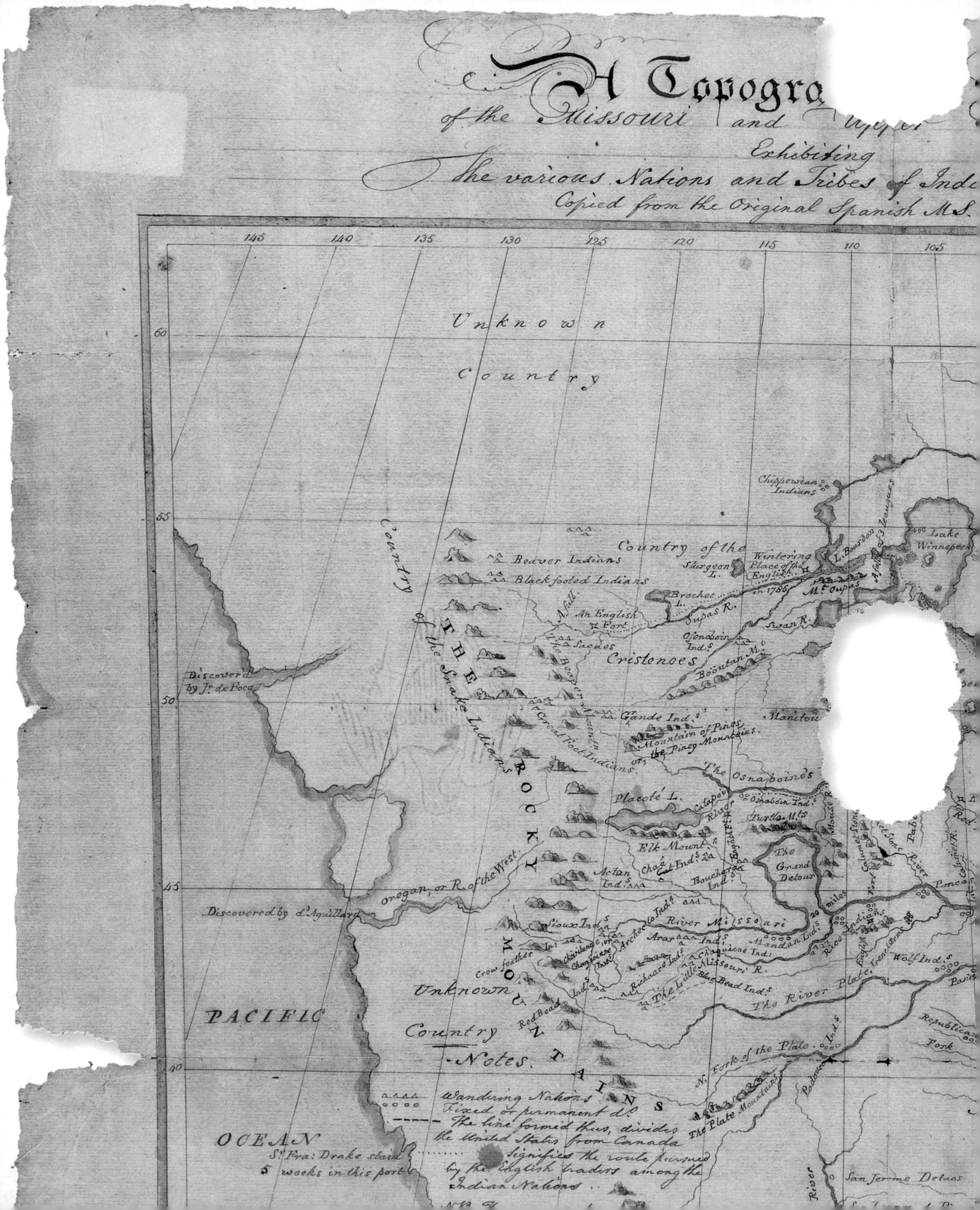

A Topogra[...]
of the Missouri and Upper [...]
Exhibiting
The various Nations and Tribes of Indi[...]
Copied from the Original Spanish M.S.

145 140 135 130 125 120 115 110 105

60

Unknown Country

55

50

45

40

Chippewian Indians

Lake Winnepeek

Country of the Sturgeon L.

Wintering Place of the English in 1786

L. Bourbon

A fall of 3 leagues

M.t Oupas

Beaver Indians

Black footed Indians

Brochet L.

Supas R.

Swan R.

A fall

An English Fort

Country of the Snake Indians

THE ROCKY MOUNTAINS

Sacues

Osnoboin Ind.s

Cristenoes

Boöutan M.t

Discovered by J.n de Foca

The Rocky Mountains

Gande Ind.s

Manitou

Mountain of Pinos, or, the Piney Mountains.

Great Foot Indians

The Osnaboine's

Placoté L.

Catapoi River

Osnoboin Ind.s

Turtle M.ts

House R.

Elk Mount.s

Chaä Cat Ind.s

English F.t

The Grand Detour

Oregan, or R. of the West.

Actan Ind.s

Bouchard Ind.s

Fort Calumet Stone

Pabe

Ponca

Discovered by d'Aguillar

Sioux Ind.s

River Missouri

20 miles

Archeolo Ind.s

Arar Ind.s

Mandan Ind.s

Ricara Indians

Chevilanqe, or Changtaane Ind.s

Chaquiene Ind:

Crow feather

Richaare Ind.s

The Little Missouri R.

Wolf Ind.s

Blue Bead Ind.s

Unknown Country

The River Plate

Red Bead

Republican Fork

PACIFIC

OCEAN

N. Fork of the Plate

Padouca Ind.s

The Plate Mountains

Notes.

Wandring Nations
Fixed or permanent d.o
The line formed thus, divides the United States from Canada
Signifies the route pursued by the English traders among the Indian Nations.

S.r Fra: Drake staid 5 weeks in this port

River

San Jerome Detuos

Swivel on the bow hoisted Sail and Set out in high Spirits for the western Expedition . . ."

—From the journal of Private Joseph Whitehouse on departing Wood River, Illinois Country, May 14, 1804

The Lewis and Clark Expedition, Thomas Mickell Burnham

THE MOST DISTANT FOUNTAIN

[1802–1842]

The season was far advanced. On bare limbs of the forest hung a few withered remnants of its gay autumnal livery, and the smoke crept upward through the sullen November air from the squalid wigwams of La Salle's Abenaki and Mohegan allies. These, his new friends, were savages whose midnight yells had startled the border hamlets of New England; who had danced around Puritan scalps, and whom Puritan imaginations painted as incarnate fiends. La Salle chose eighteen of them, whom he added to the twenty-three Frenchmen who remained with him, some of the rest having deserted and the others lagged behind.

La Salle had abandoned for a time his original plan of building a vessel for the navigation of the Mississippi. Bitter experience had taught him the difficulty of the attempt, and he resolved to trust to his canoes alone. They embarked again, floating prosperously down between the leafless forest that flanked the tranquil river; till, on the sixth of February, they issued upon the majestic bosom of the Mississippi. Here, for the time, their progress was stopped; for the river was full of floating ice. La Salle's Indians, too, had lagged behind; but, within a week, all had arrived, the navigation was once more free, and they resumed their course. Towards evening, they saw on their right the mouth of a great river; and the clear current was invaded by the headlong torrent of the Missouri, opaque with mud. They built their campfires in the neighboring forest; and at day light, embarking anew of the dark and mighty stream, drifted swiftly down towards unknown destinies.[1]

—Francis Parkman

Surveying the West

The expedition carried a copy of Le Page du Pratz's map of French-claimed Louisiana, published in 1763. English colonies are east of the "Apalachean Mountains," Spanish New Mexico lies west of an unnamed range based on the Rockies, and the Great Plains are labeled "Large Meadows." The lower Missouri River is drawn with some accuracy, but the upper course is pure fancy. Note the westward-flowing Beautiful River, perhaps the Columbia, and the path of a reported native route leading to it from the Missouri.

WHEN FRANCIS PARKMAN wrote those words 150 years ago the West was still not fully explored, but the romance of the wilderness had ignited the imaginations of Americans in the East. Robert La Salle had drifted south on his journey, becoming the first white man to see the mouth of the Mississippi River in 1682, and he claimed much of the western portion of the Mississippi basin on behalf of France, naming it "Louisiana." It was La Salle's claim that constituted the Louisiana Territory, and it was the Missouri, whose muddy, gaping mouth La Salle and his men had passed on their way to glory, that was to become the first major gateway to the American West.

Thomas Jefferson

As early as 1764, and with increasing magnitude over the next twenty-five years, isolated groups of settlers had begun pushing the frontier across the Appalachian Mountains at a rate of nearly seventeen miles per year, moving into territories in the present-day states of Kentucky, West Virginia, Tennessee, Ohio, Indiana, and Michigan, and southward into the Mississippi Territory. Impelled by the prospect of free or cheap land, and fueled by the indestructible faith in a "fresh start," they cleared forests, transformed Indian trails into roads, and dotted the land with farms and villages. By the end of 1783 there were 25,000 of them scattered throughout the Allegheny Plateau; by 1790 Kentucky alone had 75,000 inhabitants, a figure that would grow over the next fifteen years to 300,000. Ohio's population by 1804 was 120,000, Tennessee's 170,000, Alabama-Mississippi's 20,000. Indeed, by the time Thomas Jefferson was inaugurated as the third president of the United States there were more than one million settlers occupying a huge area between the

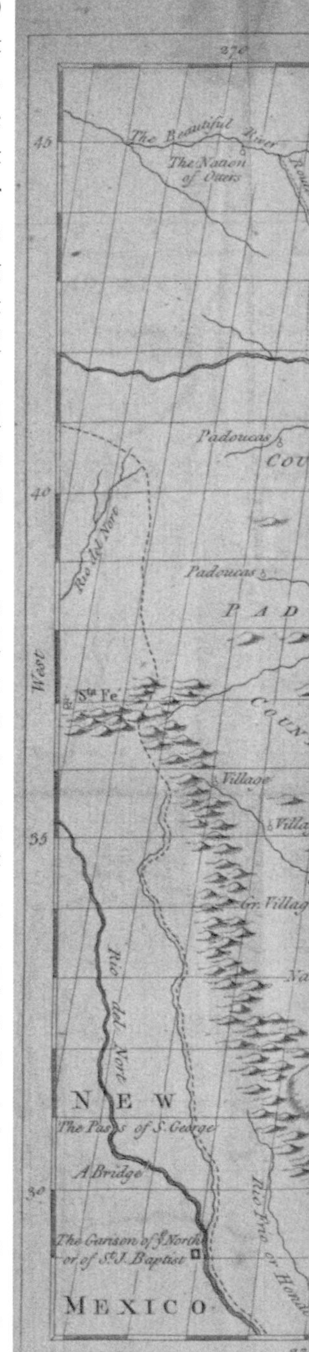

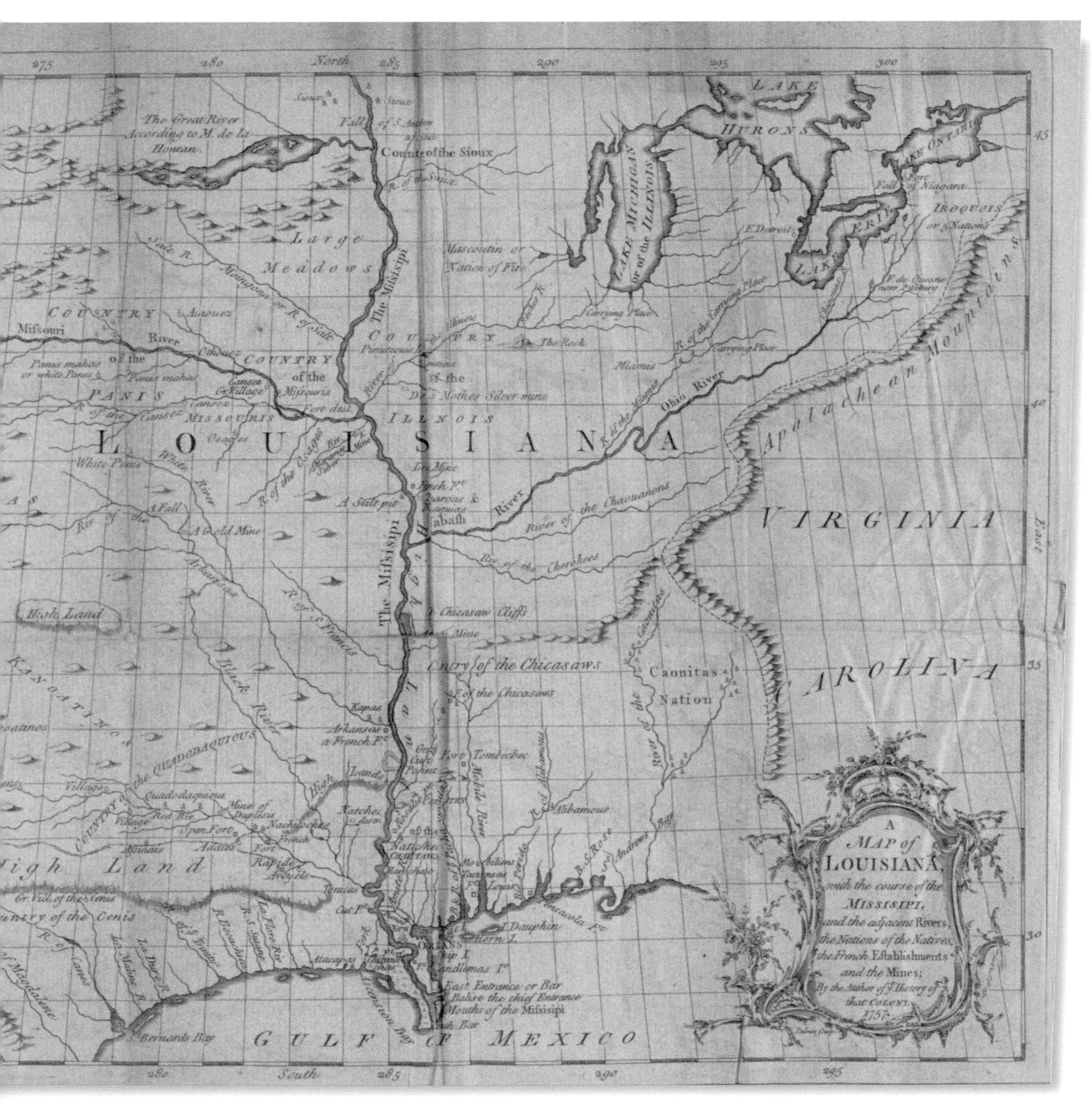
A MAP of LOUISIANA, with the course of the MISSISIPI, and the adjacent Rivers, the Nations of the Natives, the French Establishments and the Mines; By the Author of ye History of that COLONY. 1757.
LOUISIANA
VIRGINIA
CAROLINA
Apalachean Mountains
LAKE HURONS
LAKE MICHIGAN or of the ILLINOIS
LAKE ONTARIO
LAKE ERIE
IROQUOIS or 5 Nations
Fall of Niagara
F. Detroit
The Great River According to M. de la Hontan
Country of the Sioux
Large Meadows
The Missisipi
Mascoutin or Nation of Fire
COUNTRY of the Illinois
ILLINOIS
Ohio River
River of the Chaouanons
Riv. of the Cherokees
Missouri River
COUNTRY of the Missouris
MISSOURIS
PANIS
Chicasaw Cliffs
Cntry of the Chicasaws
Caonitas Nation
Fort Tombecbec
Mobile River
Arkansas a French Ft.
Black River
High Land
GULF OF MEXICO
Mouths of the Misisipi
East Entrance or Bar
S. Bernards Bay
North
South
East

The Missouri River, longest in America, drains a territory of about 580,000 square miles, far larger and more diverse than anyone in 1804 could have known. It flowed from a wonderland of glaciers, alpine lakes, and badlands studded with dinosaur bones, through grass-covered plains, deep canyons, forests, and blazing deserts.

Appalachians and the Mississippi River, many of them concentrated in the vicinity of the Ohio River and its numerous tributaries.

But beyond the Mississippi the United States had no sovereignty, nor indeed had it played any significant role in the white man's exploration of any part of that vast territory. Since 1535, when Cabeza de Vaca and his African slave, Estevan, wandered across Texas into Mexico after being shipwrecked on Galveston Island, the trans-Mississippi West was the imaginary province of the Spanish, French, and British explorers who laid claim to its various parts on behalf of their respective countries—imaginary in the sense that they did so in complete disregard for the native peoples who had been living there in one form or another for 25,000 years. Fray Marcos, Ulloa, De Soto, Coronado, Cardenas, Alvarado, Cabrillo, Junipero Serra, Onate, Joliet, La Salle, Louis de St. Denis, Bienville, Pierre de la Verendrye, Pierre and Paul Mallet—the names of these explorers and sometimes colonists go on and on but the appellations are French and Spanish, and when they are English, like Drake and Kelsey and Mackenzie, they are English or Scottish out of Great Britain.

But all this was soon to change. Thomas Jefferson had been absorbed by the prospect of westward expansion long before he was elected to the presidency of the United States in 1801, and had, in fact, secretly finagled a congressional appropriation of $2,500 in January of 1803 for an expedition to explore the upper Missouri and westward over the Rocky Mountains to the Pacific. Such secrecy was required, at least in the initial phases of planning, by the fact that not one teaspoon of the turf Jefferson wanted his emissaries to examine belonged to the United States. Indeed, until 1803, virtually all of it belonged to France and before that, Spain.

So it was almost serendipity when Napoléon Bonaparte, facing the probability of a renewed war with Great Britain and on the verge of bankruptcy after his military fiasco in Egypt, abruptly offered to sell the Territory of Louisiana to the United States for $15 million. Jefferson's envoys, Robert Livingston and James Monroe, had been sent to France merely to bargain for the city of New Orleans, whose port was essential to the unimpeded transport of American goods on the Mississippi, and for as much of West Florida as they could get. They had been instructed

to offer $2 million for that prime piece of property, and to go as high as $10 million if necessary, but when the opportunity arose to acquire an additional 828,000 square miles for an additional $5 million, they did not quibble over small change, however nonplussed they initially may have been. And in so doing they executed what must unquestionably be considered the mother of all real estate deals in the history of the New World. They doubled the size of their country with a few strokes of the pen.

Meriwether Lewis

What they bought for all that money was "Louisiana," which in 1803 consisted of nearly all of the western half of the Mississippi River drainage basin, or what is now, Louisiana, Arkansas, Oklahoma, Missouri, Kansas, Nebraska, Iowa, Minnesota, South Dakota, North Dakota, most of Wyoming and Montana, eastern Colorado, a tidbit of New Mexico, and a table scrap of Texas. Understandably the boundaries of an uncharted region roughly equal in size to the existing commonwealth were imprecise. The northern border of Jefferson's purchase was generally accepted to be the forty-ninth parallel, and its western limit the Continental Divide, although the Divide itself was as much speculation at this point in history as all the other fantasies and delusions rumored to exist west of the Mississippi. Shining mountains were said to rise five miles high in a single, unbroken ridge

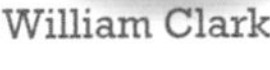
William Clark

The Missouri, placid at the start of the journey, grew more rugged near the Great Falls, where the Corps had to portage their boats. Near this spot, far left, is Sulphur Spring, now called Sacajawea Spring. Lewis, as expedition doctor, used the mineral-laden water to treat the ailing Sacajawea.

"In all your intercourse with the natives treat them in the most friendly and conciliatory manner which their own conduct will admit."—JEFFERSON'S INSTRUCTIONS TO LEWIS, JUNE 20, 1803

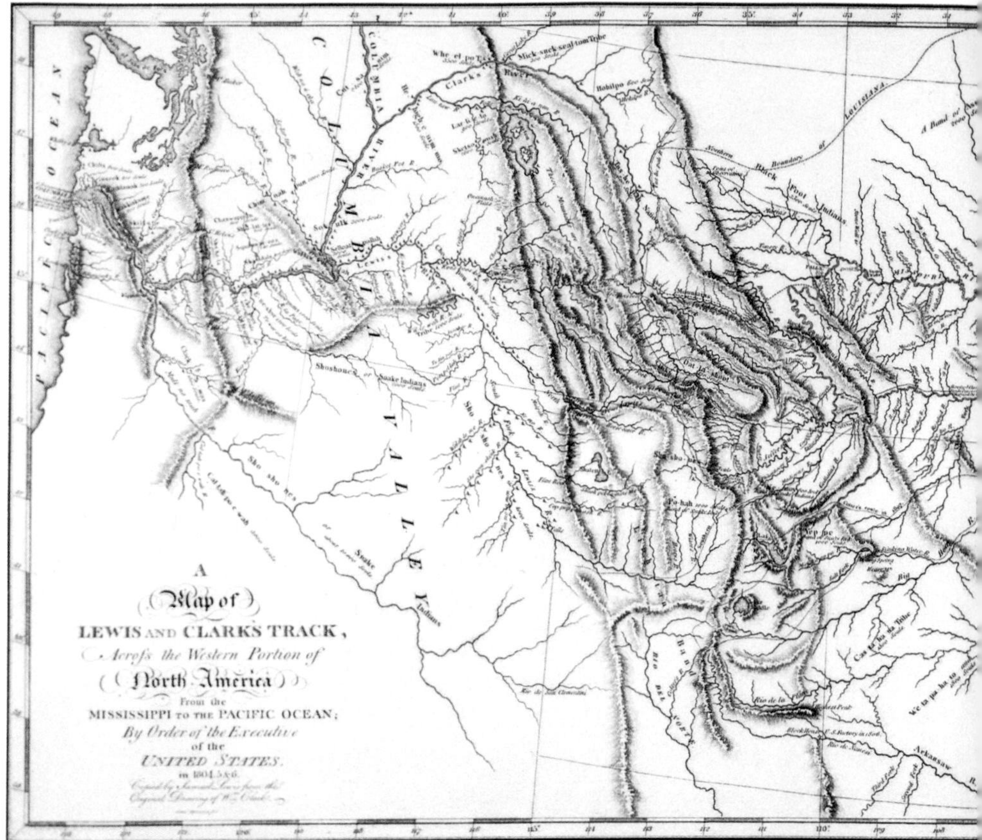

Lewis and Clark's 1814 map is a cartographic masterpiece based on field sketches, celestial navigation readings, and Clark's careful logging of distances and compass directions. Further details were filled in, less accurately, through the reports of Native Americans, early trappers, and others. Although missing such noteworthy sites as the Yellowstone geyser basins, the map is remarkable for its accuracy. It proved the lack of an easy water route across the country, but also showed the scale of opportunity offered by the West.

above an endless prairie of grass; some asserted that the Lost Tribes of Israel were still wandering about in the Great American Desert. Another myth held that a clan of Welsh Indians allegedly descended from a Welsh prince named Madoc, who never actually existed, but who was thought by the hopeful to have discovered America in 1170. Some envisioned a mountain of pure, snow-white salt extending for 180 north/south miles across the Great Plains.

What was not hallucinatory about Louisiana, as Lewis and Clark were about to find out, were its colossal dominions of grasslands, prairies, deserts, mountains, river systems, and canyon lands. Louisiana was an almost unimaginable El Dorado of natural resources, native peoples, wildlife, and unprecedented beauty, and no Americans had ever been there, though a number of Spanish, French, and British explorers had ventured up the Missouri as far as its confluence with the Platte, and a few had even traveled one thousand miles north to the Mandan villages near the present site of Bismarck, North Dakota. There the Missouri makes a rather abrupt turn to the west into territory that was then unknown to any white man, and it was most particularly this region, and

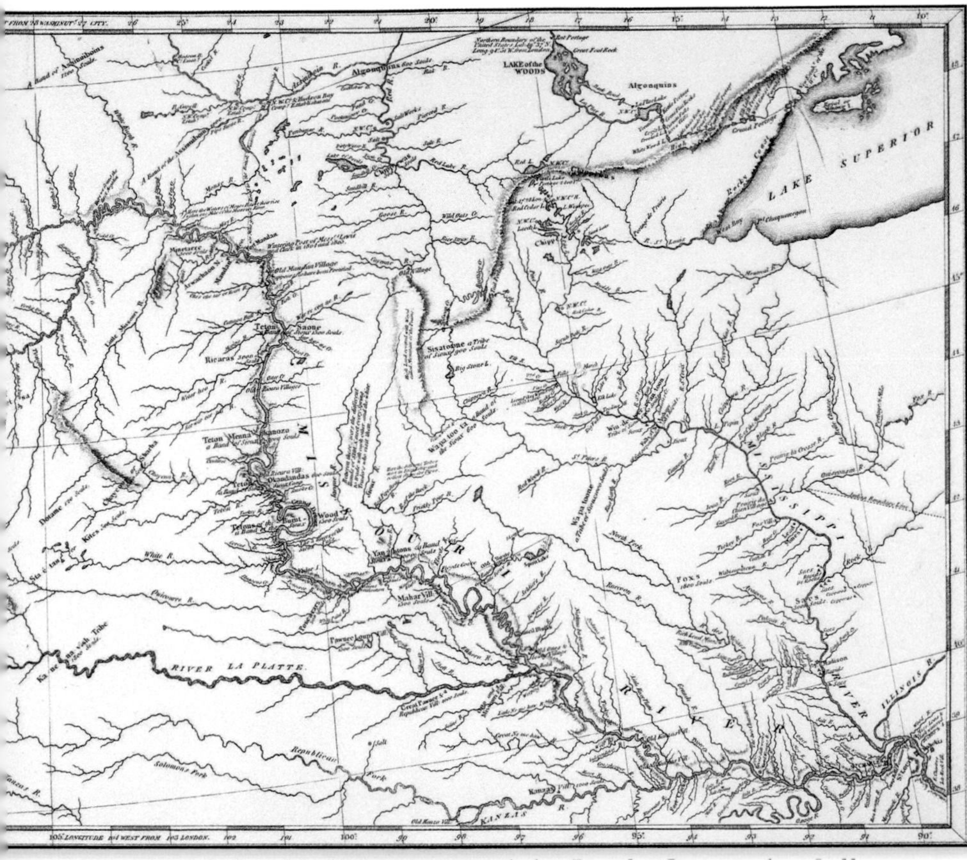

everything that lay between it and the Pacific Ocean, that Jefferson was determined to illuminate.

To that end, he conceived of what he called a Corps of Discovery, and appointed to its leadership his own personal secretary and protégé, Meriwether Lewis. Jefferson's instructions to Lewis indicate a great deal more than idle curiosity about what lies around the next bend or over the next hill. He clearly understood the inevitability of his nation's continued push westward and of its ultimate need for more land for expansion, though he seems to have been somewhat reticent to sound too imperialistic in tone. And while he was intrinsically interested in science for its own sake, he was equally cognizant of the economic benefits that would accrue from a close study of the natural resources that might be encountered along the way. However, the predominant object of the mission was, as he put it to Lewis, "to explore the Missouri river, & such principal stream of it, as, by it's course and communication with the waters of the Pacific ocean, whether the Columbia, Oregan, Colorado or

Snags (Sunken Trees) on the Missouri River, Karl Bodmer

any other river may offer the most direct & practicable water communication across this continent for the purposes of commerce . . ."[2]

In short, it was to find the elusive, though clearly existent, Northwest Passage—the waterway that would link the Mississippi Valley with the Pacific coast, and in so doing establish not only a viable trade route between the United States and the Orient, but a route along which future American expansion might easily flow into Oregon country and the Northwest. The explorers were also instructed to keep meticulous and detailed cartographic and geographic records, and copious notes detailing everything they encountered, with particular attention to the areas of zoology, botany, ethnology, and mineralogy. And further, they were to see what they could do about establishing friendly relationships with the native tribes they encountered. The rhetoric of Jefferson's charge was perhaps a bit more poetic, but it was a tall order of business in any idiom: "In all your intercourse with the natives treat them in the most friendly and conciliatory manner which their own conduct will admit. Allay all jealousies as to the object of your journey, satisfy them of its innocence, make them acquainted with the position, extent, character, peaceable, and commercial dispositions of the U.S., of our wish to be neighborly, friendly, and useful to them, and of our disposition to a commercial intercourse with them."[3]

It is small wonder that Lewis may have felt a bit overwhelmed and in need of a co-captain. He sent a letter to his old army friend William Clark expressing "an anxious wish that you would consent to join me in the enterprise," and assuring

The Missouri River of the early nineteenth century was no superhighway. Shallow and silted up in many places, it was often a tangle of snags, far left, that barred easy passage for any but the most nimble boats.

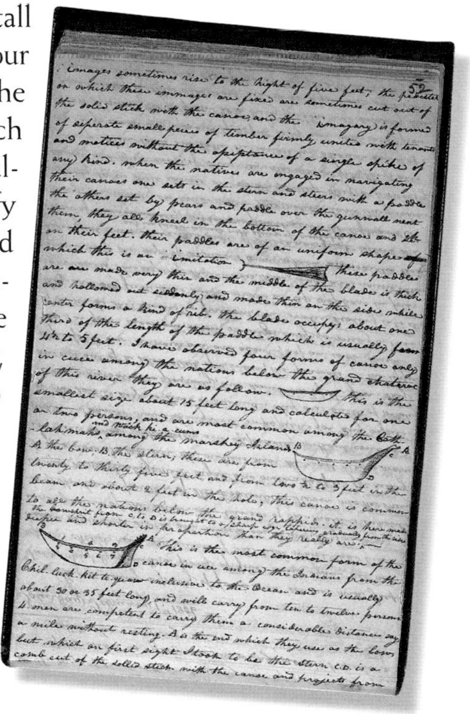

Lewis and Clark were charged with collecting and describing plants and animals along the way. The results were significant: 122 species and subspecies of animals new to science and 178 new plants were discovered. Among them were salal, Gaultheria shallon, *which Lewis collected during the soggy winter at Fort Clatsop, and bitterroot,* Lewisia rediviva, *now the state flower of Montana.*

Clark that his situation (i.e., rank and status) "if joined with me in this mission, will in all respects be precisely such as my own."[4] So began one of the most remarkable alliances in the history of exploration, a partnership marked by reciprocal trust and respect, and utterly devoid of rivalry or friction. As A. B. Guthrie has observed, "Hardships such as they endured make men cranky . . . Days of no food, of survival on stinking salmon, unknown roots, horse flesh, and dog meat. Days of frustration. Days of rain and mist and of snow and of heat, of mishaps and swarming mosquitoes. Who wouldn't quarrel, one with another? Except Lewis and Clark."[5]

Preparations took well over a year before the expedition would actually be ready to travel. Supplies had to be procured, equipment shipped, personnel selected, boats built or acquired. In Pittsburgh, Lewis purchased two flat-bottomed pirogues, one with six oars and one with seven, and had a keelboat built that was fifty-five feet long, eight feet wide, and had a thirty-two-foot mast with a square sail to augment the twenty oars used to propel it. The keelboat was capable of carrying nearly twenty thousand pounds, and would prove to be a somewhat

less-than-sprightly craft to row (or sail, or tow) against the powerful current of the Missouri, but it negotiated the Ohio passably, and delivered its captains and a growing entourage of men picked for the journey at the confluence of the Ohio and the Mississippi on November 13, 1803. A week later they were fifty miles south of St. Louis, and after innumerable delays and layovers eventually reached what would be their winter camp on the Wood River, directly across from the mouth of the Missouri. It would be another five months of planning, preparing, and waiting out the weather before the Corps of Discovery could commence in earnest their westward trek.

Finally, on May 14, 1804, William Clark set out in a heavy rain from Camp Wood and headed up the Missouri to the frontier outpost of St. Charles, where he was joined in a few days by Lewis, who had been in St. Louis completing yet additional arrangements. There they spent five days in further preparations, adding more supplies, reshifting the loads to make the boats easier to row, and adding a

REFERENCES.

Route of the Exploring Party.
Route pursued by the Spaniards.
Excursions made by Capt. Pike.
American Camps.
Spanish Camps.
Limits of actual Surveys.
At the mouth of the Canadian, on the Arkansaw River, the Ensigns armorial of France were buried in a leaden Box at the foot of a great Oak in 1742.
The Red River to A. was surveyed by T. Freeman Esq.
The Washita to B by Wm. Dunbar Esq.
The Arkansaw from C to its Mouth by Lt. Wilkinson.
The White River to D by Capt. Many.

SCALE.

GULF OF MEXICO

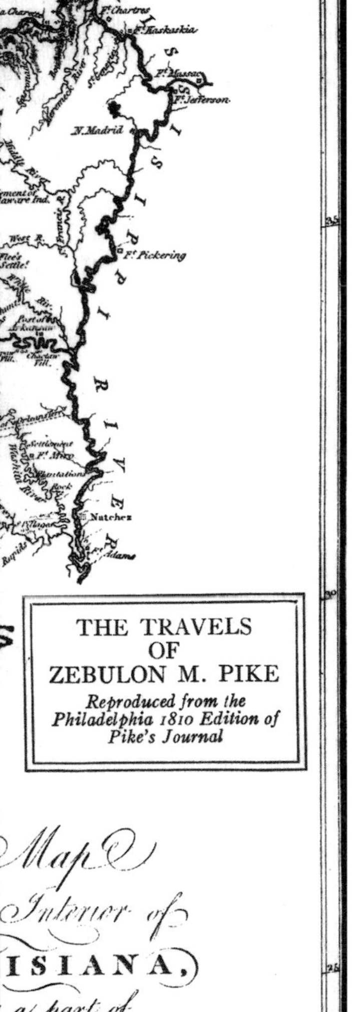

ZEBULON MONTGOMERY PIKE

[1779–1813]

Pike's first expedition was in 1805 when he led a party up the Mississippi to search out its source. He mistakenly identified Leech Lake as its headwaters and returned to St. Louis to report success. The next year, still confident in Pike's abilities, Jefferson sent him across the southwest part of the unexplored territory acquired by the Louisiana Purchase. Pike went up the Missouri and Osage Rivers to the Republican, then south to the Arkansas, which he followed to the Front Range of the Rockies, where he wintered at the present site of Pueblo, Colorado. In the spring he crossed the Sangre de Cristo Mountains and eventually emerged on the upper Rio Grande, where Spanish troops from Santa Fe discovered and arrested him. Whether he was lost or spying for the government isn't certain, but to the Spanish he was *persona non grata* either way. They confiscated his maps and notes and escorted him across northern Mexico to Nacogdoches, and dumped him on the American side of the border. But Pike had a good memory, and his published reports proved useful, if misleading in one crucial way. He is largely remembered for fathering a misconception that would endure for half a century—that the plains region he crossed was all a great American desert, and fundamentally uninhabitable.

Zebulon Pike

The Corps of Discovery underway, far right: Two dugout canoes, called pirogues, paddle beside the fifty-five-foot keelboat, pushed by an unusual tailwind on the lower Missouri River. Head winds, or no winds at all, were the general rule during this stage of the journey. Most miles were hard won by poling, rowing, and man-hauling against stiff currents. In this modern painting, a man stands at the bow fending off snags, while six others, of a possible twenty, man the oars.

couple of new members to the expedition. When they were all at last assembled, the Corps numbered forty-eight men, including Clark's black slave, York; a number of French-Canadian *voyageurs*; and the indispensable half French/half Shawnee hunter, trapper, scout, and interpreter George Drouillard (or, as the captains misspelled and mispronounced his name, Drewyer). Most of the men already had considerable experience on the frontier, and many had particular skills as carpenters, boat builders, blacksmiths, gunsmiths, and hunters. There were, one must observe, no spellers, grammarians, or proofreaders on board, as Clark's journals conclusively demonstrate. To wit: "Set out at half passed three oClock under three Cheers from the gentlemen on the bank and proceeded on to the head of the Island (which is Situated on the Stbd. Side) 3 miles Soon after we Set out to day a hard Wind from the W.SW accompanied with a hard rain, which lasted with Short intervales all night."[6]

For the next month, while covering some fourteen to twenty miles on an average day, the expedition made its way upriver almost due west across the present state of Missouri to the mouth of the Kansas River, the captains occupying themselves throughout by recording detailed descriptions of the flora, fauna, topography, temperature, and weather conditions. The terrain along this stretch of the lower Missouri was still wooded and lush, inspiring Clark to observe that the country was "butifull . . . rich & well timbered . . . well watered

Lewis and Clark, 1804, L. Edward Fisher

The 224 tattered pages of Clark's elkskin-bound journal cover the hardest part of the journey—over the Lolo Trail and down to the Pacific. Evidently, Clark kept his record on loose sheets and sewed them together during the rainy coastal winter. Also here is a page from Lewis's journal with his drawing of a sage grouse.

and abounds in Deer Elk & Bear." There were wild growing greens which "Servent York Swam to the Sand bar to geather . . . for our Dinner," and a great profusion of all kinds of fish. The river meandered along through open plains, interspersed with groves of cottonwood, sycamore, and ash, and thick vegetation providing "delisious froot such as Grapes, Plumbs, & Blue Currents."[7]

If the food and the scenery were five-star, the same could not be said for the ticks and "musquiters," which Clark complains were "Verry troublesome." So too was the river, with its heavy, debris-choked current, crumbling riverbanks, shifting sandbars, and obstructed channels. Frequently the heavily laden keelboat had to be hauled upstream by towropes from the bank, and there was the constant danger of being rammed and overturned by drifting trees:

. . . opposite the Lower point of the 2d Island on the S.S. we had like to have Stove our boat, in going round a Snag her Stern Struck a log under water & She Swung round on the Snag, with her broad Side to the Current expd. To the Drifting timber by the active exertions of our party we got her off in a fiew Mints. Without engerey [injury] and Crossed to the Island where we Campd.[8]

All of these hazards were compounded by usual hazards of the season like the the spring runoff and the sudden, violent thunderstorms that blew the boats into the banks and hung them up on sandbars. And then there were those clouds of murderous "musquiters," so thick that the men coated themselves in bear grease and lit torches in an attempt to keep them at bay.

By the twenty-first of July the party reached the mouth of the Platte River (at the present-day site of Council Bluffs, Nebraska), nearly six hundred miles upstream from their winter camp near St. Louis, and by early August they had covered another 150 miles to the confluence of the Niobrara. By now the countryside had undergone a profound change, the woodlands having given way to tallgrass prairie (so called because big bluestem grew as tall as a horse's belly), and the tall grass, in turn, having given way to the lower-growing species typical of the high plains, mixed-grass prairie—sand reed grass, little bluestem, "turkey foot," side oats.

The fauna had changed as well. Elk were now as common as deer, and the deer were mule deer, a different species from eastern whitetail

found on the lower river. Buffalo were frequently sighted, and the party's hunters killed their first one just as they crossed into the southeast corner of what is now South Dakota. On September 14, Clark killed what he and Lewis referred to as a "wild goat" (apparently an antelope) and a jackrabbit, which they compared to a European hare. Prairie dogs were a complete novelty but not exempt from extirpation:

. . . discovered a Village of Smal animals that burrow in the grown (those animals are Called by the french Petite Chien) Killed one and Caught one live by poreing a great quantity of Water in his hole we attempted to dig to the beds of one of those animals, after diging 6 feet, found by running apole down that we were not half way to his Lodge, we found 2 frogs in the hole, and Killed a Dark rattle Snake near with a Ground rat [prairie dog] in him.[9]

Buffalo were a mainstay of the Plains tribes, furnishing much more than meat and clothing. While earthen lodges like those on the bluff, far right, sheltered the Mandan during the winter, many moved into teepees when the buffalo returned in spring. Bodmer's painting daepicts Mandan women ferrying firewood across the river in bullboats made of buffalo skin.

By October, Clark's journals are abundant with references to windy, rainy, cold weather, and it was with great relief that they reached the Mandan villages near the mouth of the Knife River, where they intended to spend the winter. There were five villages in all, strung out along an eight-mile stretch and populated by three groups, the Minitari, Amahamis, and Mandan, all of whom were united by joint agricultural and hunting endeavors and by their mutual hatred of the Sioux. Lewis and Clark immediately set about establishing good relations with the tribes, smoking the peace pipe, distributing presents of tobacco, beads, ribbons, and Certificates of Good Conduct, and making grand speeches about the beneficence of the Great Father and his expectations concerning their behavior; then they began constructing a fort on the east side of the river, about two miles away from the nearest village. They concluded their labors by the end of November, by which time it was extremely cold, with ice running

Mih-Tutta-Hangkusch, a Mandan Village, Karl Bodmer

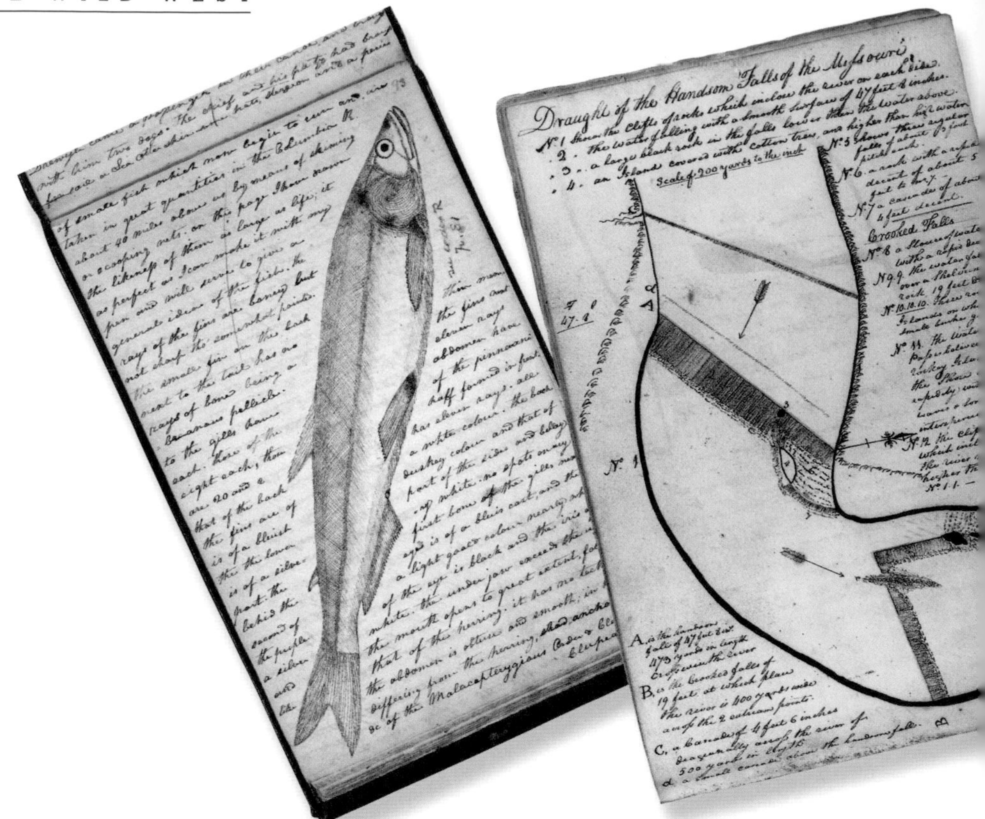

With meticulous attention to detail, Lewis and Clark diligently recorded every aspect of their journey in a series of notebooks. They often included sketches. Lewis described the eulachon, a small coastal fish: "I have drawn the likeness of them as large as life . . . I think them superior to any fish I ever tasted." Clark, the mapmaker, included a "Draught of Handsom Falls of the Missouri." The other pages are Lewis's renditions of Oregon grape and the head of a brant.

thick in the river and snow beginning to fall. And it would get worse. Clark would record 21 degrees below zero on December eleventh and 40 below on the tenth of January.

If life at Fort Mandan was not all beer and skittles, neither was it entirely dull and inactive, in spite of the bitter winter weather and repeated incidents of frostbite suffered by both whites and Indians. Hunting parties were continually going out to replenish supplies, firewood needed to be cut, clothes had to be mended and new ones made, and there was the construction of four new pirogues to replace the now burdensome keelboat they intended to send back to St. Louis in the spring. There were, moreover, frequent dances that took place in the Mandan lodges during the long winter nights—evenings that were not without their convivial moments, as the high incidence of venereal disease among the men suggests.

For the captains there were the reports to attend to, and all the specimens and artifacts they had thus far collected had to be numbered, labeled, and packed up to be sent back downriver once the spring thaw made it possible for the keelboat to travel. The survey of geographical

information they continued to gather throughout the winter, both from the local Mandan and from various French and British visitors drifting down from trading posts in the Assiniboine River area of Canada, was astonishing in its range, though much of it repeated old topographic errors and assumptions that in hindsight demonstrate that nobody, Indians included, really knew much about the terrain that lay ahead. The Corps had not yet encountered anyone who had even imagined, much less experienced, the true enormity of the Rocky Mountain range and its geophysical architecture. As Bernard DeVoto points out, "Nobody so far had had accurate ideas about this country; nobody would have very accurate ones till American trappers began to explore it twenty years later."[10]

One of the most fortuitous events of the winter was the hiring of a man named Touissant Charbonneau, a French *voyageur* who had lived with the Minitari for several years and who appeared at Fort Mandan one day to ask for a job as an interpreter. So engaged, he was presently joined by his two wives, described by Clark as "two squars of the Rock mountains, purchased from the Indians." One of these "squars" was the

THE LONG WINTER

Three groups—the Mandan, the Amahamis, and the Minitari—occupied the "Mandan Villages" that were visited by virtually every fur trapper, trader, and adventurer headed for the northern Rockies during the first half of the nineteenth century. The tribes had banded together for protection against their common enemy, the Teton Sioux, and their villages were located along a six-mile stretch of the Missouri River near the present site of the Garrison Dam in North Dakota. These five consecutive settlements were home to some 4,400 Indians, a population concentration that was unquestionably the largest in the upper Great Plains region. The Mandan were primarily agriculturists, growing tobacco, squash, pumpkins, watermelon, corn, and beans. The Minitari were more occupied with hunting buffalo, deer, elk, and pronghorn (or, as Lewis and Clark called them, goats). Their lodges, which distinguished them from all other Plains Indians, were large round domed structures thirty to forty feet in diameter with a smoke hole in the center and a four-foot doorway preceded by a ten-foot entryway. The entire edifice was held together by a system of forked posts, beams, and rafters, and the roof was covered with willow branches and interwoven grasses before being plastered over with mud or clay.

The Mandan and Minitari were friendly toward white men and were accustomed to trading with the British and French-Canadians

Mandan Dancer

whose posts lay in the Assiniboine River region some nine days to the north. The greatest hazard they seemed to pose to their pale-faced visitors was the venereal disease their promiscuous and accommodating women frequently passed on, though the same benign exchange cannot be said for European health threats to the Indian. In 1837 a smallpox epidemic nearly wiped out the entire Mandan tribe, leaving fewer than 150 survivors.

Interior of a Mandan Earth Lodge, Karl Bodmer

Mandan Peace Pipe

celebrated teenager Sacajawea, to whom more monuments have been erected in the United States than any other woman before or since, and about whom so much hagiographic prose has been written that Bernard DeVoto was inspired to remark, "many antiquaries and most trail markers have believed that Lewis, Clark, and their command were privileged to assist in the Sacajawea Expedition, which is not quite true."[11]

The men of the expedition had never encountered bears as large or ferocious as the grizzly. One of them was chased a hundred yards by a grizzly he had shot through the heart. At that time perhaps as many as 100,000 grizzly bears lived in the northern plains and Rockies.

Charbonneau would turn out to be cranky, temperamental, overbearing, and except for his occasional skills as a cook, marginally useless, but his young wife, if not quite the supernova that legend would have her, would nevertheless prove extremely valuable to the expedition once it reached the Rocky Mountains. She was a Shoshone, spoke both Shoshone and Minitari, and, before her capture as a child by a raiding band of Minitari, had grown up in what are now southwestern Montana and central Idaho in close proximity to the Continental Divide. Moreover, her brother, Cameahwait, was chief of the band of Shoshone that Lewis and Clark would encounter when they staggered out of the Beaverhead Mountains into the Lemhi Valley, still dragging their now useless canoes, and it was largely because of this fortunate consanguineous coincidence that they were able to procure both horses and valuable information about the country that lay ahead. Indeed, without the help given them by the Shoshone, the Lewis and Clark Show might have ended right there on the banks of the Lemhi.

On April 7, 1805, the keelboat started its journey from Fort Mandan back downriver to St. Louis laden with boxes of specimens, reports, maps, and letters; on the following morning the main company of explorers headed west to begin the second phase of its long journey. Leaving their winter quarters at Fort Mandan, Lewis wrote, "Our vessels

"I must confess that I do not like the gentleman and had reather fight two Indians than one bear."—LEWIS'S DIARY, MAY 11, 1805, NEAR GREAT FALLS, MONTANA

Specht

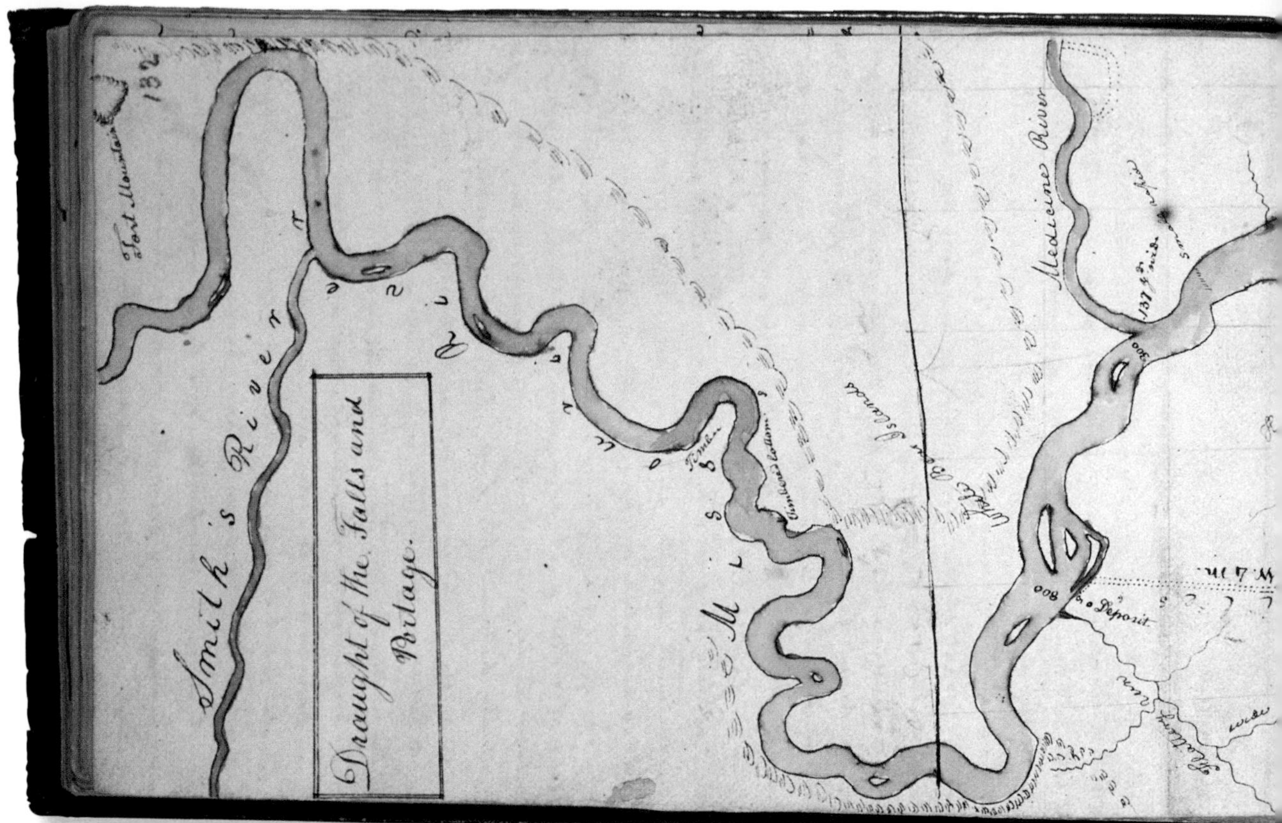

Clark's map of the Great Falls shows the eighteen-mile portage trail (double dotted line) beside the winding, blue-tinted river. It does not show the hardships of the experience: apple-size hailstones, prickly pear cactus spines, marauding grizzly bears, intense heat, and weeks of exhausting labor. They pulled the canoes on crude wagons and fell asleep during rest breaks.

consisted of six small canoes, and two large perogues. This little fleet altho' not quite so respectable as those of Columbus or Captain Cook, were still viewed by us with as much pleasure as those deservedly famed adventurers ever behold theirs; and I dare say with quite as much anxiety for their safety and preservation."[12]

His anxiety was well founded, for these cottonwood dugouts he was charitably calling canoes were narrow beamed and extremely unstable in the fast, shallow current of the upper Missouri and difficult to maneuver past the snags, drifting logs, and sandbars. For the most part the men towed them from the banks, which meant laboring through the brush along the low bluffs, or across floodplains thick with willows, or up to their rumps in icy shallows of gumbo muck under an ever-present cloud of "musquiters." The weather, which must have seemed to have been brewed in hell, was just a normal spring on the high plains—the broiling sun suddenly blacked out by a ferocious storm that would hammer the men with hail and sheeting rain, followed abruptly by more frying-pan heat and nostril-clogging mosquitoes and then an icy wind presaging snow flurries—"A verry extraordernarey climate, to behold the trees Green & flowers spred on the plain, & Snow an inch deep. The evening verry cold, Ice freesing to the Ores."[13]

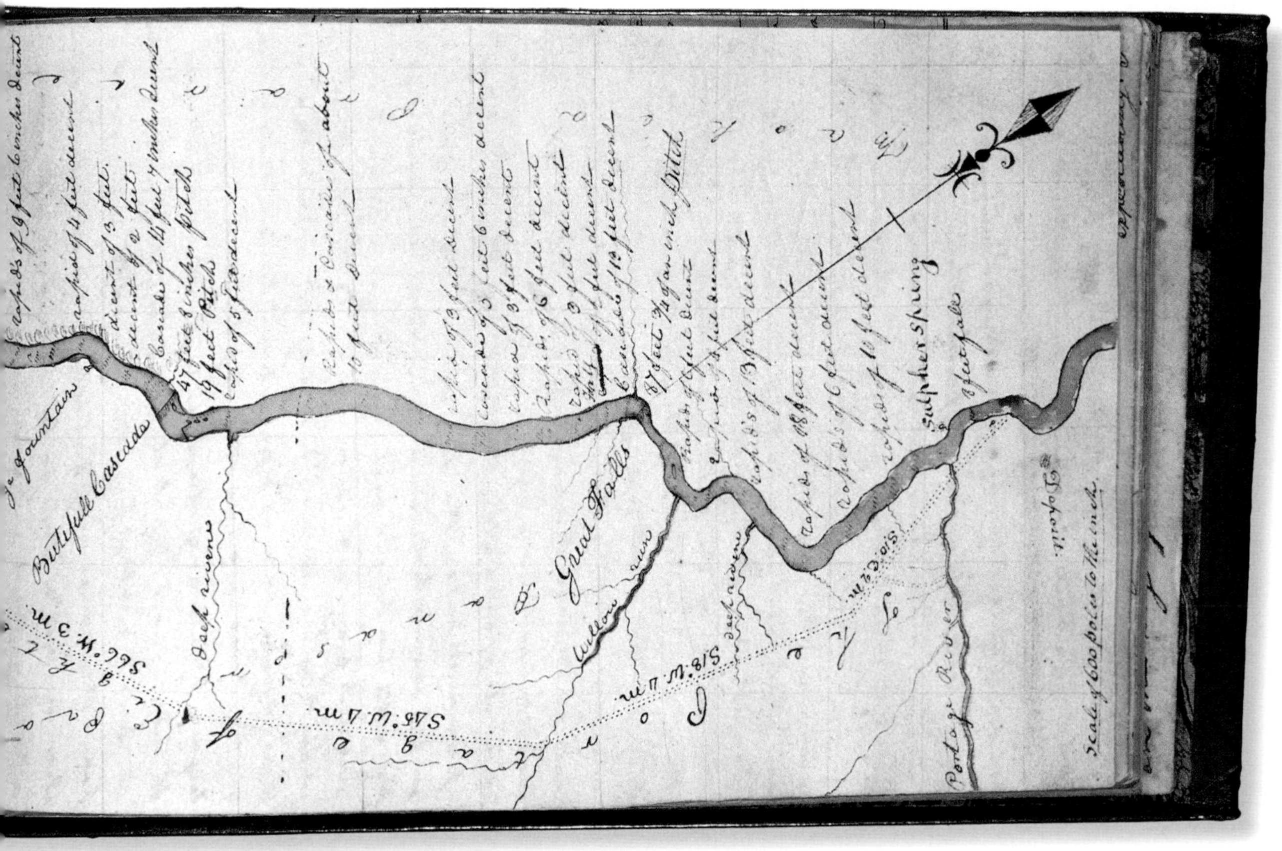

On April 28 the boats reached the confluence of the Yellowstone. Ten days later, a big river that the explorers named the Milk (because of its café au lait color) came flooding in from the north. On May 20 they arrived at the Musselshell. And after another week of backbreaking hauling they camped just below the mouth of an unnamed stream coming in from the south they christened the Judith, in honor of the future Mrs. Clark, Julia Hancock of Fincastle, Virginia. Lewis writes that for most of the time now "the men are compelled to be in the water even to their armpits . . . added to this the banks and bluffs along which they are obliged to pass are so slippery and the mud so tenacious that they are unable to wear their mockersons, and in that situation draging the heavy burthen of a canoe and walking acasionally for several hundred yards over the sharp fragments of rocks . . . their labour is incredibly painful and great, yet those faithful fellows bear it without a murmur."[14]

Once again things would get worse. The Great Falls of the Missouri, which the company reached in mid-June, pour over a series of five ledges, the first of which Lewis estimated at eighty-seven feet high. In a ten-mile stretch, the river drops four hundred feet in a murderous series of cataracts that are audible from a distance of seven miles downstream, "the whole of the water of this great river confined in a channel of 280 yards . . . from the foot of the falls arrises a continued mist which is extended for 150 yds down & to near the top of the clifts on L. Sd."[15] The portage around this nightmare would exceed in difficulty anything they had previously encountered by an exponential factor, and it would take more than two precious weeks for them to drag their canoes and supplies (the pirogues having already been left behind) some eighteen miles to the top of the falls, eighteen miles of prickly pear cactus that penetrated their moccasins and punctured their feet—eighteen miles of searing heat, violent hailstorms that bloodied their scalps, torrential rains that flash flooded ravines and turned the trail to mire. Just to keep everybody sharply alert, grizzlies and rattlesnakes now vied with the ever-present mosquitoes for numerical ascendancy.

At Three Forks, in western Montana, the expedition bore southwest up the Jefferson River. The land looks gentle, but the effort of hauling heavy dugouts through ever-shallower water, combined with the mosquitoes, cactus spines, and short rations, tested the men's strength, slowed their progress, and proved that this was country better suited for horses than boats.

To make matters worse, time was becoming a critical issue. It was already July, and the explorers had not yet even reached the Rockies. More days were lost in building new canoes to replace the pirogues, and it wasn't until the middle of the month that they were on the move again, entering the great canyon of the Missouri (or Gates of the Mountains, as Lewis would call it) on the nineteenth and reaching the forks of the three rivers that join to form the Missouri on the twenty-fifth. They named these rivers for Jefferson and his secretaries of state and Treasury, Madison and Gallatin, and after five days of careful deliberation (a mistake would have bankrupted their chances of crossing the Rockies before winter) chose the Jefferson as the one most likely to lead to the headwaters of the Columbia. Onward they went, into what would prove to be the most rugged country they would encounter on their entire journey. Clark was sick with a high fever and also hampered by an ankle wound, and his feet were so blistered he could scarcely walk. All of the men were exhausted, many of them were sick, and hunting was becoming more and more difficult.

THE WEST IN 1803

You have made a noble bargain for yourselves and I suppose you will make the most of it.

—CHARLES-MAURICE DE TALLEYRAND-PÉRIGORD, FRENCH DIPLOMAT

France, an American ally during the Revolution, seemed ready to become an enemy at the turn of the nineteenth century over American access to New Orleans, the only outlet to the sea for Americans living in the Mississippi River basin. President Thomas Jefferson was prepared to offer $3 million to buy the city. Napoléon, who was preparing for war with England, needed cash more than he needed an American colony, and offered instead the entire Louisiana Territory for $15 million.

Fifteen million dollars was an immense bounty in 1803. It was a pile of dollar bills more than three miles high, and any number of other analogies were made by opponents of the purchase to convince the public that this deal was a bad, not to mention unconstitutional, idea. One reason for the shock was the simple fact that all the minted coin in America didn't total $15 million. But the purchase would double the size of the nation, adding eight hundred thousand square miles—enough to carve out thirteen new states—and open the way for expansion to the Pacific Ocean.

The cost was hard to imagine, but it was equally difficult to comprehend the enormity of the place, as well as the diversity of its plant and animal life, native cultures, and geography. To begin to answer these questions Jefferson had already begun to dream up his Corps of Discovery.

LOUISIANA
TERRITORY
SPANISH
TERRITORY

Meriwether Lewis

Tempers were undoubtedly stretched thin, as indicated by the reprimand Charbonneau received from Clark "for Striking his woman at their Dinner."

On August 9 Lewis, leaving the main party to struggle with the canoes and gear at their own pace, continued ahead with three men in an attempt to make contact with the Shoshone, whose assistance they were not only hoping to elicit but whose knowledge of the country was absolutely essential if the explorers were to negotiate the maze of mountain peaks and passes that lay ahead. After four days of following a dwindling feeder stream of the Jefferson, the advance party reached a spring bubbling out of the ground, which Lewis joyfully described as "the most distant fountain of the waters of the Mighty Missouri in surch of which we have spent so many toilsome days and wristless nights. Thus far I had accomplished one of those great objects on which my mind has been unalterably fixed for many years, judge then of the pleasure I felt in allying my thirst with this pure and ice-cold water . . ."[16]

But the best was yet to come, though it may not have been apparent to Lewis at the time. Refreshing themselves at the spring, the men proceeded to the top of a dividing ridge and down the other side to a western-flowing feeder stream of the Lemhi River—and in so doing became the first white men to have crossed the Continental Divide anywhere between New Mexico and Alberta, Canada, and the first Americans to sample "the water of the great Columbia river."

And what did Captain Lewis think of the view from the top? One can only imagine his musings as he stood on the ridge dividing the continent and looked out on an apparently infinite landscape of . . . nothing. More of the same: "immense ranges of high mountains still to the West of us, with their tops partially covered with Snow." It had to be clear, however unwelcome and subliminal the thought, that a commercial water route from the Missouri to the Columbia was a pipe dream gone up in smoke. Lewis might still write in his journal that if the Columbia River drainage proved navigable, then "a communication across the continent by water will be practicable and safe," but in order to actually

Rivers of the Mountain West explored by the Corps—the upper Missouri, far left, the Jefferson, the Marias, the Salmon, the Snake, and others—proved too fast and shallow to serve as transport corridors as Jefferson had hoped. But they were destined to become the lifeblood of settlement, the single most precious and most fought-over commodity in the arid and semiarid West. More than gold or timber or raw land, water and the control of it have influenced regional development patterns.

believe this fantasy he had to blot from his mind all the torturous miles they had passed between the Great Falls of the Missouri—the true terminus of any serious navigation—and the spine of the Rockies on which he stood. He also had to disregard all the miles that still lay ahead before the company would reach the forks of the Clearwater in north-central Idaho, build new canoes, and take to the waterways once more.

Keelboats, like this one on the Ohio River, served as no-frills cargo haulers. Unlike flat-bottomed, boxy barges, a keelboat had a shaped hull, allowing it to be poled, rowed, or towed upstream. Deck designs varied according to need. This boat probably maximized cargo capacity. The expedition's boat had more open deck space, room for twenty oars, and a bow-mounted swivel gun.

The advance party found the Shoshone encampment the next day near the banks of the Beaverhead and made friendly, if somewhat uneasy, contact. Four days later Clark arrived with the main company, still dragging their useless canoes, and for the next twelve days they consulted with the Indians and considered their options—first and foremost being the purchase of horses to carry them north and then west to the only pass the Shoshone indicated would enable them to cross the Bitterroot Range.

It would be ridiculous to imply that once Lewis and Clark had made their way, starving, freezing, and utterly exhausted, to the Weippe Prairie at the western foot of the Bitterroots (a travail in which they were aided not only by the Shoshone, but the Flathead and the Nez Percés), their work was done. They had new canoes to make. They still had the Clearwater to descend, and the Snake, and the Columbia. But they would move rapidly down these swift-current rivers (it would take nine days to reach the Columbia, twenty-nine more to reach the sea), and while they faced dangerous rapids and difficult portages all along the way, it must have seemed a cakewalk compared to the seventy days it took them to cross the Rockies from the Gates of the Mountains to the banks of the Clearwater—a distance, as the crow flies, of half as many miles.

And yet, for people who had been away from home for well over a year and a half, and who faced a miserable, wet coastal winter in a fifty-foot-square spruce-log fort (Fort Clatsop), with little to do but make moccasins and little to look forward to but a supper of boiled roots and

Ohio-Mississippi River Keelboat, Karl Bodmer

Sunset at Columbia, James Everett Stuart

dog, "cakewalk" may not seem the appropriate word. True, Clark would rise to exuberant heights in his notebook upon first encountering what he mistakenly thought was the end of the trail ("Ocian in view! O! the joy"), but he would tone down his enthusiasm when transcribing the notes ("Great joy in camp we are in view of the Ocian, this great Pacific Octean which we been so long anxious to See"), and that joy would soon give way to a kind of sodden, waterlogged forbearance that had northwest weather as its dominant theme. On November 19 he wrote, "I arose early this morning from under a Wet blanket caused by a Shower of rain"; on November 22, "moderate rain all the last night with wind"; on December 26, "rained and blew hard last night"; and

on December 27, "rained last night as usial and the greater part of this day."[17] And, of course, come spring the party had to retrace their steps—according to my calculator, about 6,160,000 of them before they would at last reach home, two years, four months, and ten days from the time of their departure.

If the Lewis and Clark expedition failed in its primary mission (it did not discover a transcontinental water route that would link trade between the United States and the Orient, because none existed), it did the world a far greater service by laying to rest a fantasy that had endured and enthralled since the days of Columbus. But more important, their painstaking notation of the climate, topography, geology, flora, fauna, and Indian occupation of the upper Missouri River, Northern Rocky Mountains, and Columbia River drainage—which included the information that the entire area was swarming with beaver—launched the American fur trade, which, in turn, opened up the West.

The Pacific coast of Oregon welcomed the Corps of Discovery with a fog-shrouded, persistently rainy climate that, while far less severe than the previous winter in the Mandan Villages, offered the exhausted men little in the way of sunshine to celebrate their trailblazing journey across the continent.

Theirs was the first report, as Bernard DeVoto has observed, "on the United States over the hill and beyond the sunset, on the province of the American future. There has never been another so excellent or so influential." Indeed, theirs were the first footsteps in a great historical process—exploration followed by migration that was succeeded, in turn, by territorial occupation and political incorporation—a metamorphosis that would engage the nation for the next hundred years, until the trans-Mississippi expansion would culminate on February 14, 1912, with the proclamation of Arizona as the forty-eighth state, and the map of the contiguous Union would be complete.

HIGHWAY OF EXPLORATION

Lewis and Clark covered a great swath of country on their journey—about six thousand miles in two years and four months. Yet they saw only a narrow strip of the vast land. It remained for others, including former Corps of Discovery members John Colter, George Drouillard, and John Potts, to probe deeper and farther from the basin of the Missouri River, inset. Although Native Americans knew the region intimately, it was an exotic world for early trappers and explorers. At every turn, they encountered new wonders. The Big Sandy River, far right, just west of the Wind River Range, would become one of the richest trapping grounds in the Rockies. More than one hardened mountain man wrote diary entries praising its scenic beauty. The White Cliffs on the Missouri in western Montana, following page, prompted Lewis to pen one of his most famous passages: "It seemed as if those seens of visionary inchantment would never have an end."

They called it the Big Muddy, left. Compared to rivers east of the Mississippi, the Missouri was a different animal—wild and rough, given to extremes like the country from which it flowed. During spring its turbulent water swept out of the Rockies and across the plains carrying tangles of driftwood, cottonwood trees ripped out by their roots, carcasses of drowned bison, and a heavy load of sediment—hints, for anyone who could read them, of the wild and different landscapes of the West. The Snake River, inset, rising west of the continental divide, joined the Columbia, which reached the Pacific.

"I wanted to be the first to view a country on which the eyes of a white man had

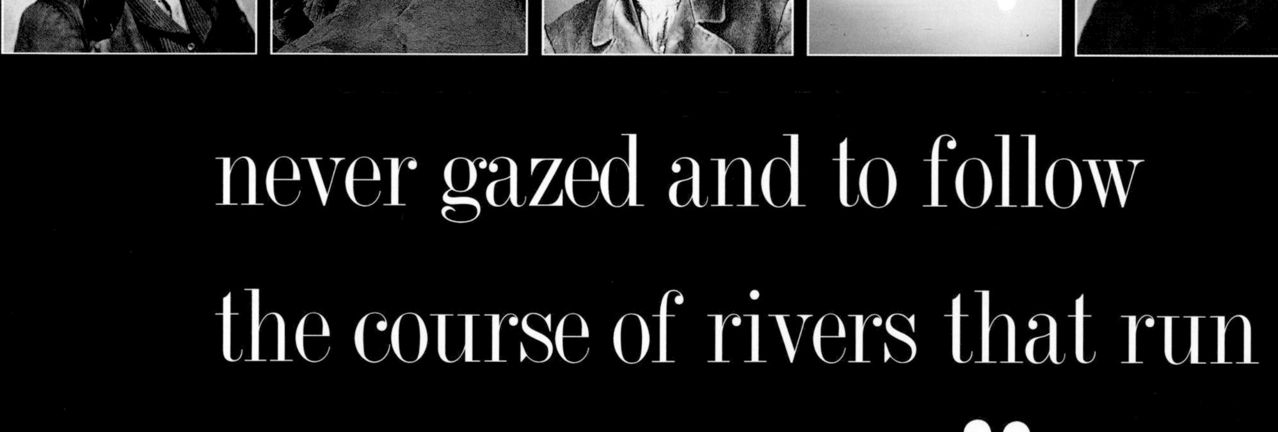

never gazed and to follow the course of rivers that run through a new land."

Setting Traps for Beaver, Alfred Jacob Miller

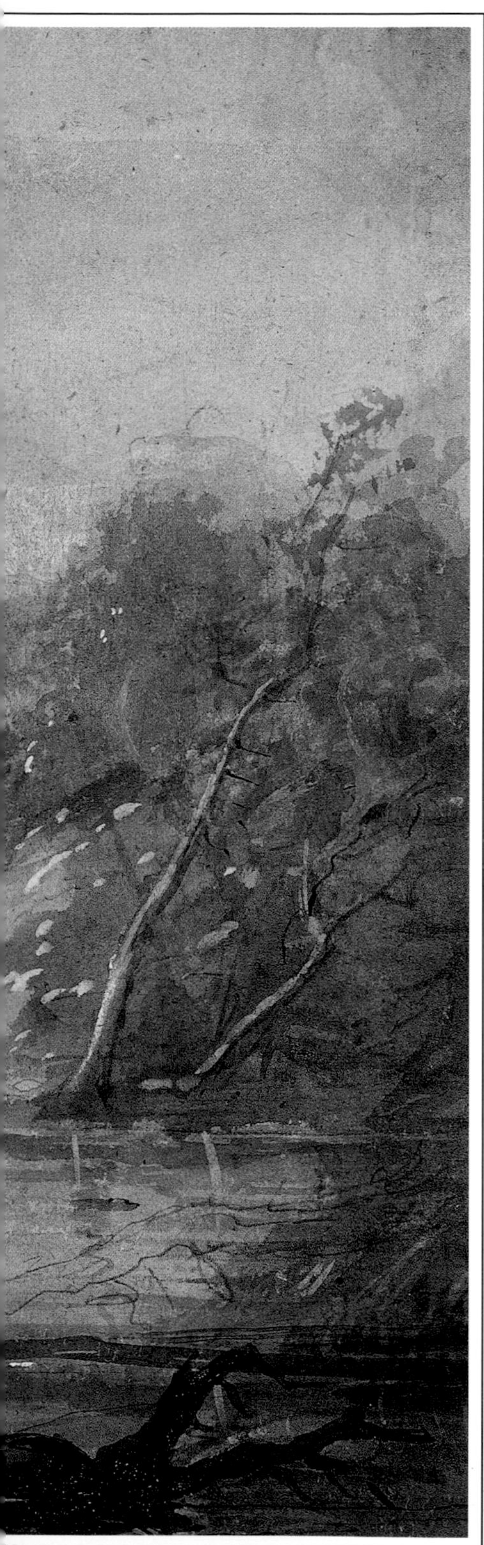

A STRANGE AND MOTLEY POPULACE

[1808–1835]

There is, perhaps, no class of men on the face of the earth, says Captain Bonneville, who lead a life of more continued exertion, peril, and excitement, and who are more enamored of their occupations, than the free trappers of the West. No toil, no danger, no privation can turn the trapper from his pursuit. His passionate excitement at times resembles a mania. In vain may the most vigilant and cruel savages beset his path; in vain may rocks and precipices and wintry torrents oppose his progress; let but a single track of a beaver meet his eye, and he forgets all dangers and defies all difficulties. At times, he may be seen with his traps on his shoulder, buffeting his way across rapid streams, amidst floating blocks of ice: at other times, he is to be found with his traps swung on his back clambering the most rugged mountains, scaling or descending the most frightful precipices, searching, by routes inaccessible to the horse, and never before trodden by white man, for springs and lakes unknown to his comrades, and where he may meet with his favorite game. Such is the mountaineer, the hardy trapper of the West; and such, as we have slightly sketched it, is the wild, Robin Hood kind of life, with all its strange and motley populace, now existing in full vigor among the Rocky Mountains.[1]

—Washington Irving

Trappers and the Fur Trade

The leading figures of the American fur trade—Astor, Ashley, Sublette, and others—were sharp-minded businessmen who made fortunes in the early days and moved on to other enterprises. Most mountain men, however, were something else. A good number were rebels and misfits who escaped beyond the reach of civil law to the unregulated freedom of the frontier, far right. A few simply preferred a different culture, finding the values of native society more to their liking than what they had left behind.

IT HAS BEEN SAID that the settlement of the American West owes itself to a hat—specifically a beaver hat—without which no self-respecting dandy of the European carriage trade would dare to have been seen. Thus, to the great misfortune of the aquatic rodent population of the Rocky Mountains (*C. Canadensis* of the family Castoridae), a nineteenth-century fashion statement gave birth to the fur trade. And in time the trade, having attracted a small, if legendary, cast of characters that managed to exterminate the rodent in something less than thirty years, evolved into the guiding business of the region. Trappers who found themselves with nothing much left to do began escorting emigrants over the rugged terrain between the eastern front of the Rockies and the Pacific coast. Others went back to the Great Plains to help eradicate the buffalo. All of this was good for western expansion, if bad for the House of Castoridae, but in the latter's case the social progression of history didn't really matter. By the time the beaver had been trapped out, silk had replaced felted fur as the hatter's fabric of choice anyway.

Prior to the explorations of Lewis and Clark, virtually nothing was known about the United States west of the Mississippi. The only other synchronous penetration of the Rockies (and it was a minor one at that) was Zebulon Pike's journey up the Arkansas in 1806–7 as far as present-day Pueblo, Colorado, where he observed but did not climb the peak named after him, and thence south to the upper Rio Grande valley. There he was arrested for trespass by the Spanish and escorted, via Santa Fe and Chihuahua, back across Texas to the Spanish-American border at Nacogdoches. Pike had nothing to do with the pursuit of the ill-fated beaver, and while his maps and attentive observations would prove useful to Texas immigrants in the mid-1820s, he is chiefly remembered for having helped propagate the myth that the southern plains were equivalent to "the sandy deserts of Africa."

Lewis and Clark provided a degree of enlightenment about a small portion of the country along the upper Missouri and across the Rockies into the Columbia basin. Their preliminary report,

Trappers Saluting the Rock Mountains, Alfred Jacob Miller

issued by President Jefferson in February 1806, fired the imagination of many men with restless feet and fanciful dreams, and the report's observations concerning the large number of fur-bearing animals just waiting to be found along the way proved an irresistible call to commerce for a number of influential merchants back in the United States. But until these merchants—or rather their hired adventurers—began retracing Lewis and Clark's steps, adding their own digressive footprints to the course of empire, the country beyond the ninety-eighth meridian remained as unrevealed to white Americans as the back of the moon.

It did not take long for things to change. Scarcely six months after Lewis and Clark had returned from their epic journey to the Pacific, a St. Louis trader named Manuel Lisa commanded the first party of fur trappers into the region of the upper Missouri. Lisa, who according to Bernard DeVoto was "the shrewdest mind in the business," owed much of his early success to the fact that he hired the former Lewis and Clark veteran George Drouillard (whose name everybody still mispronounced and misspelled Drewyer) as his head guide. Relying on Drouillard's expertise, he built the first post for the mountain trade at the confluence of the Yellowstone and the Bighorn, named it Fort Raymond, and spent the winter of 1807–8 attempting to establish contact with the local Indians.

Among Lisa's other employees were three additional members of the Corps of Discovery, the most celebrated of whom, John Colter, he sent out from Fort Raymond during that first winter to search for the Blackfeet and encourage them to come in to the post. Colter failed to attract any customers, but his toughness and resilience during the attempt provides a clear image of the kind of man it took to survive in the fur trade. Alone, living on his wits and his rifle, and traveling com pletely unexplored territory, he went up the Bighorn into present-day Wyoming, then west along the Shoshone (or the Stinkingwater, as it was then called) to the Wind River Range and over the Continental Divide into Pierre's Hole, Jackson Hole, and present-day Yellowstone

The Missouri River, far left, remained a starting point for further exploration of the West, but the fur trade carried trappers and other explorers up the great river's tributaries and across the mountain ranges in search of beaver. The Missouri basin was rich in fur-bearing mammals, and enterprising businessmen from the East were quick to exploit the bounty.

"I have often been asked why we exposed ourselves to such danger. My answer has always been that there was a charm in the life of a free mountaineer from which one cannot free himself, after he once has fallen under its spell."—BILL HAMILTON, MOUNTAIN MAN

National Park. He was the first white man ever to lay eyes on any of these spectacular locations. As Hiram Chittenden said in his classic study *The American Fur Trade of the Far West,* "This very remarkable achievement—remarkable in the courage and hardihood of this lone adventurer and remarkable in its unexpected results in geographical discovery—deserves to be classed among the most celebrated performances in the history of American exploration."[2]

Mountain men explored thoroughly and brought back reports of varying reliability. Jim Bridger described the Grand Canyon of the Yellowstone, far right, as an enormous echo chamber. He said a man about to fall asleep at the mouth of the canyon could shout "Wake up!" and in the morning his voice would come back to rouse him. Stories like Bridger's might explain why Yellowstone went unrecognized until the early 1870s. Geysers, mudpots, petrified trees, and obsidian mountains seemed too fantastical to be true.

Louis, Rocky Mountain Trapper

Colter did eventually find the Blackfeet, though at the time he was traveling with a band of their most intransigent enemies, the Crow, and wound up killing several of them when a skirmish broke out between the two old adversaries. It may be overstating matters to argue, as some historians have, that this cemented the murderous hatred demonstrated by the Blackfeet tribe toward all American fur trappers in years to come. But it certainly did nothing to sweeten their inherently bellicose disposition—nor did it persuade them to drop in on Lisa's trading post to conduct business.

And it didn't win Colter himself any points either when a year or so later, the Blackfeet caught him camped near the Three Forks in an area they thought of as their own hunting ground. They killed his partner, John Potts, stripped Colter of his clothes, and told him to run for his life, indicating that chasing him down and lifting his scalp would provide them with a fine afternoon's entertainment. Unfortunately there is no record of their proportionate amusement when he outstripped all but one of their warriors, then turned on the Indian and speared him with his own weapon.

Hightailing it barefoot across a rocky plain choked with prickly pear cactus, Colter eventually came to the Madison River and dove into its frigid waters, hiding himself in a tangle of driftwood until his furious pursuers were constrained by darkness. Silently emerging from hiding, he swam downstream to a point where he was able to crawl from the water and strike out eastward across the prairie. Seven days later Colter showed up on the Bighorn at a fort built by Manuel Lisa, buck naked and very much the worse for wear, but alive—and a clear inductee for any future Mountain Man Hall of Fame.

Colter may have been the first white man to see the Grand Tetons, Jackson Hole, and the Yellowstone country, but he was soon followed by others, as the trappers began to spread throughout the northern Rockies. In the summer of 1808, Lisa formed a partnership with William Clark, Pierre Chouteau, and Andrew Henry, which they incorporated into the Missouri Fur Company, sending several parties that year and the next up the Missouri to the Yellowstone River. In 1809 David Thompson, a trader and explorer for the Hudson's Bay Company, established two posts

Relations with Indians were often testy. In the etching, left, a trapper leads his horse past a hostile Indian camp visible beyond the tip of his rifle. The horse is blindfolded to keep the animal quiet. He is crossing the stream at a point where the rushing water will muffle the horse's hoofs. His weapons are ready, and his eye is peeled. Many a trapper lost his life at the hands of Indian enemies, but as history would soon prove, the ultimate advantage lay with the invaders.

FORT BRIDGER

There were a number of famous trading posts west of St. Louis during the period 1807 to 1845, among them Fort Lisa, Fort Tecumseh, the Mandan Villages, Fort Union, Three Forks of the Missouri, and Bent's Fort or Fort William. None, perhaps, was more famous than Fort Bridger, built by the illustrious mountain man Jim Bridger on the Black Fork of the Green River in southwest Wyoming. Its purpose, as Bridger explained in a letter to Pierre Chouteau Jr., on December 10, 1843, was somewhat different from that of most of its predecessors:

I have established a small fort with a blacksmith shop and a supply of iron in the road of the emigrants on Black's Fork of Green River which promises fairly. They, in coming out, are generally well supplied with money, but by the time they get there are in want of all kinds of supplies. Horses, provisions smith work, etc., bring ready cash from them, and should I receive the goods hereby ordered will do a considerable business in that way with them. The same establishment trades with the Indians in the neighborhood, who have mostly a good number of beaver among them.[3]

Jim Bridger

Bridger was correct in his assessment, and for ten years his establishment was on the main route of the emigrants heading west. Many of them seemed to have had somewhat higher expectations for the fort's spartan accommodations than the site actually provided. "The buildings are two or three miserable log cabins," wrote one, "rudely constructed and bearing but a faint resemblance to habitable houses." Another dismissed the fort as "a shabby concern." But everyone who

The Cliffs of Green River, Wyoming, Thomas Moran

went there found its wealth of supplies welcome and essential to the successful continuance of their journey. Fort Bridger remains one of the most important landmarks in the history of the West. Today it is a state historical site where, in an ironic twist that would set poor Mr. Bridger to spinning in his grave, alcohol, firearms, horses, and camping are strictly forbidden.

in present-day western Montana and northern Idaho (Salesh House and Kullyspell), and in 1810 Henry led another party of the newly formed Missouri Fur Company up the river to the Three Forks, where he built a post, only to be driven out in the spring by the rancorous Blackfeet.

A letter written from the Three Forks by Pierre Menard to one of the Missouri Fur Company partners narrates that unfortunate conflict, and gives a dramatic picture of a day in the oft-romanticized life of a carefree, self-reliant trapper:

It must be a tall tale. In this wildly dramatic rendition, right, a white horse and a black horse, a red man and a white, gallop in frantic combat over a precipice. The Indian's horse breathes fire, vultures gather, and no doubt the mountain man, grimly clutching a trapped beaver, ultimately survives to tell the story.

Three Forks of the Missouri
April 21, 1810

Mr. Pierre Chouteau, Esq., Dear Sir and Brother-in Law:—I had hoped to be able to write you more favorably than I am now able to do. The outlook before us was much more flattering ten days ago than it is today. A party of our hunters was defeated by the Blackfeet on the 12th inst. There were two men killed, all their beaver stolen, many of their traps lost, and the ammunition of several of them, and also seven of our horses. We set out in pursuit of the Indians but unfortunately could not overtake them. We have recovered forty-four traps and three horses, which we brought back here, and we hope to find a few more traps.

Menard goes on to explain that those who were attacked had been left behind to guard the camp while the rest of the men were out tending to the traps, as was the usual practice among teams of trappers, and he identifies the casualties as one James Cheeks and a man named Ayers.

Besides these two, there are missing young Hull who was of the same camp, and Freehearty and his man who were camped about two miles farther up. We have found four traps belonging to these men and the place where they were pursued by the savages, but we have not yet found the place where they were killed.

"Law sakes! Mr. Meek, didn't you never get killed by none of them Indians and bears?"

"Oh, yes, madam," said I gravely, "I was frequently killed."—STEPHEN HALL MEEK, MOUNTAIN MAN

The Death Struggle, Charles Deas

Long Jakes, 1844; The Rocky Mountain Man, Charles Deas

In the camp where the first two men were killed we found a Blackfoot who had also been killed, and upon following their trail we saw that another had been dangerously wounded. Both of them, if the wounded man dies, came to their death at the hand of Cheeks, for he alone defended himself.

This unhappy miscarriage causes us a considerable loss, but I do not propose on that account to lose heart. The resources of this country in beaver fur are immense. It is true that we shall accomplish nothing this spring, but I trust that we shall next Autumn. I hope between now and then to see the Snake and Flathead Indians. My plan is to induce them to stay here, if possible, and make war upon the Blackfeet so that we may take some prisoners and send back one with propositions of peace—which I think can easily be secured by leaving traders among them below the Falls of the Missouri. Unless we can have peace with these [men] or unless they can be destroyed, it is idle to think of maintaining an establishment at this point.[4]

Unfortunately, the next autumn did not prove any more tranquil than its preceding spring, and Henry and his men crossed over the Continental Divide to the north fork of the Snake (now called Henry's Fork), where they spent the winter exploring the country around Jackson Hole. In short, while the mountains were not exactly overrun by fur trappers by the year 1810, a few had already explored as far south of the upper Missouri as Yellowstone country and had even crossed the Continental Divide into the Green River Valley. And with one major exception, the American fur trade would remain largely confined to the upper Missouri and its tributaries for the next twelve years.

That exception was in the Pacific Northwest. Along the coasts of what are now Oregon, Washington, and British Columbia, explorers and sea traders from Spain, Portugal, Russia, and England had been engaged in their respective and often overlapping pursuits for many years before the first Americans appeared. The Northwest Territory was rightly, if unenforceably, Spain's by virtue of her explorations in 1774 and 1775. But once English captain James Cook showed up in 1778 and engaged in a vigorous barter with the natives for sea-otter pelts, commercial voyages from the various nations became commonplace. Sailing into one of the many coastal sounds with a hold full of cheap baubles and trinkets, merchant mariners would trade for the sea-otter furs that were so highly valued in the Orient—and in turn would trade the furs in Canton for the tea, silk, porcelain, and exotic spices so highly valued in the Occident. Their profits, needless to say, were enormous.

By the time Charles Deas painted this portrait of Long Jakes in 1844, far left, the time of the mountain men was past. Their heyday lasted less than two decades, from the early 1820s to the late 1830s. Beaver hats went out of fashion, and at the same time, mountain men ran themselves out of business by overtrapping. Unlike the Indians who had sustained their cultures for thousands of years, the trappers hunted for profit with no apparent regard for the future.

EXPLORERS' WANDERINGS

I was also led on by the love of novelty common to all, which is much increased by the pursuit of its gratification.

—Jedediah Smith

In the years after Lewis and Clark returned home the West was crisscrossed by fur trappers, some of whom became explorers or guides. Jedediah Smith's foray into Spanish territory may have been unofficial—and certainly alarming to the Spanish authorities—provided a mouthwatering glimpse of the central valley of California. Zebulon Pike, whose journeys cannot accurately be rendered because his papers were lost when he was captured by the Spanish, and Stephen Long, who also lost his notes in the field, both had set out to find the sources of the Arkansas and Red Rivers—Pike in 1806, and Long in 1819. Both men wandered far from their destinations and returned to describe the plains as an uninhabitable wasteland, a description that kept settlers away in droves for years. Of all the journeys in the generation following the Corps of Discovery, perhaps Robert Stuart's accidental discovery (or rediscovery, since it was already known to many fur trappers) of the South Pass—a wide and easily passable gap in the Rocky Mountains, was the most important. Stuart's 1812 route eastward from Astoria in search of help for the Astoria settlers eventually became the Oregon Trail.

Bonneville—1832–34
Bradbury—1808
Fremont—1838
Patties—1827–29
Smith—1826–28
Stuart—1812
Wyeth—1832–33

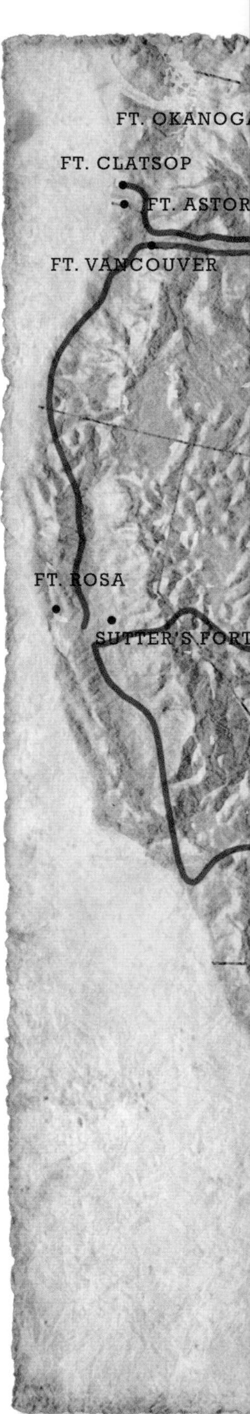

FLATHEAD POST
FT. MACKENZIE
FT. BOISE
WALLA WALLA
FT. MANDAN
FT. BOISE
FT. HENRY
FT. PLATT
FT. LARAMIE
FT. ATKINSON
FT. LISA
SARBY'S POST
FT. UINTAH
FT. LEAVENWORTH
ST. LOUIS
CHOUTEAU'S POST
BENT'S FORT
TAOS
SANTA FE

The Trapper's Last Shot, T. Dwight Booth

American merchants, quite naturally, saw no reason that they shouldn't get in on the action. In 1788, under the command of Captain Robert Gray, the first Yankee ship showed up off the northwest coast, thus adding a fourth nationality to the varying claims of sovereignty in the region. But it was during Gray's second trip in 1791 that he made his way into the history books for a more significant achievement. Like everyone in his line of work, the captain was on the constant lookout for evidence of a Northwest Passage that would connect the eastern United States with the Pacific Ocean, thereby making trade with the Orient significantly easier than circling halfway around South America. Sailing south from Nootka Sound on May 11 he spotted an area of white water he knew to be characteristic of waves breaking over shoals at the mouth of a major river. He drove his ship across the sandbars and forced his way into the estuary of what he deduced must be the great and elusive River of the West. What conclusions Gray actually drew concerning the prospects of his discovery remain unrecorded. The facts are simply that he landed, claimed the territory for the United States despite prior Spanish claims of which he was well aware, named the river after his ship, the *Columbia Redidiva*, and went back to his primary interest—trading with the coastal Indians for furs.

An overland advance into Oregon country by American explorers would not occur until Lewis and Clark arrived in 1805—disproving in the process the theory of a Northwest Passage and inadvertently vindicating Gray's lack of curiosity. Like Gray, they claimed the region for the United States, and after a miserable winter spent in a hastily built fort on the Netul River returned to the Mississippi Basin by essentially the same route they had come. Theirs was a temporary visitation. A "permanent" land-based occupation of the territory would not be attempted until 1811, when John Jacob Astor formed the Pacific Fur Company and sent his

It was a profession of limited opportunity and much danger. Historian David Lavender in his book, The Rockies, *estimates that all told, there were about one thousand mountain men. Of those, some 280 were killed by Indians or natural hazards. Being caught alone by enemies, left, was a quick route to either death or legend. One who survived was Tom Fitzpatrick, whose epic one-man escape from the Blackfeet made him a legend; it also turned his hair white.*

ship, the *Tonquin,* around the horn to the mouth of the Columbia to establish a settlement he would call Astoria. Astor launched an overland party from St. Louis about the same time. The land expedition, under the guidance of its inexperienced leader, Wilson Price Hunt, bogged down in present-day Idaho along the canyon of the Snake River, split into several floundering groups, and did not arrive (piecemeal, and minus five members who perished en route) until late winter/early spring of 1812.

John Jacob Astor

In his painting Mt. Hood from the Dalles, *right, John Mix Stanley offers an allegory of the West. A stunning landscape, lush with promise and crowned by a peak of unearthly beauty, surrounds a brightly lit white man's house and a scene of riverside commerce. Displaced to the shadowy edge of the scene are Native Americans and their quickly vanishing way of life.*

Astoria was a shaky prospect from the outset, beset by competition from the British Northwest Company, plagued by difficulties with the local Indians, and demoralized by the fog-shrouded, rain-drenched environment. Everyone there detested the miserable climate, and regarded the indigenous population, addicted as it was to thievery, beggary, and prostitution, with an equivalent loathing. Moreover, war between the United States and Britain had broken out in 1812, and fearing a takeover by an armed British naval force (the HMS *Raccoon* did, in fact, arrive off the coast on November 30, 1813, to "secure" the area), the Americans prudently sold out to the Nor'Westers and beat it back to more temperate climes.

The Pacific Fur Company's only significant contribution to American expansion in Oregon country occurred a year earlier when one of its employees, Robert Stuart, headed east during the winter of 1812 to inform his employer that the *Tonquin* had been blown up in an altercation with the natives, and that both trade goods and the conveyance for pursuing trade had been abruptly eliminated. Stuart's route took him far south of the course laid by Lewis and Clark, over a portion of southwestern Wyoming that would become known as South Pass—

Mt. Hood from the Dalles, John Mix Stanley

essentially a low, rolling meadow over the Continental Divide at a place where the elevation is only 7,550 feet. The remarks attributed to Stuart about the ease of his passage are responsible in large part for its becoming the highway of choice for future emigrants to Oregon and California. As the *Missouri Gazette* reported on May 15, 1813, "By information received from these gentlemen [Stuart and his companions], it appears that a journey across the continent of North America might be

THE FASHION THAT OPENED THE WEST

Throughout much of Europe the felt hat was in high fashion from about 1550 to 1850, though the beaver, from which the felt was made, was extinct in western Europe by 1600 and nearly extinct in Russia and Scandinavia shortly thereafter. North America eventually provided a new source of raw material—until by the mid-1840s the beaver on that continent was as scarce as its European counterpart.

The making of a beaver hat was a complicated process involving the removal of a pelt's guard hairs to produce a wool called fluff (only the soft underfur could be used), and a brushing of the stripped pelt with nitrate of mercury to stain the tips a yellowish-red. Over time the mercury vapor often attacked the nervous system of the hat maker, distorting his speech, causing twitching and lurching, and giving rise to the term "mad as a hatter." This material was then mixed and carded and weighed, the amount needed for a single hat varying between eight and twelve ounces. The fluff was matted into a bat by a process called bowing, manipulated into a triangular shape called a capade or gore, and wrapped in a leather-hardening skin. Heat, pressure, and moisture were applied. Two triangular bats were then

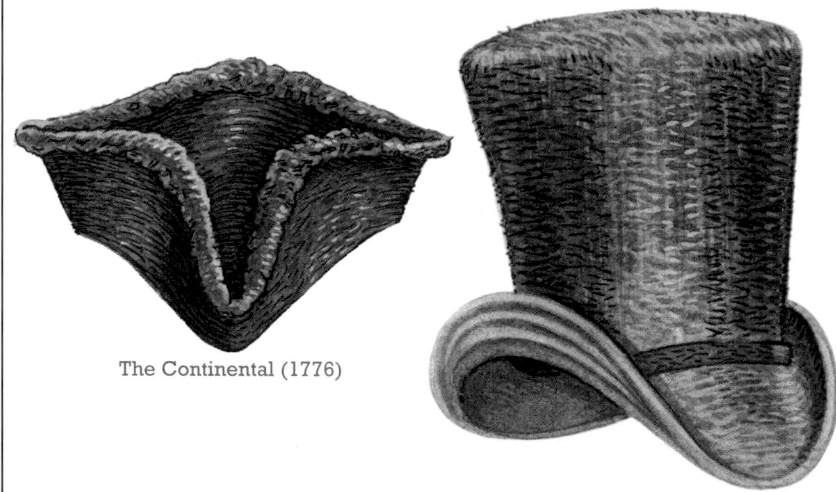

The Continental (1776)

The Wellington (1812)

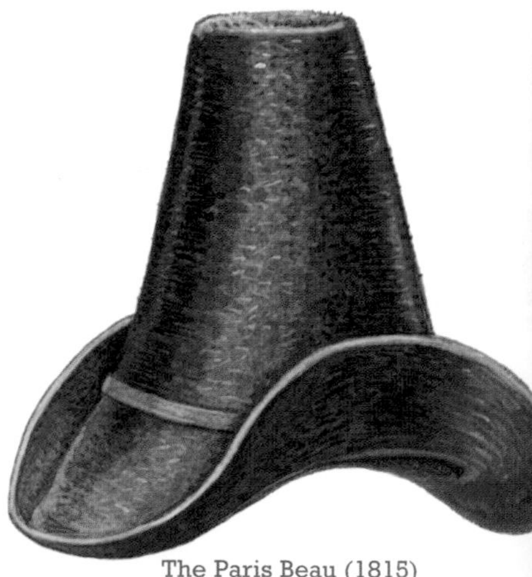

The Paris Beau (1815)

condensed, and the result was a large cone that looked like a dunce cap, which needed more shrinking and toughening.

The final step before shaping and finishing was called planking, in which the dunce cap was immersed in a hot solution of diluted sulfuric acid, wine sediment, and beer grounds, then rolled on sloping planks, which ultimately reduced the felt to half its previous size.

Shaping and finishing the hat consisted of forcing the shrunken cone over a wooden form and cutting the portion that extended below the mold with a rimjack to create a brim. Then came stiffening, waterproofing, steaming, ironing, brushing, and ironing once again. Small wonder that when a gentleman talked about his "beaver," he referred to the item on his head and not a small, furry, aquatic rodent with which he was unacquainted.

The D'Orsay (1820)

The Regent (1825)

The beaver's thick coat provided waterproof insulation and helped make it possible for the mammal to survive under the surface of frozen ponds all winter in the harsh climate of places like the Snowy Range, below. Since they lived in the dams that created the ponds, beaver could let some water out once the surface had frozen, creating an air space under the ice. But the coat that served the beaver so well also invited its doom and made fur traders like John Jacob Astor rich.

performed with a waggon, there being no obstruction on the whole route that any person would dare call a mountain in addition to its being much the most direct and short one to go from this place to the mouth of the Columbia River."[5]

But South Pass would have to wait another eighteen years before it would begin to fulfill its role as the main route for settlers headed west. The first wagons would not cross it until the spring of 1830, when William Sublette led a party to the annual fur trappers' rendezvous at the head of the Wind River, and it wasn't until 1841 that the first large wagon train of settlers would make the crossing. For the time being, mountain men remained free to continue their itinerant activities in relative isolation.

Their objective was occasionally exploration for its own sake, although most of the useful geographical and biological information they acquired remained personal intellectual property, shared occasionally with a few comrades but infrequently recorded for posterity. Most of the passion, of course, was for a twenty-five- to forty-pound sack of hair with a fuzzy face, buckteeth, a paddle for a tail, and an undercoat of fine, soft fur, suitable for rendering into felt—*C. canadensis:* the American beaver.

Indian mythology to the contrary, the beaver, though a talented architectural engineer, adroit at damming streams and building mud-plastered houses along the edges of the pools that back up behind their dams, are not overly endowed with cunning or intelligence, and trappers had little trouble killing them by the hundreds of thousands. Stealth and a pair of iron jaws baited with a musky secretion taken from the beaver's sexual glands was all it took. The trapper kept this elixir, called *castoreum,* or "medicine," in a plugged bottle that he carried on his person at all times, where, according to DeVoto, it tended to "perfume him, vocationally." When setting his snare the trapper daubed a little "medicine" on an arched bait stick that

C. Fiber,—— Common Beaver.

he positioned above the trap's trigger mechanism, then submerged its jaws in water just deep enough that the beaver would drown itself in its frantic efforts to escape. A trap pole driven into the streambed and secured by a five-foot length of chain prevented the unhappy hostage from dragging its attachment up onto the bank, where it could gnaw off its leg or foot and escape.

One man working alone and setting the average number of six traps a day for two months in the spring and three in the fall could bring in around nine hundred pelts. And since the average pelt (or "plew") weighed a pound and a half, at four dollars a pound for prime goods he could theoretically clear over $5,400 in a season.

Except that, unfortunately, it did not work that way. The ratio of traps set to beaver caught was probably closer to ten-to-one, not all skins were prime by any stretch of the imagination, and the price they brought fluctuated wildly. At one point it fell to as low as a dollar a pound. Moreover, the trapper had to be constantly alert and concerned that his own greasy locks did not wind up as a decoration for the tepee of some bellicose Blackfoot while he was otherwise preoccupied with the business of his trade.

Beavers have more important work to do than simply provide raw material for fur-felt. They shape the mountain landscape by damming streams to create ponds in which to build their lodges, right. The ponds help protect the beavers from predators and provide an easy way to float their preferred food—green willow and aspen—from the cutting place to home. Over time, the ponds fill with silt and make the transition from marsh to meadow to rich forestland.

Many an "old coon" has commented on the lack of wisdom exhibited by engaging in this kind of adventure alone. Alexander Ross, a fur trader with the Hudson's Bay Company from 1813 to 1825, explains in his narrative *The Fur Hunters of the Far West*:

There is . . . much anxiety and danger in going through the ordinary routine of a trapper's duty! For the enemy generally is lurking about among the rocks and hiding places, watching an opportunity, the hunter has to keep a constant lookout. And the gun is often in one hand, while the trap is in the other; but when several are together, which is often the case in suspicious places, one half set the traps, and the other half keep guard over them. Yet notwithstanding all the precautions some of them fall victims to Indian treachery.[6]

It was customary, therefore, for a large party of trappers to break into groups of two, three, and four, spreading out during the day in as much as a twenty-mile radius and reconvening at night for safety, although safety was a relative concept. Plews were dressed in camp—skinned, dried, folded with the hair inside, and bundled—and either cached or moved along with the party when it sought out new territory.

The system for transporting pelts back to the States, and for resupplying these roving bands of mountain men, was first developed by William H. Ashley, who in 1822 joined in partnership with Andrew Henry to form what would eventually become the greatest name in the trade, the Rocky Mountain Fur Company. Improving on a Hudson's Bay Company practice of having widely ranging trappers return to a fixed base, Ashley originated the rendezvous system whereby all parties involved in fur trapping and trading met at a designated time and place in the mountains during the summer months to conduct business. George Frederick Ruxton painted a consummate portrait of that commercial exchange in his nineteenth-century narrative *Adventures in Mexico and the Rocky Mountains*:

At a certain time, when the hunt is over, or they have loaded their Pack animals, the trappers proceed to the 'rendezvous,' the locality of which has been previously agreed upon; and

Our Camp, Alfred Jacob Miller

THE RENDEZVOUS

During the summer when beaver shed their fur and their pelts were valueless, trappers took advantage of the break to pack up the year's cache of pelts and trundle the load out of the mountains to a trading post to sell so they could buy necessities for another winter in the wild. In 1825, fur trader General William Ashley set out to corner the market in beaver pelts and at the same time establish himself as a one-stop shop for the supplies trappers would need for the coming year. He decided to go to the trappers rather than waiting for them to come to him—and to his competitors. He established an annual rendezvous, held at a prearranged spot in the mountains of Idaho, Wyoming, or Utah, where trappers and Indians could bring their goods for trade or sale. This arrangement allowed him to come out of the mountains with the beaver pelts as well as the cash he had paid for them. The scheme made Ashley rich, and the rendezvous went on for fifteen years—always a rowdy gathering characterized by drinking, gambling, and the inevitable eruptions of violence. By the time the trappers had conducted their business and set out for another lonely year's work, they were once again impoverished.

From Indians, who had long ago figured out how to survive and thrive in the West, mountain men learned a great deal. They made friends, learned native languages, adopted Indian dress and other customs, and sometimes married Indian women. In this painting by Alfred Jacob Miller, right, the couple seems to be headed for a special occasion. He carries freshly killed geese and wears full buckskins. She wears bright clothing and rides sidesaddle on a richly decorated horse.

here the traders and agents of the fur companies await them, with such assortment of goods as their hardy customers may require, including generally a fair supply of alcohol. . . . The dissipation of the 'rendezvous,' however, soon turns the trapper's pocket inside out.

The goods brought by the traders, although of the most inferior quality, are sold at enormous prices—coffee, twenty and thirty shillings a pint cup . . . tobacco fetches ten and fifteen shillings a plug; alcohol, from twenty to fifty shillings a pint; gunpowder, sixteen shillings a pint cup; and all other articles at proportionately exorbitant prices. . . .[7]

The annual rendezvous was in part a consequence of the discovery of South Pass, that opening through the mountains that extended the trappers' range to include virtually all of the interior West. The old system of returning to the upper Missouri posts to unload furs and resupply became increasingly time-consuming and impractical, even during the short summer season, when the poor quality of the pelts did not warrant hunting. Moreover, the journey through Indian and grizzly bear country could be extremely dangerous. If you were going to be gouged by your employer and effectively fleeced of your earnings anyway (the markup on goods supplied by the traders was as much as 2,000 percent), why not kick back in the mountains for a week or two and have a little fun—although "having a little fun" in the company of six hundred men who had just survived a year of isolation, deprivation, and extreme discomfort had its own risks.

Horse races and wrestling matches occasionally led to fistfights, which sometimes led to duels, generally rifles at twenty paces, which resulted in a modest reduction to the trapping population by at least one, if not both, contestants. Well, why not? Fun is fun. A mountain man had little use for savings, had no intention of returning east and settling down to grow old and fat amidst the comforts of civilization, and had no use for possessions other than ammunition, lead, traps, and maybe a new skinning knife. So he might as well buy another trinket for the squaw and one more kettle of raw alcohol and stay drunk for as long as the spree lasted. There might be no tomorrow.

By 1824 the fur trade had moved far beyond the upper Missouri and spread throughout the intermountain region and

Captain Walker or a Bourgeis and His Squaw, Alfred Jacob Miller

Kit Carson, William Ranney

into the interior West. There were many participants who made critical path-finding discoveries, some of whom remain unknown and uncelebrated, others of whom have become household names like Jim Bridger, Jim Beckwourth (or Beckwith), John Colter, Thomas Fitzpatrick, William Sublette, William Ashley, Kit Carson, Nathaniel Wyeth, Joseph Walker, Peter Skene Ogden, and Jedediah Smith. Between the western slopes of the Continental Divide and the Pacific Ocean it was Walker, Ogden, and Smith who made the greatest impact. And among this triumvirate it was Smith who stood, if not head and shoulders, at least a shave and a haircut above the rest.

Jedediah Strong Smith first went up the Missouri in 1822 as a rookie in the employ of William Ashley. By 1825 he was Ashley's partner; a year later (along with William Sublette and David Jackson) he bought Ashley out and formed the Rocky Mountain Fur Company, the most famous of all such enterprises in North America. His rise in the fur trade was meteoric, and its explanation lies in the superior level of competence he exhibited at all aspects of a mountain man's life. Smith was a crack shot, a ferocious Indian fighter, tough as a nail, and immediately apparent as a leader of men. He was also something of an oddity in that he didn't drink, smoke, or use profanity, and he apparently retained a rare degree of celibacy when it came to bedding down with amorous Indian squaws. Chittenden compared him to Stonewall Jackson, calling Smith a rare combination of "the most ardent belief in and practice of the Christian religion and undaunted courage, fierce and impetuous nature, and untiring energy."

Christopher Houston Carson, far left, better known as Kit, fled a saddle-making apprenticeship at age fourteen and spent the next decades becoming perhaps the most famous mountain man of them all. When the beaver were gone he turned to guiding, as illustrated in this 1854 painting. That led to other stints as an army officer, Indian agent, and rancher.

"I have met honest mountain men. Their animal qualities, however, are undeniable . . . they are just what uncivilized white man might be supposed to be in a brute state, depending upon his instinct for the support of life."—George Frederick Ruxton (ca. 1846)

Smith is credited with having "rediscovered" South Pass when he and Tom Fitzpatrick led a group of trappers over the Divide in 1824, and it was his extensive travels both south and west of the Three Forks—Clark's Fork, Pierre's Hole, and the upper Snake—that linked various isolated explorations of the labyrinthine terrain between South Pass and Lewis and Clark's North Pass. But his greatest expedition would take him far to the west of the Rocky Mountains and would distinguish him as the leader of the first party of Americans to reach California by an overland route.

James Beckwourth

Charles Stewart Stobie came late to the fur trade but did his part to build its legend. Raised in the East and trained as a painter, he moved to Denver in 1865 and soon made a name for himself as a scout, Indian fighter, and artist. He made friends with James Beckwourth, above, one of the true old-timers and a famous liar. Stobie, far right, was often the subject of his own paintings and photographs, as in this dandified 1866 portrait shot in Denver.

Leaving the rendezvous on the Bear River in Cache Valley on August 16, 1826, Smith and sixteen companions (two of whom would drop out during the first month) traveled south along the Wasatch Front following the Sevier River for about one hundred miles, then angled west and southwest following what, 160 years later, would become Interstate 15 through the Virgin River canyon to Las Vegas. No bright lights or casinos greeted them, just the muddy, swirling Colorado River, along which they continued until they arrived at a village of Mohave Indians near present-day Needles. Recuperating for fifteen days among these friendly natives (who would become less friendly in subsequent years), Smith and his men bought horses to replace those they had lost, then headed due west, straight across the blistering wasteland of the Mohave Desert, eventually crossing the San Bernardino Mountains at a place near Cajon Pass. On the twenty-seventh of November, 104 days after their departure from Cache Valley, they staggered, exhausted and emaciated, into the San Gabriel Mission, where they were met by its Franciscan proprietor, Father José Bernardino Sanchez.

Father Sanchez was not especially pleased. Not only did his visitors look like precursors of the Hell's Angels, they were Americans, and therefore trespassers on Mexican soil. Moreover, they were riding stolen horses bearing the mission brand, they were armed to the teeth, and they were *Protestants,* a fellowship as unacceptable in California as it was in Mexico and Mother Spain. Sanchez did not know what to do with them. He eventually solved his dilemma by passing the buck, sending Smith under guard to explain his unauthorized and illegal presence to

Charles Stewart Stobie

Wind River Country, Alfred Bierstadt

the Mexican governor of California in San Diego, José Maria de Echeandia.

José Maria was as suspicious of and perplexed by the intruders as Father Sanchez had been, and Smith's accounting of how he happened to be in California was evasive to say the least. It made no mention of exploration as a motive, nor did it refer to the search for a nonexistent river (the Buenaventura) that was alleged to connect the California seacoast with the Rocky Mountains, and it didn't say anything about continuing to trap for beaver. What Smith told his interrogator was that he and his men had accidentally wandered into Mexican territory because they had run out of provisions, and their horses had been too exhausted to retrace the difficult route they had come. He was not particularly apologetic. What he wanted now, he said, was to resupply; then he would return to the Great Salt Lake by way of the Columbia—which meant, of course, continuing his trespass all the way north to the forty-second parallel.

The answer was six weeks in coming, and it did not include any sightseeing up through California into Oregon country. The governor was aware that no Americans had ever seen California, apart from its coast, and feared that they might take a fancy to what they witnessed. History taught that what Americans took a fancy to they had a habit of appropriating, sooner or later. So Señor Smith could just depart the way he had arrived—across the Mohave. And so he did—at least as far as the east side of Cajon Pass. Then he turned north, crossed the transverse range of the Tehachapis, and headed straight up the great

In the first half of the nineteenth century, lands west of the Continental Divide were in dispute. Spain claimed the entire West Coast and the Southwest. Britain, Russia, and the United States added their claim to Oregon country (now Washington, Oregon, and Idaho). Wyoming's Wind River Range, left, was a favorite haunt of mountain men. During most of the fur trade era this was Spanish territory unless you asked the native people, who claimed a far older sovereignty.

Jim Baker

central valley, trapping fifteen hundred pounds of beaver pelts along the way, marveling at the scenery, the amiable natives, and the mild climate, until he reached the confluence of the Stanislaus and San Joaquin Rivers.

It was now mid-May, and if the party was going to make the annual rendezvous back at Bear Lake in Utah that summer they were going to have to cross the mountains soon. Finding the snow still too deep for the heavily loaded horses, Smith left the main group camped beside the Stanislaus, and with two companions began what would be the first crossing of the Sierra Nevada ever accomplished by white men. They floundered through four to eight feet of snow over what is present-day Ebbetts Pass (8,700 feet), and emerged eight days later somewhere south of Walker Lake at the western edge of the Great Basin. From there it was due east across the desolate high desert of Nevada and the utterly barren salt flats of what was once Lake Bonneville. Parched and starved, with cracked, swollen lips and emaciated bodies, they arrived at Bear Lake some forty-three days from their departure, having completed what one historian referred to as "one of the greatest single exploits in the whole history of western exploration."

California was now a reality. Not only was it reachable by an overland route, its wonders had been fully revealed: the land was lush, well

Death Valley, shown at far left from Zabriskie Point, was hardly beaver country, but it was the sort of place that mountain men loved to discover and tell stories about. Unfortunately for a party of immigrants who came this way in 1849, Jedediah Smith had gone another way. The immigrants, having heard rumors of a shortcut from Utah to California, nearly met their death here, hence the name. Had Smith found the valley, it might have been a famous place—famous enough for families traveling overland to avoid.

"I started into the mountains, with the determination of becoming a first-rate hunter, of making myself thoroughly acquainted with the character and habits of the Indians, of tracing out the sources of the Columbia River and following it to its mouth; and of making the whole profitable to me, and I have perfectly succeeded." —JEDEDIAH SMITH

Harry Yount stands among wind-stunted conifers at Berthoud Pass, Colorado, far right. The big spacious land would soon begin filling up with people chasing other dreams, most significantly miners and prospectors drawn by the 1859 Colorado gold rush. Gold fever began with a small discovery in what is now Denver, spread like wildfire through the mountains, and laid the foundations for cities, highways, railroads, and other developments that followed. The short, bright, era of mountain men was over.

watered, temperate in climate, and rich in wildlife, fish, and fowl. Americans now knew for a fact that however difficult the journey, it could be made. They knew, moreover, that on the other side of that barren wilderness between the Rockies and the Sierra lay Paradise, and that nobody there was going to seriously oppose them. Writes Maurice Sullivan, Jedediah Smith's first biographer: *One wonders what would have happened to a band of Mexicans riding into Missouri on horses stolen from the Missourians; showing by their manner that they were contemptuous of the Missourians; fraternizing with the native enemies of the settlers; renaming the rivers, insisting on choosing their own course through the territory, and, as they went, gathering the natural wealth of the country.*

In the end this tolerance of invasion lost the magnificent empire of the Pacific slope. Jedediah Smith had opened the gate, and Mexico was never able to close it."[8]

SCENES FROM A DREAM LANDSCAPE

The travertine terraces of Mammoth Hot Springs, in northern Yellowstone National Park, send up clouds of warm steam to mingle with the colors of sunset. It was a fortunate twist of fate that kept the wonders of Yellowstone hidden for so long. Lewis and Clark missed it entirely, although Clark came within fifty miles and spoke with Indians who must have known of its existence. John Colter skirted the area in 1807–8, but apparently missed the geysers. Other mountain men, including Jim Bridger and Osborne Russell, spent considerable time here, yet reports of hot springs and geysers were ignored or treated as tall tales. Not until 1870, when the Hayden Survey returned with reliable evidence, did the country take notice. By then, the mood was right to create a national park devoted to the protection of aesthetic values. Other beauty spots soon joined Yellowstone on the protected list, including the Big Thompson River in Rocky Mountain National Park, following page.

Mountain men used the word "hole" to describe flat-floored valleys ringed by mountains. Davey Jackson—trapper, business partner of Jedediah Smith, and relative of President Andrew Jackson—took a particular liking to one notable hole at the head of the Snake River, left and inset. On the east rose the Gros Ventre Range; to the west, a soaring wall of crags called the Trois Tetons. Jackson spent enough time here that his friend William Sublette dubbed the valley "Jackson's Hole." No doubt many Indians and trappers appreciated this view of the Snake River and Tetons long before the establishment of Grand Teton National Park.

BOUNDARIES OF TEXAS.
Political, Conventional, and Natural.
The Boundary between the United States and Mexico, as laid down in Onis' Treaty of 1819, marked thus,
The Political Boundary of Texas Proper, under the Spanish Regime.
The Political Boundary of Texas Proper, under the Mexican Republican Regime.
Territory absolutely in possess
Texians.
Boundaries of the Mexican States of Chi
Coahuila, and Tamaulipas,
OSAGE TERRITORY
INDIAN TERRITORY
Osage Indians
Creek Indians
Cherokee Indians
ATTACHED TO ARKANSAS
Kioway Indians
Chactaw Indians
SANTA FE
FORMERLY NEW MEXICO
MEXICO
Comanches Indians
Caddo Indians
FANNIN
NACOGDOCHES
Shawnee Indians
Cherokee Indians
ROBERTSON
Lepan Indians
Comanche Chief Town
Droves of Wild Cattle & Horses
Elevated Prairies
AUSTIN
COLORADO
JACKSON
MATAGORDA
HARRISBURG
JEFFERSON
GULF OF MEXICO
NEW MAP OF TEXAS
1841.
MATAMORAS
Longitude West from Greenwich
Longitude West from Washington

“[It is] our manifest destiny to overspread the continent allotted by Providence for

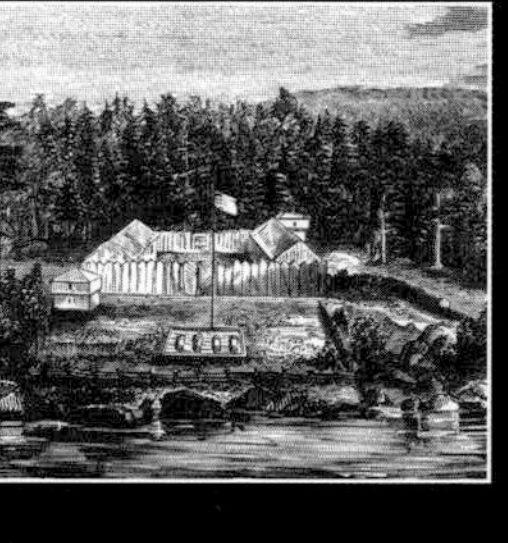

the free development of our yearly multiplying millions.”

The Attack on an Emigrant Train (detail), Charles Wimar

I

TO OVERSPREAD THE CONTINENT

[1812–1849]

Clash of Destiny

It would seem that the White race alone received the divine command, to subdue and replenish the earth; for it is the only race that has obeyed it— the only race that hunts out new and distant lands, and even a New World, to subdue and replenish . . .

Civilization or extinction, has been the fate of all people who have found themselves in the trace of the advancing Whites, and civilization always the preference of the Whites, has been pressed as an object, while extinction has followed as a consequence of its resistance . . . The van of the Caucasian race now top the Rocky Mountains, and spread down on the shores of the Pacific. In a few years a great population will grow up there, luminous with the accumulated lights of the European and American civilization. Their presence in such a position cannot be without its influence upon eastern Asia . . .

The sun of civilization must shine across the sea; socially and commercially the van of the Caucasians, and the rear of the Mongolians, must intermix. They must talk together, and trade together, and marry together. . . . Moral and intellectual superiority will do the rest; the White race will take the ascendant, elevating what is susceptible of improving— wearing out what is not. . . . And thus the youngest people, and the newest land, will become the reviver and the regenerator of the oldest . . . It is in this point of view, and acting upon the social, political, religious condition of Asia, and giving a new point of departure to her ancient civilization, that I look upon the settlement of the Colombia river by the van of the Caucasian race as the most momentous human event in the history of man since his dispersion over the face of the earth.[1]

—Senator Thomas Hart Benton, 1846

Eastern farms, like this one in nineteenth-century Indiana, right, prospered in a more favorable environment. There were trees for building cabins and fences, adequate rainfall to grow crops without irrigation; good pasture, thick topsoil, and a long growing season. In contrast, much of the West was a harsh place characterized by extreme temperatures, scarce water, unrelenting winds, vast treeless plains, rough topography, and scorching deserts. Those who went had better be prepared for a different sort of life.

IF A SATELLITE camera were capable of warping time back to the year 1810, and possessed the ability to project imaginary boundary lines down on Earth five hundred miles below, it would show that the North American continent west of the Mississippi and below the forty-ninth parallel was divided into two roughly equal parts: the territory acquired by the Louisiana Purchase in 1803 (plus the Oregon country), and a vast dominion owned by Spain. Spanish sovereignty over lands that would eventually become a part of the United States—or to put it another way, lands that would eventually be filched, purloined, swindled, squatted upon, and commandeered by the United States—included a portion of present-day southern Oregon; all of California, Nevada, Utah, and Arizona; half of Colorado; most of New Mexico, and most of Texas without its panhandle.

Prior to 1803 the area we call Texas was largely the province of various Indian tribes—the Caddos, Kichais, Wacos, and Tawaconis in eastern Texas, and the Comanche and Apache groups on the western plains. The former, Caddoan speakers from whom the word *Texas* is derived (meaning "allies" or "friends"), were primarily agricultural people and generally friendly toward Europeans; the latter were nomadic buffalo hunters and raiders, and decidedly hostile. There was also the remnant of a thin line of missions and presidios on the northern border of the Spanish frontier in the vicinity of (or along) the Rio Grande, settlements that had been so relentlessly harassed by the Apache and Comanche that they were largely abandoned during the latter half of the eighteenth century. Their primary purpose, as with all Spanish missions, had been to subdue and convert the heathen, a task at which they had been spectacularly unsuccessful. As Walter Prescott Webb observed, "The wild Comanche and Apache were not amenable to the

INTRODUCTION.

It was not the intention of the compilers of this map to add a Guide, but from the numerous incidents which have lately sprung up regarding the Gold fields of Western Kansas, they found it impossible to lay down the location of every place which they deemed useful without rendering the topographical part crowded and indistinct. They have therefore introduced a few pages, giving the neccessary outfit for four men, six months in the mines; the distances to the principal camping places along the routes; and also the different mail stations &c. along the route to California.

List of outfits for four men six months.

TEAM, WAGON AND FIXTURES:

2 Yoke of Oxen	$120.00
1 Wagon	65.00
Wagon- Cover, Yokes and chains	10.00
	$195.00

TOOLS:

4 Steel Picks with handles	$5.00
4 Shovels	3.00
1 Pit Saw	7.00
2 Axes	2.00
1 Hatchet	65
1 Saw File	25
2 Gold Pans	1.50
1 Chisel	30
1 Auger	25
1 Hand Saw	1.00
1 Drawing Knife	50
25 lb of Nails @ 5cts.	1.25
2 Gimlets	15
2 lb Quicksilver and retort	3.00
Sheet Iron for Long Toms	75
	$26.60

CAMP FIXTURES AND FURNITURE:

8 Pair of Blankets	$24.00
1 Camp Kettle	1.00
4 Tin Plates	30
4 Spoons	15
1 Coffee Pot	50
1 Camp Stand	1.00
4 Cups	35
1 Dipper	15
1 Large Spoon	15
1 Large Fork	15
1 Frying Pan	35
1 Dutch Oven	70
1 Bread Pan	30
1 Coffee Mill	40
1 Wooden Bucket	25
4 Knives	1.00
	$30.75

PROVISIONS:

6 Sacks of Flour at $3	$18.00
400 lb of Bacon at 10cts.	40.00
100 lb of Coffee at 11cts.	11.00
6 lb of Tea at 75cts.	4.50
100 lb of Sugar at 7cts.	7.00
100 lb of Salt	1.00
6 lb Ground Pepper	1.00
1 Ten Gallon Water Keg	1.00
2 Bushels of Dried Fruit	2.50
2 Bushels of Beans	2.00
250 lb Pilot Bread @ 5cts.	12.50
25 lb of Rice	1.50
1 Box of Soap	1.00
	$103.00
Team	195.50
Tools	26.60
Camp Fixtures	30.75
	$355.85

SUNDRIES:

3 Gallons of Brandy,
12 lb Gunpowder,
25 lb of Lead,
10 lb of Shot,
2000 Gun Caps,
2 dozen Box of Matches,
15 lb of Candles,
1 Whet Stone,
30 lb of Rosin.

Settler's Farm in Indiana, Karl Bodmer

gentle philosophy of Christ nor were they tamed by the mysteries and elaborate ceremonials of the church. The war-whoop was sweeter to them than evening vespers; the crescent bow was a better symbol of their desires than the holy cross; and it was far more joyful, in their eyes, to chase the shaggy buffalo on pinto ponies than to practice the art of dry-farming under the direction of a black-robed priest."[2]

In the aftermath of the Louisiana Purchase, American migration into Spanish Texas began with freebooters illegally drifting westward out of Louisiana and Missouri in pursuit of large herds of feral horses they hoped to catch and trade. Quite naturally they cast an appraising

MANIFEST DESTINY

The phrase "manifest destiny" is generally attributed to a journalist named John O'Sullivan, who used the term during a commentary in the *United States Magazine and Democratic Review* in July 1845. Mr. O'Sullivan was miffed by what he had in a previous essay identified as the "tyranny of kings, hierarchs, and oligarchs"—a reference primarily to Great Britain, which in its Proclamation of 1763, had attempted to prevent any American settlement beyond the Appalachian Mountains. In the second editorial he was once again chastising those he saw as acting with "the avowed object of thwarting our policy and hampering our power, limiting our greatness and checking the fulfillment of our manifest destiny to overspread the continent allotted by Providence for the free development of our yearly multiplying millions."

The idea, championed by most Americans who gave it any conscious thought at all, was that God had ordained Anglo-European expansion across the North American continent, and that one could get on the bus or off the bus, but either way the bus was leaving for points west. "The American realizes that 'Progress is God,'" thundered the visionary futurist and land speculator William Gilpin. "The pioneer army perpetually . . . strikes to the front. Empire plants itself upon the trails."[3] Senator Thomas Hart Benton waxed even more bombastically in his conviction that *"the divine command" to subdue the American earth had been bestowed on the white man alone: "The Red race has disappeared from the Atlantic coast; the tribes that resisted civilization met extinction. This is a cause of lamentation with many. For my part, I cannot murmur at what seems to be the effect of divine law. . . . Civilization, or extinction, has been the fate of all people who have found themselves in the trace of the advancing Whites, and civilization, always the preference of the Whites, has been pressed as an object, while extinction has followed as a consequence of its resistance. . . ."*[4]

In fact, there were many opposed to the

The Oregon Trail, Albert Bierstadt

presumptions of a manifest destiny. The political position of the Whig party was that if America grew too large it would fail as the great experiment in self-government upon which it was founded, and for starters they solidly opposed the annexation of Texas. But there was too much destiny in the manifesto. The Whig candidate, Henry Clay, lost the 1844 election to James K. Polk, an avowed and unequivocal believer in territorial expansion; and by the time Polk's term was up, the bus had arrived not only at the Texas terminal, but in Oregon and California as well.

The Plaza and Church of El Paso, Sarony, Major, and Knapp after A. de Vaudricourt

eye on the countryside as they passed through it. Political boundaries meant little to these greedy filibusters, and the Spanish, oddly enough, seemed not only to tolerate them but to invite their presence, hoping, no doubt, that they might prove an obstacle to the unrelenting Indian raiders who continued to make life miserable for the rancherias along the crumbling northern frontier. The local Spanish authority was hard pressed to keep the drifters at bay, especially since Spain's political center in the New World was some eight hundred miles to the south in Mexico City.

In 1820 Moses Austin, a Connecticut Yankee cum Missouri miner and trader, persuaded the Spanish governor of Mexico to give him a large land grant in southeastern Texas, ground upon which he promised to locate a colony of three hundred Anglo settlers, all of whom, he assured the governor, would be Catholics, and all of whom would comport themselves as loyal Spanish subjects. Austin would die before he could get his project off the ground, and within the year Mexico would revolt from Spain and establish itself as a republic, but "manifest destiny" was not to be so easily deflected.

The Spanish extended their influence in the New World through a system of mission churches, far left. As agencies of both church and state, the purpose of missions was to represent colonial power, convert native people to Catholicism, and convince them to adopt the Spanish agrarian way of life. The first mission in east Texas was Francisco de los Tejas, built in 1690.

Mexico's colonization policy turned out to be a simple continuation of Spain's, and Austin had a son who developed into an even more competent *empresario* than he himself had been. Stephen Austin inherited his father's vision and resolve, and in 1822, on well-watered and fertile land he personally picked out between the Brazos and Colorado Rivers, established the first legal settlement of Americans in Mexican territory.

In 1845, the United States annexed Texas and claimed the Rio Grande as the international border. This was a double insult. Mexico had never recognized Texan independence, and saw the Nueces River, 150 miles north of the Rio Grande, as the Texan border. Two years of war forced Mexico to accept the American view.

To employ an old cliché, it was an opening of the floodgates. Homesteaders began pouring in, and by 1823 there were, in addition to those legally planted by Austin and other authorized *empresarios* who followed in his footsteps, three thousand illegal immigrants in Texas. Then, in 1825, Mexico effectively drove a stake through its own heart by passing a colonization law offering land to any foreigner who could demonstrate that he was a Christian, morally upstanding, and in possession of "good habits." Within five years there were seven thousand Americans in Texas, more than double the number of Mexican residents, though in many cases the sum and substance of their habits was not exactly what their grantors had had in mind. Increasing demands for greater political liberty and more free trade with the United States, along with a quarrelsome disdain for Latinos and a penchant for insurrection, began to greatly disturb the host country—as did the illegal importation of a large number of slaves.

Alarmed by what they had brought upon themselves, the Mexican government tried in 1830 to slam the door by prohibiting any further American immigration and canceling all outstanding land grant contracts. The result was an *increase* in migration, so much so that by 1835 there were thirty thousand Americans in the territory—more than twice the number of Mexicans and Indians combined. No sooner had they arrived than many of these new inhabitants began clamoring for still more economic and political independence. Some, like Stephen Austin, argued that such liberties ought to be sought within the context of the Mexican Republic itself. Others, like the radical William Travis, wanted autonomy from Mexico.

Stephen Austin

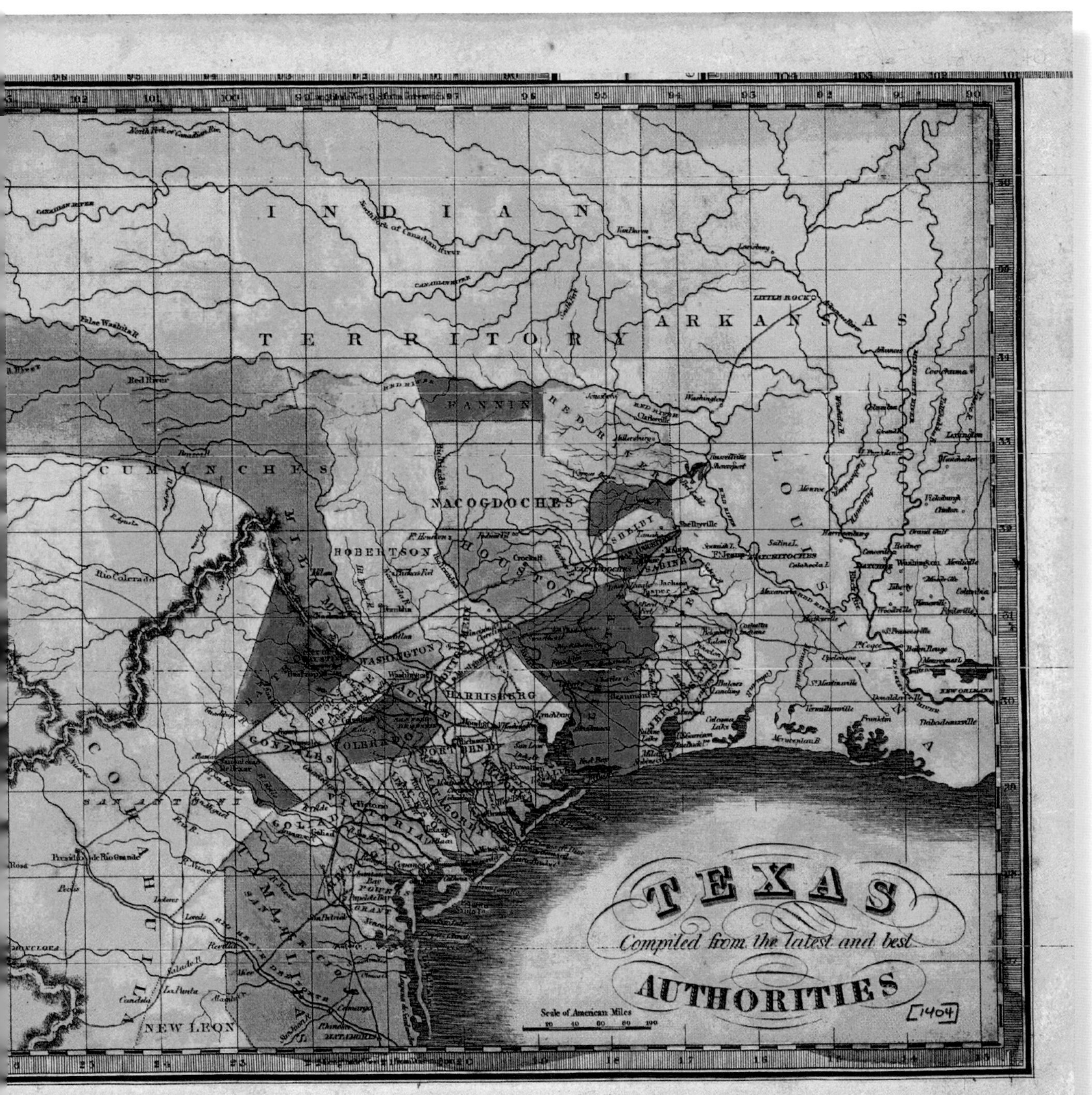
INDIAN
TERRITORY
ARKANSAS
LOUISIANA
CUMANCHES
NACOGDOCHES
FANNIN
ROBERTSON
HOUSTON
SHELBY
WASHINGTON
HARRISBURG
AUSTIN
GONZALES
COLORADO
GOLIAD
COAHUILA
TAMAULIPAS
NEW LEON
LITTLE ROCK
NEW ORLEANS
Rio Colorado
Red River
TEXAS
Compiled from the latest and best
AUTHORITIES
Scale of American Miles
[1404]

Antonio López de Santa Anna Pérez de Lebron was a man of shifting political philosophy. He fought with the Spanish army in support of the Crown before switching sides in 1821 to become a revolutionary hero. Between 1833 and 1855 he became head of Mexico eleven times, first as a federalist president, finally as a corrupt dictator.

Mexico itself was on the verge of a civil war between those who wanted a decentralized federalist government and those who wanted the provinces to be controlled from and by Mexico City. When General Antonio López de Santa Anna took power in 1833 and established himself as a reactionary dictator, revolts began to break out everywhere. One of Santa Anna's initial acts was to dispatch soldiers to reopen the custom house and garrison at Anahuac, a few miles southwest of present-day Laredo. This not only frightened those Texans who favored independence from Mexico (and ultimate annexation to the United States), it gave them the excuse they needed to advance their revolutionary cause. Led by William Travis, a small party of thirty men marched on Anahuac dragging a cannon in their wake and successfully demanded its surrender.

Santa Anna was not amused. He was even less amused by a second skirmish that occurred three months later in Gonzales, just west of San Antonio. Enough was enough. In reprisal, he marched north with an army of 4,000 men, intending to crush forthwith all resistance to his authority. Although it cost the lives of 1,544 of his own troops to do so, he wiped out the 183 men he found waiting for him at the Alamo Mission in San Antonio, including William Travis and recent arrivals Davy Crockett and Jim Bowie. At the Texan outpost at Goliad he captured 371 additional defenders of the revolutionary movement, all of whom he summarily executed. Then he divided his forces into columns and advanced eastward from the Colorado to the Brazos to San Felipe de Austin, destroying Texan farms and ranches as he went.

"We were surrounded by some gross, proud, and victorious men. Anyone who knows the character of the North Americans can judge what our situation must have been!"—José Juan Sánchez Navarro, with the army of Santa Anna, 1835

Antonio López de Santa Anna

THE ALAMO

In April of 1833 a convention of Texas settlers voted to separate from Mexico, which led to the presentation of a "resolve" to Mexican president Antonio Lopez de Santa Anna by Stephen Austin asking for independent statehood. Santa Anna's response was to arrest Austin and throw him in jail for eight months, where he languished until September of 1835. A war with Mexico, or so it was concluded by the Texan rebels, was the only logical response. Accordingly, in December of 1835 they attacked the Mexican garrison at San Antonio and captured it, holding it for some two months until an infuriated Santa Anna showed up with a force of several thousand troops to take it back. The Texans retreated to the old Mission of San Antonio de Valero, known as the Alamo, and held Santa Anna off for two weeks while the Mexican artillery methodically reduced the walls of the stronghold. Early in the morning of March 6 the Mexican infantry attacked and the 183 rebels were overwhelmed and slaughtered to a man.

A letter appealing for help, written by William Travis during the siege, is often referred to as a sample of the defiant and heroic courage exhibited by the Alamo's defenders. Given that the odds were something like twenty to one against them it might just as appropriately be regarded as a suicide note. "The enemy has demanded a surrender at discretion," Travis wrote. "Otherwise the garrison are to be put to the sword if the fort is taken. I have answered the demand with a cannon shot, and our flag still waves proudly from the walls. I shall never surrender nor retreat."

Dawn at the Alamo, Henry Arthur McArdle

James Bowie

William Travis

Davy Crockett

SAM HOUSTON

Born near Lexington, Virginia, in 1793, Sam Houston moved at age thirteen to the mountains of Tennessee, where he spent much of his time with the Cherokee Indians, by whom he had for some reason been adopted. During the War of 1812 he served as a sergeant in the American army and was gravely wounded at the Battle of Horseshoe Bend on the Tallapoosa River in Alabama, where Andrew Jackson defeated the Creek Nation and forced them to cede two-thirds of their territory to the United States. Houston's twenty-fifth birthday found him studying law back in Tennessee. Soon thereafter he was admitted to the bar and settled down to open a law practice in the town of Lebanon. He was elected to Congress in 1823, reelected in 1825, and in 1827 became the governor of Tennessee.

Then things took a turn for the worse. Houston's wife, Eliza Allen, suddenly left him in 1829 and he abruptly resigned the governorship, leaving Tennessee for Oklahoma, where he rejoined the Cherokee and commenced a secondary, though earnest, relationship with the bottle. Eventually he wandered down through Arkansas to Texas. He was elected to the Convention of 1833 as the delegate from Nacogdoches. A strong supporter of the resolution for sovereignty, he was also a member of the 1836 convention that declared Texas independent of Mexico and was elected by that congress as commander-in-chief of the revolutionary troops.

Initially, being commander of the Texas militia was unrewarding and disagreeable. Things did not go well at the Alamo (183 defenders dead); they went even worse at Goliad (371 captured and shot). Houston suffered a rasher of reproach for backpedaling from Santa Anna's superior army, but at last redeemed himself at the San Jacinto River, when he maneuvered the Mexicans into an inescapable position and attacked them from two sides, killing about 630, taking another 730 prisoner, and capturing Santa Anna himself. Santa Anna had no choice but to surrender, and Houston secured Texas its independence. He was elected president of the republic that year—a resurgent political career that would endure until 1861, when, after the people of Texas had voted to secede from the Union, he refused to join the Confederacy and was removed from the office of governor. He died two years later and is buried at Huntsville, where his monument is only slightly less impressive than the state's notorious penitentiary.

Sam Houston, Stephen Seymour Thomas

Surrender of Santa Anna, William Henry Huddle

This splitting up of Santa Anna's army was a serious mistake. Although the Texans were frantically retreating, they were at the same time welding together a considerable resistance force under the command of Sam Houston—a force that numbered about nine hundred men by the time it stopped fleeing and took a stand at the San Jacinto River.

Houston surprised Santa Anna, whose disdain for his adversary was catastrophically misplaced, and whose subdivided regiment left him with only a few hundred more soldiers than he faced in opposition. He would have the dubious honor of watching 630 of them slaughtered to the tune of "Remember the Alamo" before surrendering the remaining 730 and signing a treaty that preserved his hide. But as part of the bargain, the treaty granted Texas its independence.

Santa Anna's defeat plunged his political career straight into the toilet for a number of years, and although the government that replaced his denounced his San Jacinto treaty as an invalid document signed under duress, Mexico never again was able to exert influence or authority over the newly declared Republic of Texas. Oddly enough, it would be almost a decade before the United States would fully accept the territory into the Union and grant it statehood. Sectional differences confounded the argument in Congress for a number of years, with many Northerners fearing the addition of such a large slave-holding state, particularly one made up of feisty freebooters and frontiersmen, but in the end a joint resolution favoring annexation was passed by both houses, and signed into law on March 1, 1845, by President John Tyler.

Unlike Texas, ownership of Oregon country had always been an ambiguous matter, with four nations proclaiming sovereignty at the beginning of the nineteenth century—Spain, Russia, England, and the United States. Spain bowed out in 1819 when the United States agreed to the establishment of the northern boundary of California along the forty-second parallel, and Russia withdrew in the aftermath of treaties in 1824 and 1825, with both England and the United States ceding claim to any lands lying below 54° 40′ north latitude. That left

In William Henry Huddle's rendition of Santa Anna's surrender after the battle of San Jacinto, left, Sam Houston lies wounded in the ankle surrounded by his army of rebel frontiersmen. He greets the conquered Mexican dictator, who had been captured a day after the battle wearing a corporal's uniform, evidently for disguise. Santa Anna hurriedly signed papers ordering all Mexican troops to withdraw south of the Rio Grande. In the subsequent Treaty of Velasco, Santa Anna accepted Texan independence.

Sam Houston

The Santa Fe Trail, right, rattled its way across eight hundred miles of deserts, plains, and mountains from the Missouri settlements to the Spanish capital of New Mexico. It was pioneered by Indian trader William Becknell, who drove a mule train to Santa Fe in the autumn of 1821. Until then, the Spanish government had forbidden entry by foreigners to the frontier regions. Mexican independence changed that policy, but the journey remained a hard one until 1878 when the railroad reached Santa Fe.

the British and the Americans, and actually the only turf in dispute between these two countries was a triangular area bordered on the north by the forty-ninth parallel (the Canadian boundary) and on the south by the Columbia River. The United States had always been willing to accept the former as its northern boundary, and England was only interested in ownership of the Columbia because it believed that control of the river dictated control over the northwest fur trade all the way back to the Rocky Mountains.

Claims of ownership rested, in part, on discovery. The British offered up (by sea) Captain James Cook in 1778 and Captain George Vancouver in 1792 and (by land) Alexander Mackenzie, who crossed the Canadian Rockies from Lake Athabasca, Saskatchewan, to Bella Coola on the Pacific in 1793. The American claim countered with Captain Robert Gray in 1788 and again in 1791, and Lewis and Clark in 1805–6. Possession also depended greatly on settlement—of Astoria, the outpost established by John Jacob Astor's Pacific Fur Company in 1812 and sold to the British North West Company in 1813, and Fort Vancouver, built by the British Hudson's Bay/North West Company in 1825.

The truth is that all these claims were largely academic; citizens of both nations operated under an agreement of

The Pioneers, H. D. Bugbee

joint occupation. Both trapped, traded, settled, and farmed almost entirely without conflict. If the Hudson's Bay Company, with its series of posts from Fort Vancouver north into Canada, existed as a kind of de facto occupational force in the region, it was a most benign force that offered unselfish and bountiful assistance to early settlers of both nationalities, a kindness that was accepted without any corresponding gratitude on the part of many American pioneers, particularly those of the missionary persuasion.

Compared to the windblown, cactus-studded aridity of the mountainous interior, the West Coast was a stunningly rich and well-watered paradise. Together, the Sierra and the Cascades capture moisture moving in from the Pacific and cast a great rain shadow over lands to the east. The Pacific Ocean also moderates temperatures, resulting in ideal growing conditions. The redwoods of northern California, left, are not only the tallest trees in the world, they are symbols for the vast natural wealth the region offered.

Missionary activity began in Oregon country in the aftermath of the arrival in St. Louis during October 1831 of four northwest Indians. Three Nez Percés and one Flathead had traveled east from the Rocky Mountains with a group of returning fur traders primarily to see what the land of the white folks looked like. They had no apparent motive other than inquisitiveness, though like the mythical cat their curiosity turned out to be ill-fated. Two of them took sick and died in Missouri; the other two expired on their way back to Oregon country. But a young Wyandot Indian named William Walker, a Christian who had heard about but had never actually encountered these Indians, wrote an utterly fabricated account of the motives for their journey to a Wyandot agent in Ohio named G. P. Disosway, claiming they had come on a pilgrimage in search of religious enlightenment. They wanted to obtain a copy of the white man's "Book of Heaven," he said, and were desperate for conversion.

It is not known what motivated Mr. Walker. His anecdote was complete nonsense, as was the preposterous illustration he provided demonstrating how the Flatheads tie a board to their children's heads at birth in order to deform their skulls. (They don't, and their heads aren't flat.) Disosway, however, was sufficiently moved to send Walker's letter to the Methodist *Christian Advocate and Journal*, and its subsequent publication in that periodical so stimulated the faithful that within a year the first servants of the Lord made their appearance at Fort Vancouver ready to undertake the next "great awakening." Wisely, they chose the fertile and mild climate of the Willamette Valley as the best place to set up shop. But they soon lost interest in the few wretched Indians they found who had not already been eliminated by white man's diseases,

Despite Whitman's comment, the Columbia River valley was a densely populated region long before the arrival of white settlers. During the annual salmon runs, Native Americans gathered at traditional fishing grounds, right. In a matter of weeks, they could catch and dry a large portion of their annual food needs. This left ample time for other pursuits, including trade, art, horse-breeding, the acquisition of wealth, and development of ritual. The first Europeans to enter the area, including Lewis and Clark, were relatively impoverished in comparison.

deeming them "stupid, melancholy, and . . . doomed." For solace they turned their attention to more mundane matters like agricultural production and colonization.

In 1837 the Methodist Board of Missions sent twenty additional evangelists to help out in Oregon, and in 1840 a group of nearly fifty souls known as "the great re-enforcement" set forth, among them teachers, mechanics, farmers, and a physician. Again settlement proved more important to these people than their religious work. This was a good thing, since their longed-for converts seemed to turn their Protestant stomachs, and the Indians' sentiment toward such nose-averted proselytizing as they did receive graduated from stupor to coolness to outright hostility. As the wife of one Reverend Cushing Eells sourly observed, "we have been here almost nine years and have not yet been permitted to hear the cries of one penitent or the songs of one redeemed soul." Small wonder.

The first missionaries may have made few converts among the Indians, but the same cannot be said of their influence on the folks back home. A flood of come-all-ye propaganda, plus news of their success with both agricultural and cattle-raising ventures in the Willamette Valley, caused a widespread infection called "Oregon fever" throughout the United States, particularly along the Mississippi Valley, where there had been a prolonged period of hard times and depressed farm prices. As a consequence, in the spring of 1843 there began what has since been called "the great migration," an assemblage of people from all parts of the Midwest, men and women of all ages from Kentucky, Tennessee, Ohio, Illinois, Missouri, and Indiana. "The destiny of the American people is to subdue the continent," fulminated the inveterate booster

"The Indians have in no case obeyed the command to multiply and replenish the earth, and they cannot stand in the way of others doing so."—Marcus Whitman, 1844

Salmon Fishing at Kettle Falls, artist unknown

Emigrants Entering Oregon, artist unknown

Wagon-borne white settlers made deep impressions on the land, carving their names at places like Oklahoma's Inscription Rock, right, and leaving tracks of iron-rimmed wheels throughout the West, below. In a typically romantic painting, previous page, emigrants enter the paradise of Oregon. With the snowy mountains behind them, along with all the difficulties of a long journey, they emerge to claim their just reward. Even the Indians, watching curiously and quietly on fine horses, seem to approve their arrival.

William Gilpin, "to rush over this vast field to the Pacific Ocean . . . to change darkness into light and confirm the destiny of the human race. . . Divine task! Immortal mission."[6] The emigrants set out a thousand strong from Independence, Missouri, on the twenty-second of May in 120 wagons, accompanied by over five thousand cattle and oxen, and arrived more or less without catastrophic incident in the Willamette Valley in late November, six months later. The following year another fifteen hundred made the journey; the year after that, three thousand.

By 1845 there were nearly six thousand Americans in Oregon country, most of them settled south of the Columbia River. The Hudson's Bay Company was still fully in control of the region above the forty-second parallel, but as the number of emigrants grew, so grew the concerns of the English. Their new neighbors seemed on the whole an aggressive and unruly lot, and the danger that they might begin to leak into British territory north of the Columbia was real—so real, in fact, that the Hudson's Bay Company (often derisively referred to by the American rabble as the HBC, or "Here Before Christ") decided to abandon Fort Vancouver and move its headquarters to Fort Victoria on Vancouver Island. The beaver had been nearly wiped out along the Columbia and there was less reason to argue, less impulse to defend territory that was no longer of serious economic interest.

In short, when Britain's de facto occupational force evacuated the very sod that the two countries had been disputing for over half a century, there wasn't much left to quibble about. And since possession is nine-tenths of the law, it was but a short diplomatic hop to settle the U.S./Canadian boundary at the forty-ninth parallel—a demarcation to which the Americans had always been willing to agree, and an obvious extension of the border east of the Continental Divide. The treaty confirming these terms was signed by the United States and England in June of 1846, and while it would take two years of homeland bickering between the pro- and anti-slavery forces in Washington, a bill was finally passed in 1848 officially creating the Oregon Territory.

The annexation of Oregon was similar to that of Texas—traders, followed by filibusters, followed by settlers, followed by federal maneuvers to protect

Miller

Fort Vancouver, owned by the Hudson's Bay Company, was located on the Columbia River about a hundred miles upstream from the coast. Although England gave up its claim to the territory in 1846, the company maintained a commercial presence there until 1860.

and legitimize what had already been acquired by occupational fiat. However tickled the government in Washington may have been by the illegal invasion of its citizens into territory it didn't possess, it was at least covert in its approval of the process of conquest in Texas and Oregon. California presented a slightly different paradigm in this regard, though initially many of the patterns were the same.

Long before there was any formal endeavor to wrest California from Mexican hands—either by purchase or, failing that, by force—Americans had known of its fabulous environment. And they had made themselves a factor in its developing economy, initially through a busy shipping traffic in sea-otter furs and whaling, and thereafter in the purchasing of hides and tallow. This latter commerce took agents of the New England merchants underwriting western trade far from the coast and deep into the interior, where the astonishing fertility, magnificent climate, and abundant resources of the region were not lost upon them.

Until 1826, American invasions into California had emanated entirely from the west— that is to say, from the sea. Jedediah Smith led the first overland expedition south from the Wasatch Mountains in Utah

to the Mohave settlements near present-day Needles, and then straight across the desert to the San Gabriel Mission east of Los Angeles. He repeated the journey in 1827, following essentially the same route he had taken the year before, though with far more disastrous consequences than the mere annoyance he had created among the Mexican authorities for his initial trespass. For reasons that have never been adequately explained, the Mohave Indians, who had played genial host to Smith's party the year before, had an "insidious change of heart." After three days of apparent hospitality, they suddenly butchered ten of his men in what seemed to be an unprovoked, surprise attack. Nine men escaped, including Smith, and eventually made it across the desert and up the San Joaquin Valley to their old camp on the Stanislaus. But bad luck followed. In a dispute over a stolen ax, five more were killed by Umpqua Indians in Oregon on their return journey to the Rocky Mountains.

Overland penetration, however, had been made. Smith's second expedition was followed in 1828 by another party of fur hunters led by Sylvester Pattie and his son, James Ohio. The Patties came into California from the southwest, blazing a route from Santa Fe to the

THE MORMONS

We have been hunting during the past twenty-six years for a place where we could raise Saints, not merely wheat, and corn. . . .

—BRIGHAM YOUNG, 1856

From the time of Joseph Smith's first visions near Palmyra, New York, when the angel Moroni appeared and revealed the location of the golden tablets upon which were written the Book of Mormon, to the arrival of Brigham Young's Pioneer Company in the Valley of the Great Salt Lake, the Church of Jesus Christ of Latter-day Saints was a faith on the move. For seventeen years the Mormons endured escalating persecution by their neighbors—first in Kirtland, Ohio; then in Independence, Missouri; next in Far West, Missouri; and finally in Nauvoo, Illinois. The same violence that drove them from one midwestern town to another intensified until it culminated in the murder of Smith and his brother Hyrum, and ultimately forced the Latter-day Saints to flee once and for all into the wilderness. They would establish the Kingdom of God in some isolated part of the West as far away from their oppressors as they could get.

At least in part, what seems to have infuriated the "gentiles" about Mormonism can be found in the etymology of the word *gentiles* itself, which is late Latin for "pagans." No self-respecting Puritan's ancestor was going to sit quietly by and be contemptuously dismissed as a heathen. Moreover, the very genesis of Mormonism (as described by Joseph Smith) conveyed a kind of challenging hubris. At age fourteen, Smith was searching Scripture in an attempt to decide which of the many Christian sects was

Winter Quarters, C. C. A. Christensen

"right," and which church he should join (Baptist, Presbyterian, Methodist, or Shaker), when the Lord and His Beloved Son appeared before him in a vision and told him, in so many words, to join none of the above—they were all an abomination. Shortly thereafter, the angel Moroni surfaced and instructed Smith that he had been singled out to restore the true gospel of Jesus Christ on earth.

As Wallace Stegner gently put it in his book, *The Gathering of Zion*, "A chosen people is probably inspiring for the chosen to live among; it is not so comfortable for outsiders to live with."[7] The very idea of special selection, when the specially selected believe themselves to be the sole possessors of the Lord's truth, is likely, to strike outsiders at best as more than a little smug, at worst as insufferably arrogant. But there were other issues as well. To the Mormons, church and state were conceptually synonymous, not separate, as ordained by the nation's Founding Fathers. Authority and control were imposed by a patriarchal hierarchy in accordance with the revealed will of God, not by the will of the people in democratic referendum; rules of conduct were dictated by divine command, and arrived at through revelation. Indeed, revelation was the justification for the doctrine of plural marriage, a practice that in the pluralistic environment of the Midwest (where the Mormon Church may have been growing but was hung by a political thread) led to the Mormons' final undoing.

If it was an undoing. For those who embraced the faith, suffering and torment were seen as tests of constancy, an expression of worthiness. The exodus from Nauvoo, followed by hard months on the trail and a daily confrontation with exhaustion, hunger, disease, and death, was a willing penitence before absolution. "For every early Saint," Stegner writes, "crossing the plains to Zion in the Valleys of the Mountains was not merely a journey but a rite of passage, the final, devoted, enduring act that brought one into the Kingdom."[8]

This was a different sort of migration than any seen before, one motivated by impulses utterly distinct from those of the explorers, trappers, and gold-seekers who preceded and paralleled it. "These emigrants were convinced that they went not merely to a new country and a new life, but to a new Dispensation, to the literal Kingdom of God on earth."[9] These were not individuals in search of personal attainment, nor disparate families traveling together for the sake of mutual safety. The Mormon migration was a community on the march, an all-for-one and one-for-all social organization that was organized systematically, utterly subjected to rules and order, and almost militaristic in its discipline—and, one should add, the most successful of all the pioneering groups who made the overland journey.

The first Saints left Illinois during the winter of 1846, some 3,285 families with their wagons, animals, and household goods. Crossing Iowa to the Missouri they wintered over at Kanesville, then in April began the journey up the Platte, moving across the plains of Nebraska into Wyoming and reaching Fort Laramie in early June. From Fort Laramie they crossed South Pass to Fort Bridger, then climbed laboriously over the Wasatch Mountains and descended into the Salt Lake basin. An advance party, including an ailing Brigham Young, arrived at the mouth of Emigration Canyon on June 24, 1847, and looking out across the alluvial fan of Emigration Creek at the broad valley nestled between the Oquirrhs and the Wasatch, declared the search for Zion at an end.

There is no reliable record that Brother Brigham ever actually uttered his famous phrase, "this is the place," but it has been suggested that if he didn't, he should have. Because it *was* the place, and over the next twenty-one years (the overland emigration by trail ended in 1868), some 47,000 additional converts, a large portion of them European, would make the arduous journey into the Kingdom. This number included a few thousand who walked the entire way while pushing handcarts that held all their belongings in front of them. For all the Latter-day Saints who kept the faith, it would turn out that the concepts of manifest destiny and millennium were but "variant spellings for the same thing."

Brigham Young

Eagle Creek Falls became a famous beauty spot in Oregon's Columbia River gorge. Scenes like this one defied belief when described to easterners, although many of the same listeners took Zebulon Pike and James Ohio Pattie at their word when they characterized the Spanish-held southwestern plains as a "desert." Eventually, heavy traffic on the Oregon Trail and the Santa Fe Trail revealed the truth about both areas to prospective emigrants.

Santa Catalina Mission below San Diego. There they were immediately taken into custody by the Mexican authorities, who were fed up with American intruders, particularly those who consistently treated Mexican laws and customs with vainglorious disdain—which is to say, every single intruder they had thus far encountered. Sylvester died in jail. James Ohio was released only because of an epidemic of smallpox, or so he claimed in *The Personal Narrative of James O. Pattie, of Kentucky*, a book that historian David Lavender has called a "mishmash of tall tales that were shaped for him by a ghost writer."[10] James Ohio just happened to have (or so he said) a quantity of smallpox vaccine in his possession that he was willing to make available in exchange for his freedom. Somehow he succeeded in treating, he reported, a total of 22,000 people with this inestimable stash.

Word of these expeditions filtered back to the Rocky Mountains, and before long other fur traders were following the routes that had been pioneered by Smith and the Patties and scouting new ones. Joseph Walker led a party across the desert west of Salt Lake to the headwaters of the Humboldt River, then over the Sierra and into the San Joaquin Valley, probably by way of what is now Donner Pass. Ewing Young and William Wolfskill discovered a route from Taos to the Sevier River, and then essentially followed Smith's trail to Cajon Pass and into the Los Angeles basin. This thoroughfare became a regularly traveled

San Francisco, right, began 1848 as a quiet Mexican mission town of about nine hundred souls. Then Mexico ceded California to the United States, and gold was discovered in the Sierra foothills. Within a year, as represented in this 1849 illustration, the flood of gold-seekers pushed the population above 10,000. Eventually the mountain gold ran out, but the city's boom lived on.

Carl Wimar

Missouri-Santa Fe-California trade route known as the Old Spanish Trail, along which American goods moved from St. Louis to the Far West and exotic merchandise from the Orient was transported in reverse to the East.

As was the case in Texas and Oregon, many of the early traders opted to settle down and become permanent California residents. Many of them became Mexican citizens, quickly converting to Catholicism in order to grease the skids on their land grant applications, eligibility for which required both religious and electoral reformation. One such adventurer, John August Sutter, arrived at Monterey in July of 1839 with a portfolio of letters of recommendation, a visionary's spiel, and an exotic foreign accent (he was Swiss). He charmed Governor Juan Bautista Alvarado into an offer of the land grant of his choice, in exchange for which Sutter promised to establish a colony of his countrymen in such a manner and location as to provide a buffer between English and Russian encroachment from the north and American encroachment from the east. He never made good on this promise, in spite of the gift of (ultimately) nearly 150,000 acres on which he planted grain and raised cattle, built a tannery, a mill, and a distillery, and generally comported

SAN FRANCISCO

himself in the manner befitting a feudal lord. In the end, Sutter would transform California more than he or Alvarado could ever have imagined, for it was in the tailrace of his mill on a branch of the American River that one of his employees, James Marshall, discovered gold. That date was January 24, 1848, and within a year the American population in California would increase by one hundred thousand.

Well before this transformation, however, the annexation of Texas by the United States in 1845 had caused Mexico, which had never

recognized the treaty granting Texas its independence, to break diplomatic relations with its northern neighbor. President Polk immediately added insult to injury by proclaiming the border between the two countries to be the Rio Grande instead of the long-accepted Nueces, which lay 150 miles to the north. Polk sent troops to Matamoros at the mouth of the Rio Grande to back up this assertion and blockaded its harbor with a gun ship. During the several skirmishes that ensued along the disputed line of demarcation, a small number of Americans were killed, and that was all Polk needed to send Congress a declaration of war. "Mexico has passed the boundary of the United States, has invaded our territory and shed American blood on American soil," he said, thereby ratifying in one sweeping, disingenuous statement both the unilateral annexation of Texas and the redrawing of its boundary. Congress agreed, and promptly authorized $10 million and fifty thousand soldiers toward the forthcoming war with its southern neighbor.

In the first eight months of 1849, John Sutter's trading post exploded from two cabins to more than three hundred crude canvas shelters. Contrary to the neat scene at left, Sacramento was a squalid but important boomtown located on major travel routes and surrounded by some of the richest agricultural land on the continent. The crumbling Spanish mission at Monterrey, below, was by this time symbolic of the demise of Mexican authority in California.

Political dissension in California had long existed between those Hispanic colonists who favored a federalist system and those who preferred a centralized government located in Mexico City. By 1844 it seemed that the federalists had the upper hand, although it was not clear which of the various power brokers would finally emerge as supreme leader. Into this mix, and with increasing agitation for an assertion of United States sovereignty, came a growing number of Americans. These Americans varied, as Bernard DeVoto observed, "from worthless beachcombers, deserters from the ships, resident horse thieves, and Diana's foresters up to a small, respectable, and potentially valuable company of ranchers, merchants, and traders."[11]

John C. Fremont led what today would be called a full life. A Georgia native expelled from college for "incorrigible negligence," he found his calling as an army officer and explorer, first with Nicollet to the northern plains, then to Oregon, the Rockies, Nevada, and California. Court-martialed, convicted, and pardoned, he left the army and took up exploring western railroad routes. He went on to be a Republican presidential nominee, Civil War general, governor of the Territory of Arizona, writer, promoter, and finally a military pensioner.

And into this mix, as well, came Brevet Captain John Charles Fremont of the United States Corps of Topographical Engineers, making a repeat appearance in California, his first visit having been an unauthorized and nearly disastrous crossing of the Sierra to Sutter's Fort in 1844 to purchase horses before returning to St. Louis from a scouting expedition to Oregon. Considering his point of departure and his announced destination, one might suspect Fremont of having gotten himself lost. Sutter's Fort is not on the most direct route between the Columbia and Mississippi Rivers. But he had Kit Carson as his guide on this zigzag junket, and it is highly unlikely that Mr. Carson was lost, so it is unclear what the brevet captain was really up to.

His second visit, in 1845, is equally shrouded in mystery. It has never even been clear under whose authority Fremont was in California, but there he was, with sixty-eight tough fighting men under his command, requesting permission of Don José Castro, the new military authority, to winter in the San Joaquin Valley. Castro agreed, albeit reluctantly, accepting Fremont's word that he would stay away from the coast. But Fremont promptly broke his word, forsook the San Joaquin Valley, and took up residence a good way to the west of it near San Jose, twenty miles from the coast, whereupon Castro ordered him to leave California. Fremont defied this directive, taking a stand atop Gavilan Peak, where he postured and thundered and flew Old Glory from a pole before deciding, after three days, that his position was not just tactically dubious but legally indefensible.

in the Clerk's Office of the District Court of the Southern District of New York.
COL. FREMONT
THE AMERICAN STANDARD ON THE ROCKY MOUNTAINS.

Christopher "Kit" Carson

Volcanic Mount Shasta, far right, was a familiar landmark for early explorers of northern California. In 1827, Peter Skene Ogden described "a mountain equal in height to Mount Hood or Vancouver." He called it Mt. Sastise, after a local Indian tribe, providing the first written record of the name.

With pompous dignity, he moved out and headed for Oregon, quite possibly starting a rumor on his way that Castro was about to expel *all* American settlers from California.

Alas, Oregon was not on Fremont's itinerary for long. At Klamath Lake, Archibald Gillespie of the United States Marines intercepted him with a packet of letters, the contents of which have never been revealed, prompting Fremont to turn around and head back. Whether he was ordered to do so by the government in Washington or, in the words of one historian, "saw in the situation an opportunity to make John Charles Fremont the Sam Houston of California," he wound up aiding and abetting, if not instigating, what was, by any standard of measurement, a pipsqueak revolution on the part of a few American settlers around Sacramento that became known as the Bear Flag Revolt.

On June 14, 1846, the Bear Flaggers, anxious over expulsion rumors perhaps originated by Fremont, stormed the alleged fort of a longtime American sympathizer, General Mariano Vallejo, and commandeered his horse herd. There were no soldiers to overwhelm at this "fort." It was, in fact, Vallejo's house, and he was soundly asleep. Awakened and informed that he was a prisoner of war, he kindly offered brandy all around and attempted to ascertain what war he was a prisoner of. Most of the revolutionaries got roaring drunk, but the sanctity of the occasion

"The Californians are an idle, thriftless people, and can make nothing for themselves. The country abounds in grapes, yet they buy, at a great price, bad wine made in Boston. . . ."

—Richard Henry Dana, from *Two Years Before the Mast*, describing California in 1835

The Bear Flag Rebellion of 1846 lasted only a few weeks and accomplished little except to sour relations between Mexican and American residents of California. It was led by John C. Fremont beneath the hastily drawn banner of the California Republic featuring a star and a grizzly bear. The banner was replaced by the Stars and Stripes after the American Navy captured Monterey, but a modified version became the official state flag.

was preserved by a Yankee schoolmaster named William Ide, who made a speech declaring the founding of the California Republic. Another settler named William Todd painted a homemade flag made out of a petticoat—red stripes with a star in the left-hand corner, and what one wag described as a hog standing on its hind legs, though it was meant to be a bear. Vallejo was hustled off and incarcerated at Sutter's Fort, which Fremont, with absolutely no authority to do so, had seized in the name of the United States.

There is more to this comic horse opera, but all of it is as absurd as its opening act. The real action, unknown to the Bear Flaggers, whose republic would last barely a month, was occurring far to the south, where the United States was already at war with Mexico over the southern border of Texas. Word of the armed conflict at Matamoros reached the commodore of the Pacific Fleet, John Sloat, in June. By early July, Sloat had sailed under orders into the harbor at Monterey, which was the capital of Alta California. Without opposition, Sloat declared California to be a possession of the United States. Two days later Commander John Montgomery seized San Francisco. After two more days a naval party took Sutter's Fort. Down came the Bear Flag, up went the Stars and Stripes. California, for all intents and purposes, belonged to the United States.

The *Californios*, initially not inclined or equipped to resist, were eventually provoked by the repressive occupation of Sloat's replacement, Commodore Robert Stockton, and his newfound ally, J. C. Fremont, chairperson of the newly defunct California Republic. They managed to maintain control of Los Angeles for more than three months before eventually surrendering to General Stephen Kearny on January 10, 1847. The engagement in California was over. A little over a year later, the real Mexican War ended with the signing of the Treaty of Guadalupe Hidalgo, the terms of which

John C. Fremont

recognized Texas as a U.S. possession and ceded California, along with the rest of the Southwest, in exchange for $15 million and the assumption of all American claims against Mexico. The Gadsden Purchase in 1854 of some additional thirty thousand square miles south of the Gila River in Arizona and New Mexico would complete the map of what is now the continental United States of America. And the discovery of gold would populate it.

THE TOWERING PRIZES

From the Chisos Mountains along the Rio Grande, right, to the northern plains of Montana; from the Mississippi across the Rockies to the Sierra and the Cascades, following page, and on to the Pacific, all the land was American. Yet it would take many years for the nation to understand what had been won. In 1854, Yellowstone was still a blank spot on the map. Yosemite was an obscure valley. The Colorado River through the Grand Canyon, inset, had yet to be run, and vast sections of the interior remained uncharted.

The exploration of America was not all military and commercial conquest. Scientists, photographers, painters, and poets marveled at the natural scene and inspired the nation with their work. Among the most influential was John Muir, a Scottish immigrant who lost his heart to California's Sierra Mountains, left, which he called the "Range of Light, the most divinely beautiful of all the mountain-chains I have ever seen."

"Your laws extend not into our country, nor ever did. You talk of the law of nature

and the law of nations, and they are both against you."

Watching the Wagons, Frank McCarthy

CHILDREN OF ONE GOD

[1825–1899]

Native Resistance

*Y*ou say: Why do not the Indians till the ground and live as we do? May we not, with equal propriety, ask, Why the white people do not hunt and live as we do? You . . . think it no injustice to warn us not to kill our deer and other game from the mere love of waste; but it is very criminal in our young men if they chance to kill a cow or a hog for their sustenance when they happen to be in your lands. We wish, however, to be at peace with you, and to do as we would be done by. We do not quarrel with you for killing an occasional buffalo, bear or deer on our lands when you need one to eat; but . . . your people hunt to gain a livelihood by it; they kill all our game; our young men resent the injury, and it is followed by bloodshed and war.

This is not a mere affected injury, it is a grievance which we equitably complain of and it demands a permanent redress.

The great God of Nature has placed us in different situations. It is true that he has endowed you with many superior advantages; but he has not created us to be your slaves. We are a separate people! He has given each their lands, under distinct considerations and circumstances; he has stocked yours with cows, ours with buffalo; yours with hog, ours with bear; yours with sheep, ours with deer. He has, indeed, given you an advantage in this, that your cattle are tame and domestic while ours are wild and demand not only a larger space for range, but art to hunt and kill them; they are, nevertheless, as much our property as other animals are yours, and ought not to be taken away without our consent, or for something equivalent.[1]

—CORN TASSEL, CHEROKEE ELDER

IT IS DIFFICULT to know how much, if any, of this speech by the Cherokee elder *Onitositah* (Corn Tassel) was fully digested by the United States commissioners who came in 1785 to sign yet another "peace treaty" with his tribe. Among other things, *Onitositah* was insisting that his audience accept and respect the irreconcilable differences between Indian and Anglo ways of life, but many postrevolution Euro-burghers believed in the inevitable and "humanitarian" assimilation of native tribes into the white culture and agreed with Thomas Jefferson that this social transformation would occur through "a coincidence of interests . . . between those who have lands to spare, and want other necessaries, and those who have such necessaries to spare, and want lands."

History owes much to the Swiss artist Karl Bodmer, who in 1833 traveled up the Missouri River as far as Fort Mackenzie, in Blackfoot territory on the northwest Montana plains. His portraits of Native Americans and illustrations of life on the plains provide an invaluable historic record of conditions before conquest. This painting, far right, shows an encampment of the Piegan, one of three tribes in the Blackfoot Confederacy.

The Indians, as it was commonly understood then, were "primitives." They had no written language; they were pagans; they believed the land to be communal property and exploited it only for hunting (in other words, wasted its resources), rather than putting it to its true and proper use, agricultural cultivation. Inasmuch as it was the inexorable nature of humankind to gravitate from savagery to enlightenment, it was considered entirely justifiable, even benevolent, for the civilized to liberate the barbaric from the prison of their own nescience. If, in the process of transforming hunters and gatherers into subsistence farmers, thousands of acres of land became "surplus," and thereby freed up for white settlement, well, what a serendipitous paradox! If the Indian resisted what was clearly in his best interest, well, sometimes it was necessary to kill the savage in order to civilize him. The consequences were, sadly, of his own making.

Encampment of the Piegan Indians, after Karl Bodmer

CBodmer.

Of course most frontiersmen, unlike their Jeffersonian counterparts, were scarcely burdened by these philosophical antilogs. They regarded the Indians as little more than noxious impediments to expansion and wanted them wiped off the face of the earth as quickly as possible, no hand wringing about it—or at the very least removed to its geographical equivalent, the trans-Mississippi West. Their animosity toward the native tribes was almost as profound as their displeasure with a newly formed government that seemed in its nonsensical "expansion with honor" rhetoric to suggest the same restraints on freedom they had long suffered under British rule. They weren't going to be restrained any longer. They were on the move, and they were hungry for land.

Bodmer's portrait of the Piegan chief Mehskehme-Sukahs *(Iron Shirt), far left, reflects the pride of a nation at the peak of its power. The Blackfeet—well mounted and equipped with trade goods from British posts in Canada—ruled the northern plains along the base of the Rocky Mountains. Bodmer visited before the devastating 1837 smallpox epidemic.*

And so in Georgia, where Corn Tassel had delivered his pointed rejoinder to the 1785 treaty commission, this combination of pioneer recalcitrance and a federal awareness that settlers could not be controlled, plus a growing insistence on state's rights, led to the gradual extraction of five southeastern tribes—the Creeks, Choctaws, Chickasaws, Seminoles, and Cherokees—and culminated in the infamous Indian Removal Act of 1830. Over the following nine years the remnants of the five "civilized tribes" were dislodged by treaty, fraud, coercion, and, finally, force from their territories and relocated far west of the Mississippi in present-day

"A few years more, and white men will be all around you. They have their eyes on this land. My son, never forget my dying words. This country holds your father's body. Never sell the bones of your father and your mother." —TUEKAKAS (CHIEF JOSEPH'S FATHER), 1871

Oklahoma. It was the only humane thing to do, argued President Jackson: "Can it be cruel in the Government, when, by events which it cannot control, the Indian is made discontented in his ancient home—to purchase his lands, to give him a new and extensive territory, to pay the expense of his removal, and support him a year in his new abode[?] How many thousands of our own people would gladly embrace the opportunity of removing to the West on such conditions?"[2]

It is a rhetorical question—the answer to which is *none*. How many of Mr. Jackson's "own people" would have joined with the Choctaw, whom Alexis de Tocqueville had observed crossing the Mississippi River in the winter of 1831, "among them the wounded, the sick,

newborn babies, and old men on the point of death. They had neither tents nor wagons, but only some provisions and weapons. I saw them embark to cross the great river, and the sight will never fade from my memory."[3] Or with the Creeks, driven from their homes by white settlers before they could even prepare for their bitterly accepted expulsion. Marched west in 1836 by the army, some of them in manacles, they lost an estimated 45 percent of their population in the process of migration.

Or with the Cherokee. The Cherokee, described as the most "civilized" of the "civilized tribes," resisted removal (thereby giving lie to the humanists' argument that assimilation would be the natural consequence of cultural refinement) and contested the State of Georgia's authority

Four Bodmer portraits offer a sample of prairie dress and appearance. Pictured from left to right are Loch-Kiaiu *(Distant Bear), of the Piegan tribe; a Shoshonean woman, name unknown;* Makuie-Poka *(Child of the Wolf), a Piegan; and* Mandeh-Panchu, *a Mandan. The Piegans were prairie nomads who followed the buffalo herds and diligently guarded their land from encroachment by outsiders. The Shoshones were mountain people, in part because they lacked the weaponry to take on their fierce Blackfoot neighbors. The Mandan lived a more settled life based in earth-lodge villages along the Missouri River. They hunted buffalo on horseback but also grew crops.*

During the winter of 1838–39, the Cherokee, right, were forced to abandon the southern Appalachians and move across the Mississippi. Thirteen thousand began the journey; some four thousand died along the way. Although they had adopted many aspects of white culture—not only wagons, but a written language and a republican constitution—they were unable to evade wholesale exile.

The Trail of Tears, Robert Lindneux

over them in the U.S. Supreme Court, where they won. But Georgia, backed by an intractable President Jackson, ignored the court and continued to encourage the theft of the Cherokee's land, livestock, and homes. Eventually a small minority, persuaded that they had no choice but to relocate, entered into secret negotiations with the state, and a treaty was signed and ratified by one vote in Congress. Still, the majority of the Cherokee continued to resist, appealing to the government for a nullification of what they insisted was a fraudulent agreement and enduring a ferocious persecution at the hands of white settlers while they awaited redress.

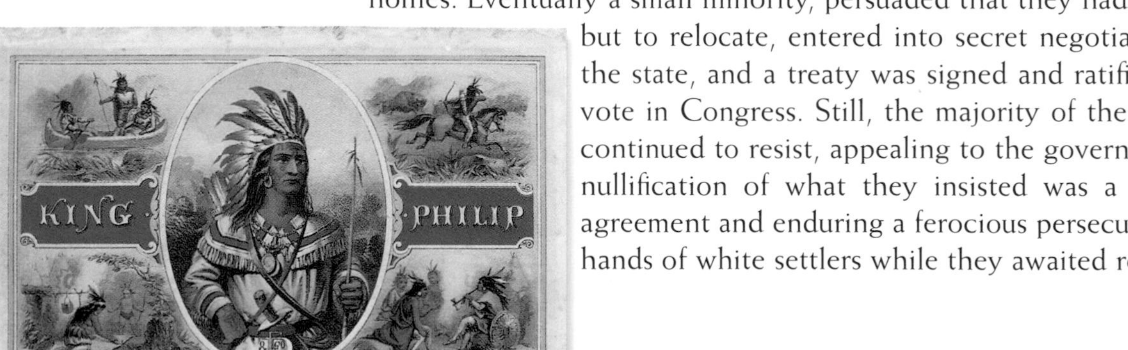

Redress came in the form of seven thousand troops under the command of General Winfield Scott, who rounded the Cherokee up, imprisoned them, and eventually marched them west on a journey that became known as the Trail of Tears (*Nunna daul Tsunyi*, "the trail where we cried"). Like the Choctaw before them, the number of those who perished along the way from sickness, starvation, exposure, and exhaustion was enormous (estimates vary between four and eight thousand), and even President Jackson, one presumes, might not have considered this an opportunity to be embraced. One wonders that it did not inspire in the "savage" heart a greater enthusiasm for bloody reprisal.

THE PRAIRIE

Armed conflicts between Indians and whites during the late eighteenth and nineteenth centuries were most certainly spine-tingling in detail and far more compelling than the "coercive bargaining efforts" made by the whites. The Chivington massacre of the Cheyenne at Sand Creek, the Sioux massacre of Captain Fetterman's troops near Fort Kearny, the annihilation of General Custer and the Seventh Cavalry at the Battle of the Little Bighorn, and the extermination of the Sioux at Wounded Knee all make for better reading (not to mention histrionics) than, say, the Northwest Ordinance of 1787, or the 1823 agreement at Camp Moultrie, Florida, or the Fort Laramie Treaty of 1868. But for all its romantic allure, open warfare was not only less prevalent than our national mythology would have it, it was far less devastating to Native Americans than the 374 bloodless treaties that were negotiated over a period of ninety-three years from 1778 to 1871 (every one of them broken by American citizens)—treaties that ultimately fleeced *all* the tribes of all their lands and their freedom.

There is no better symbol for the cultural differences between white and Native Americans than the buffalo. Indians saw it as a gift of the Creator to be hunted with gratitude and respect. Almost every part of the animal had a practical use. Whites too often slaughtered wastefully, taking only what they could immediately use or sell.

While originally the "treaty" may have been conceptualized to define legitimate alliances for trade and defense between Europeans and Indians, by the middle of the eighteenth century it had become little more than a conscience-salving method for grabbing off real estate that the whites

HUNTING BUFFALO

Often the Indians of the upper Missouri, before they had wide access to the horse and the rifle, used to drive great herds of buffalo over a precipice. As Meriwether Lewis described it in his journal entry of May 29, 1805, the most active and fleet young man of the tribe would put on a buffalo skin with the head and horns still intact and position himself so that when the hunters appeared, he could pop up and run like mad toward a chosen cliff. The startled buffalo would blindly follow, and the decoy would try to time his arrival at the edge of the

cliff precisely, drop into a prescouted crevasse just below the lip, and let the herd thunder over to its death. In this way, the most active and fleet young man became the toast of the tepee, the life of the feast—unless, as sometimes happened, he turned out not to be fleet enough, in which case the thundering herd made a rug out of him.

The Buffalo Hunter, Frederic Remington

Hunting Buffalo, Alfred Jacob Miller

desperately wanted but to which they had no legitimate claim. As the anthropologist Peter Nabokov put it, "treaty making had degenerated into a hollow formality for inexpensively obtaining what would otherwise have required a military expedition to seize, and for conveniently removing Indians to backwater reservations, where once confined, they could be schooled in the ways of white American civilization."[4]

Noted chiefs of the Sioux tribes are pictured in a New York newspaper, far right. Indian leadership was a matter of influence and advice, not command. People would follow a chief as long as they believed in his judgment and skill. A chief had no power beyond what he had earned through the respect of his tribe.

In truth, the treaty was about as abstruse to Native Americans as the concept of ownership of land, and its misleading language and rhetorical allusions to the "Great White Father" and his "children" were, for the most part, indecipherable. When the Sioux and Northern Cheyenne agreed to move to fixed reservations in Dakota Territory in exchange for hunting rights east of the Bighorns and a closing of the Bozeman Road through the Powder River country, the Lakota war leader, Red Cloud, remembered, "In 1868 men came out and brought papers. We could not read them, and they did not tell us truly what was in them . . . When I reached Washington the Great Father explained to me what the treaty was, and showed me that the interpreters had deceived me." Similarly, the Sauk chief Black Hawk, protesting an agreement that ceded tribal lands east of the Mississippi to the United States, said, "I touched the goose quill to the treaty, not knowing, however, that, by that act, I consented to give away my village." And the great Nez Percé leader Chief Joseph, speaking before a full house of Congress in 1879, made ironic reference to his "confusion" in regard to the treaty of 1863 that allegedly conveyed his tribal lands in the Wallowa region:

"We are all the children of one God. The sun, the darkness, the winds are all listening to what we have to say."—Geronimo

NOTED CHIEFS OF THE SIOUX TRIBES.

[FROM PHOTOGRAPHS BY THE PHOTOGRAPHERS OF THE HAYDEN EXPEDITION.]

Chief Joseph

I believe that the old treaty has never been correctly reported. If we ever owned the land we own it still, for we never sold it. In the treaty councils, the commissioners have claimed that our country had been sold to the Government. Suppose a white man should come to me and say, "Joseph, I like your horses, and I want to buy them." I say to him, "No, my horses suit me, I will not sell them." Then he goes to my neighbor, and says to him, "Joseph has some good horses. I want to buy them, but he refuses to sell." My neighbor answers, "Pay me the money, and I will sell you Joseph's horses." The white man returns to me, and says, "Joseph, I have bought your horses, and you must let me have them." If we sold our lands to the Government, this is the way they were bought.[5]

Chief Joseph, known to his people as Hin-mah-too-yah-lat-kekt, *was the charismatic leader of the Wallowa band of the Nez Percé. The attempt to defend their traditional homeland ended in a struggle not for land but for their lives. Joseph earned the respect of his enemies, including General John Gibbon, below, years after his defeat, but he was never allowed to return home.*

Between the very first treaty that the government of the newly formed commonwealth entered into with the Iroquois in 1784 and the Indian Appropriation Act of 1871 declaring an end to tribal sovereignty, the history of covenants between the United States and Native Americans has been one long litany of deception and loss.

A few examples will suffice. At that first treaty, signed at Fort Stanwix, New York, the six Iroquois Nations, in exchange for a permanent peace with the United States, relinquished claims to large areas of western New York, Pennsylvania, and Ohio. The remaining part of Ohio, and a good chunk of Indiana, was ceded in 1795 at the Treaty of Greenville by the remnant Northwest tribes (Shawnee, Potawatomi, Ottawa, Ojibwa, Delaware, and Miami) after they had been decimated by General "Mad" Anthony Wayne at the Battle of Fallen Timbers. The Creeks were likewise forced to surrender some twenty-three million acres of their territory in Georgia and Alabama when they signed a treaty in 1814 after being overwhelmingly defeated by Andrew Jackson at the Battle of Horseshoe Bend. By 1839 all of the southeastern Indian lands had been confiscated through one treaty or another, and the five "civilized tribes" forced to relocate west of the Mississippi River onto land set aside "for as long as the grass shall grow" as Indian Territory. Apparently the grass stopped growing in 1887. As a consequence of the Allotment Act of that year (which dissolved all native tribes as legal entities), "Indian Territory"

John Gibbon

THE INDIAN PONY

Horses first arrived in North America with the Spanish during the sixteenth century. Whether they reached the Southwest with Coronado in 1540 or DeSoto in 1541 will never be known for sure, but what is certain is that many of them escaped, or were abandoned because they were in such bad shape they were no longer useful, and they flourished in the plains environment. The Kiowa in Missouri were mounted as early as 1682, the Comanche by 1714, and the Sarci on the Canadian plains by 1784. By the latter half of the eighteenth century, the horse was dispersed over the entire country.

The impact that a horse culture had on the Plains Indian was to intensify and facilitate a number of traits already inherent in their traditional way of life, which was seminomadic, nonagricultural, often warlike, and primarily dependent on the buffalo for almost everything—food, clothing, lodging. The horse simply enabled them to roam farther and faster; it made them more effective hunters and far more formidable in battle, whether they were fighting among themselves or with the encroaching white man. It may also have ultimately done them in. Equine grazing requirements broke up the social and cultural patterns (and eventually the sense of a common spirit) of bands that had originally lived in assemblies of eight hundred to nine hundred people. Since the average number of horses per person was twelve, and the maximum number of horses the plains grasslands could support in any given place was 250 to 300, people splintered into smaller and smaller groups. As the volume of both people and horses grew, competition for grass, water, game, and winter shelter became intense. Long before Anglo-Americans began crossing the region in significant numbers, high-plains and low-plains tribes fought bitter battles for control of the middle ground. And a new conse-

Roping Wild Ponies, Artist Unknown

quence of reconstructing life as a horse culture became apparent: Mounted Indians could kill one another with far greater efficiency than ever before.

How else to explain an 1855 census of Southern Cheyenne, Arapahoe, and Comanche that showed for every three women there were only two men?

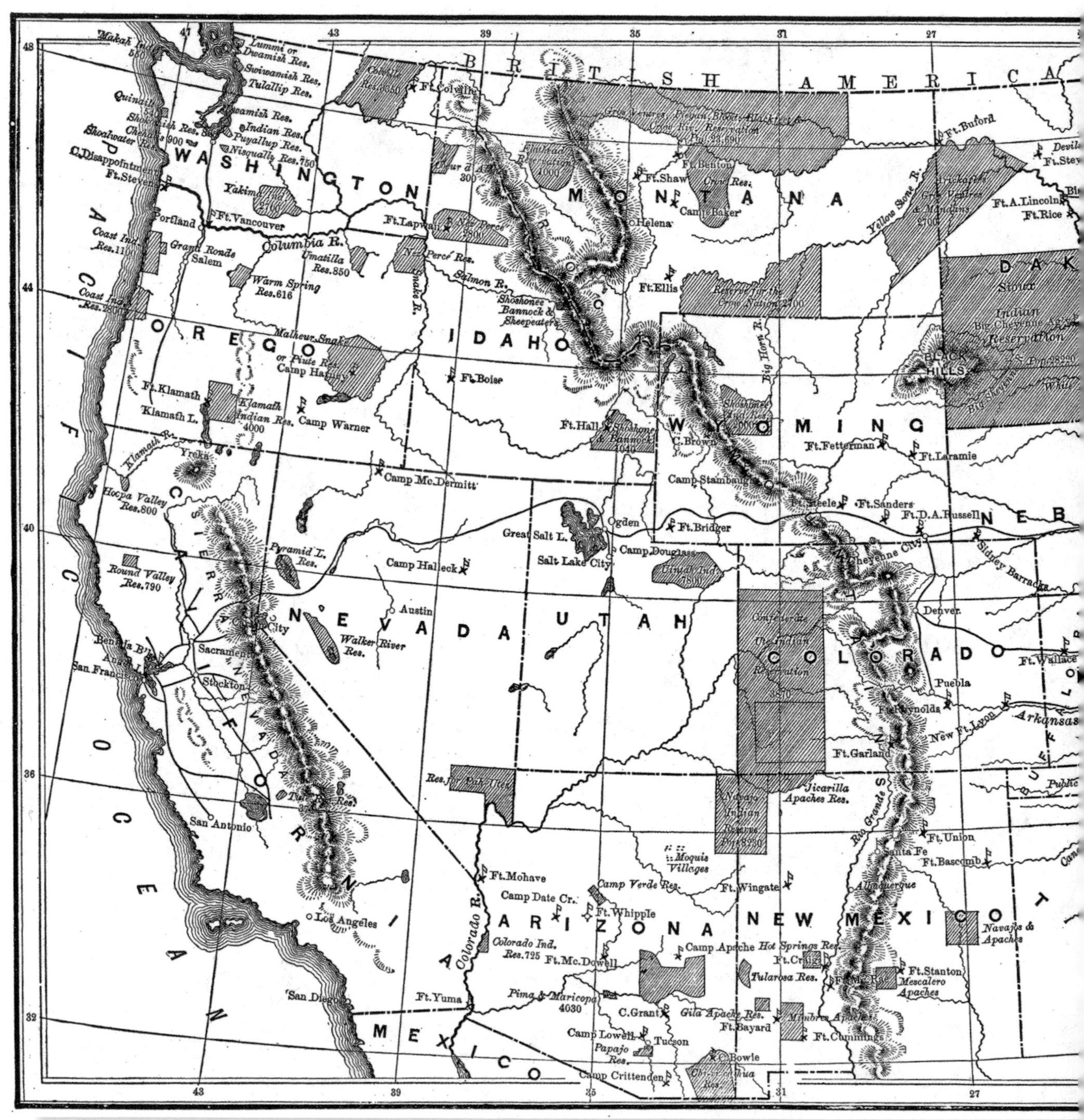
BRITISH AMERICA
PACIFIC OCEAN
WASHINGTON
OREGON
IDAHO
MONTANA
WYOMING
NEVADA
UTAH
COLORADO
CALIFORNIA
ARIZONA
NEW MEXICO
MEXICO
SIERRA NEVADA
Swiwamish Res.
Tulallip Res.
Indian Res.
Puyallup Res.
Nisqually Res. 750
Shoalwater B.
C.Disappointment
Ft.Stevens
Ft.Colville
Yakima Ind.
Portland
Ft.Vancouver
Ft.Lapwai
Columbia R.
Grand Ronde
Salem
Umatilla Res. 850
Warm Spring Res.616
Coast Ind. Res.1100
Coast Ind. Res.2800
Nez Perce Res.
Salmon R.
Snake R.
Shoshonee Bannock & Sheepeaters
Malheur Snake or Piute Res.
Camp Harney
Ft.Boise
Ft.Klamath
Klamath Indian Res. 4000
Klamath L.
Camp Warner
Yreka
Hoopa Valley Res.800
Camp Mc.Dermitt
Pyramid L. Res.
Round Valley Res.790
Camp Halleck
Austin
Carson City
Walker River Res.
Sacramento
San Francisco
Stockton
San Antonio
Los Angeles
San Diego
Ft.Yuma
Ft.Mohave
Camp Date Cr.
Ft.Whipple
Colorado R.
Colorado Ind. Res.725
Ft.Mc.Dowell
Pima & Maricopa 4030
C.Grant
Camp Lowell
Tucson
Papajo Res.
Camp Crittenden
C.Bowle
Camp Verde Res.
Camp Apache
Hot Springs Res.
Tularosa Res.
Gila Apache Res.
Ft.Bayard
Ft.Cummings
Ft.Craig
Ft.Mc.Rae
Ft.Stanton
Mescalero Apaches
Navajos & Apaches
Moquis Villages
Ft.Wingate
Albuquerque
Santa Fe
Ft.Union
Ft.Bascomb
Rio Grande
Jicarilla Apaches Res.
Navajo Indian Reserve
Res. for Pah-Utes
Ft.Garland
Ft.Reynolds
Puebla
New Ft.Lyon
Arkansas
Denver
Ft.Wallace
Cheyenne City
Sidney Barracks
Ft.Sanders
Ft.D.A.Russell
Ft.Steele
Ft.Bridger
Ogden
Great Salt L.
Salt Lake City
Camp Douglass
Camp Stambaugh
C.Brown
Ft.Hall
Ft.Fetterman
Ft.Laramie
Big Horn R.
Ft.Ellis
Helena
Camp Baker
Ft.Shaw
Ft.Benton
Crow Res.
Ft.Buford
Yellow Stone R.
Ft.A.Lincoln
Ft.Rice
Black Hills
Big Cheyenne Ag'y
Sioux Indian Reservation
Confederate Ute Indian Reservation
Reserve for the Crow Nation 2700
48
44
40
36
32
47
43
39
35
31
27

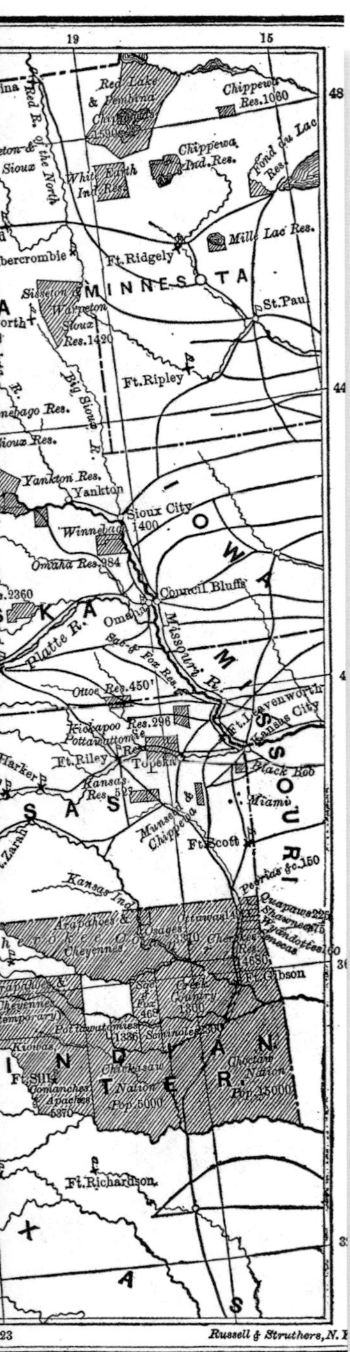

would shortly wind up almost entirely in the hands of eager white homesteaders.

At a treaty-making council in Walla Walla in 1855, and under at least three separate agreements promising economic help, schools, annuities, and permanent reserves, a number of Northwest tribes were coerced into ceding the bulk of their lands in Oregon country. When they realized they were being flimflammed they revolted, and a series of bloody wars broke out that lasted for three years and ended predictably, with the Yakimas, Palouses, Wallawallas, Spokanes, and Coeur d'Alenes being crushed. All but their small remaining reservations were subsequently opened to settlement by Americans.

The Nez Percé, who had remained aloof from these disputes but whose territory on the borders of Oregon, Washington, and Idaho was being steadily overrun by gold miners, were forced, in spite of their peaceful demeanor, to negotiate a new treaty in 1863 confining them to an area one-tenth the size of their original reservation. But the Joseph band under "old" Chief Joseph refused to move, and for fourteen years (during which Joseph died and was replaced by his son) remained precariously in the Wallowa Valley. Finally, in 1877, when the federal government succumbed to pressure from white settlers and gave "young" Joseph thirty days to gather his people and vacate the premises, years of controlled passivity gave way to explosive anger. During a series of attacks on

An 1874 map, far left, indicates major Indian reservations two years before Custer rode into the Little Bighorn valley. Indian lands have been much reduced, and in some cases relocated, since then. In the northern plains, the Sioux would lose the Black Hills and most of the land around them. In the south, Indian Territory (populated by relocated Cherokee and other tribes) would vanish and become Oklahoma.

In 1805, Lewis and Clark marveled at the abundance of game along the upper Missouri River: "We can scarcely cast our eyes in any direction without percieving deer Elk Buffaloe or Antelopes." Karl Bodmer, in 1833, witnessed similar scenes, right. Buffalo, or bison, once ranged clear to the East Coast. In the mid-1700s, they were common in Kentucky. Yet by the time Bodmer painted this view in the Missouri Breaks, wild buffalo had vanished east of the Mississippi.

white homesteaders, at least fifteen white men bit the dust before U.S. troops were dispatched to quell the violence and bring in the perpetrators.

Fleeing toward Canada, where he hoped to find safety for his people, Chief Joseph led four different army units on a twisting 1,700-mile chase through Idaho and Montana, fighting them off during a dozen encounters. With the remnants of his people starving and freezing to death, he finally yielded to Colonel Nelson Miles and General O. O. Howard on October 5, just thirty miles short of the Canadian border. "Hear me, my chiefs!" he said in his famous announcement of surrender, "I am tired; my heart is sick and sad. From where the sun now stands I will fight no more forever." Ignoring his appeal to be returned to the Wallowa, Joseph and his defeated band were sent initially to Oklahoma, then to Colville, a miserable reservation in northeastern Washington, where he died in 1904.

For the Native American peoples living in California, eighty years of Hispanic rule, the mission system, and the same panoply of European diseases that decimated tribes throughout North America had reduced the territory's population by the mid-1840s to less than one-third of its estimated original number. But the discovery of gold in 1848, and the massive influx of newcomers who descended upon the region over the next five years, was a far greater catastrophe than all the bubonic plague, smallpox, cholera, and legions of black-robed friars the hapless natives had ever seen.

Buffalo and Elk on the Upper Missouri, Karl Bodmer

THE GREAT CHIEFS

Cochise [1812–1874] Born in southeastern New Mexico in 1812, Cochise was a Chiricahua Apache who, until 1861, was passably friendly toward Americans and even worked for a time for the Butterfield Overland Stage at its Apache Pass station. His hatred for whites began when he and five other Indians were falsely accused of kidnapping the child of a white rancher near the station and, despite their denials, were seized and arrested. Cochise escaped, but in retaliation six of his people, including several relatives, were hanged. From that moment until he was eventually run down and captured by General George Crook in 1871, he sought revenge through a ferocious campaign of hit-and-run raids across the Southwest—raids that transformed a good many ranches into smoking ruins and a good many cowboys into corpses. After his surrender he was confined to a reservation in New Mexico, from which he again escaped. Finally, when a Chiricahua Reservation was established in southeastern Arizona in the summer of 1872, Cochise turned himself in for the last time, dying there in June of 1874.

Cochise

Geronimo [1829–1909] Considered one of the most dangerous of the Southwest's Indian "predators," Geronimo learned his trade as a young participant in Cochise's band of marauders, and like Cochise eventually became chief of the Chiricahua Apache. When his people were forcibly moved onto a barren reservation at San Carlos in east-central Arizona, Geronimo led a revolt, fled from confinement, and resumed terrorizing settlers along the Arizona/Mexico border. Captured by General Crook in 1886 and returned to the San Carlos Reservation, he fled again, disappearing this time into the mountains of Sonora. Crook caught him for a second time, and Geronimo escaped for a third time—back into Sonora. Finally it was General Nelson Miles's turn. Miles managed to hang on to his captive when he trapped him at Skeleton Canyon in Arizona in 1886 and had him deported to Florida as a prisoner of war. Eventually Geronimo

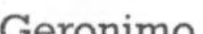

Geronimo

wound up at Fort Sill, Oklahoma, where he repented his sinful ways by becoming a prosperous farmer and converting to the Dutch Reformed Church (which eventually ousted him for habitual gambling). As a sideline, he sold pictures of himself at expositions and fairs.

Crazy Horse
[1849–1877]

Of all the prominent leaders who resisted the Anglo invasion of the Great Plains, Crazy Horse is arguably the most famous. Born into the Oglala tribe in 1849, he was already a prominent young warrior and leader by the time Red Cloud began his three-year dispute over the Bozeman Trail (1865–68) and was a major factor in the obliteration of Captain William J. Fetterman's brigade at Fort Kearny in 1867. Following the 1886 Fort Laramie Treaty that guaranteed the Sioux their ancestral lands in the Dakotas, Crazy Horse continued to fight the encroachment of whites into the Black Hills, and when the federal government finally caved to white pressure and ordered all Lakota bands out of the area, he became one of the chief leaders of the ensuing resistance. In June of 1876 he fought off General Crook's forces at the Battle of the Rosebud, and eight days later joined with Gall and Sitting Bull to annihilate General Custer's troops at the mother of all Indian/Anglo confrontations, the Battle of the Little Bighorn. Forced in May of 1877 to surrender to the superior force of General Nelson Miles, Crazy Horse was stabbed to death by a soldier some four months later while allegedly resisting arrest for leaving the reservation without authorization.

Sitting Bull
[1834–1890]

Like Crazy Horse, Sitting Bull was a Lakota chief and a symbol of defiant resistance to the military powers trying to move the Sioux out of their sacred territory in the Black Hills of Dakota Territory (territory guaranteed them by the Fort Laramie Treaty of 1868). When the commissioner of Indian Affairs declared that all Lakota must be on newly established reservations by January 31, 1876, Sitting Bull, among others, refused. Summoning Lakota, Cheyenne, and Arapaho bands to his camp on Rosebud Creek, he conducted a sun dance during which he had a vision of soldiers falling into his camp from the sky like grasshoppers. The vision is said to have inspired Crazy Horse to attack General Crook on his march up the

Sitting Bull

Rosebud, but the vision's fulfillment seems better realized by Custer, whose petite force of 265 men must have appeared to have just "fallen from the sky"—and right into the waiting arms of 2,500 Sioux and Cheyenne warriors.

After the Battle of the Little Bighorn, Sitting Bull escaped with his band into Canada but, unable to survive in a world where the buffalo no longer roamed, they were forced to surrender four years later. Sitting Bull was initially incarcerated as a prisoner of war at Fort Randall, though he was eventually returned to his tribe at the Standing Rock Reservation. Although an affable and dignified man, he defied reservation rules and regulations and refused to abandon traditional Indian ways. On December 15, 1890, fearing that he might join a newly resurgent Ghost Dance movement, the authorities sent a delegation of Lakota policemen to bring him to the Standing Rock headquarters, and during the ensuing "scuffle" he was shot and killed—murdered, some have claimed, by one of his own people.

Red Cloud [1822–1909] Born near what is now North Platte, Nebraska, to an Oglala Sioux mother and a Brule father, Red Cloud initially rose to prominence among his people for his great bravery in conflicts with other Plains tribes, but it is the three-year war he fought against the United States in an attempt to close the Bozeman Trail for which he is best remembered. The Bozeman Trail (also known as the Bozeman Road) ran east of the Bighorns from the South Platte in Colorado to the goldfields near Bannock, Montana, cutting directly across Lakota tribal lands. In order to protect caravans of miners and settlers, the army built three major forts along the trail and filled them with garrisons of soldiers. Seeing this encroachment as a preamble to the destruction of the Lakota way of life, Red Cloud launched a series of raids that made travel along the trail extremely hazardous and life inside the

Red Cloud

forts highly stressful and exhausting. The annihilation of Captain Fetterman's column of eighty men outside Fort Phil Kearny in December of 1866 helped convince the government that a military solution to the problem was not only unlikely but would come, if at all, at such a cost as to be impractical. They conceded the point, therefore, to Red Cloud. Indeed, the Treaty of Laramie, by which possession of the territory from the Bighorns to the Black Hills was guaranteed to the Lakota Nation, and the forts along the Bozeman Trail were to be abandoned and destroyed, was the only de facto concession of defeat that an Indian tribal leader ever extracted from the U.S. government.

The problem was not simply one of overwhelming numbers, though the figures are alarming enough just by themselves. There were about 200,000 Indians in California in 1848, and about 5,000 whites; within one year the number of whites had increased to between 50,000 and 80,000; in five years they had soared to over 300,000. The really bad news was that a good many of these "Argonauts" harbored such a murderous hatred of Indians that even in the murky annals of sociopathology, one searches helplessly for their motivation and how to account for the wholesale slaughter of thousands of defenseless people who were essentially "friendly" unless provoked, and even when provoked (as they constantly were) so poorly equipped they were hardly a threat.

Burial at Wounded Knee, December, 1890, far right. Black Elk, a Sioux medicine man, recalled in Black Elk Speaks, *"I can still see the butchered women and children lying heaped and scattered all along the crooked gulch. . . . And I can see that something else died there in the bloody mud. . . . A people's dream died there. It was a beautiful dream."*

What madness explains hunting parties riding out several times a week and bagging fifty or sixty Indians at a time, with nothing more at issue than a good day's fun? Or groups of self-appointed "volunteers" setting fire to entire villages and killing everybody who tried to escape—women, children, babies, old men? It was genocide without ideology, politics, theology, or metaphysics, and it was undertaken with such cold-blooded zeal that one might regard the reports as hyperbolic if they weren't so frequent and from such reliable sources, like the renowned historian Hubert Howe Bancroft. Bancroft wrote that while California had not a single respectable Indian war to its credit, it could boast "a hundred or two of as brutal butchering, on the part of our honest miners and brave pioneers, as any area of equal extent in our republic. The poor natives of California had neither the strength nor the intelligence to unite in any formidable numbers; hence, when now and then one of them plucked up courage to defend his wife and little ones . . . sufficient excuse was offered for the miners and settlers to band and shoot down

any Indians they met, old or young, innocent or guilty, friendly or hostile, until their appetite for blood was appeased."[6]

The fact remains that in a matter of two decades, from 1850 to 1870, the native populations in California plummeted from 200,000 souls to about 31,000, and by the end of the nineteenth century to 15,000—whole clan-based societies like the Yuki were systematically slaughtered, until by 1880 there were fewer than 200 of them left, or the Yana, who probably numbered around 3,000at the onset of the gold rush and were essentially exterminated by 1872. (The lone survivor,

Ishi, who was discovered starving and naked in a slaughterhouse in Oroville, California, in August of 1911, died in 1916, bringing a definitive close to the Yana's existence on this earth.) An 1860 edition of the San Francisco *Bulletin*, reporting on a number of appalling massacres around the state, declared: "In the Atlantic and Western States, the Indians have suffered wrongs and cruelties at the hands of the stronger race. But history has no parallel to the recent atrocities perpetrated in California. Even the record of Spanish butcheries in Mexico and Peru has nothing so diabolical." Now that is a serious indictment.

Romantic notions about Native Americans began early and showed up in strange places. Around 1888, Allen & Ginter brand cigarettes were packaged with portraits of "celebrated" Indian chiefs, far right. As with baseball cards, smokers were encouraged to collect all fifty. This poster advertises the collection.

By the beginning of the nineteenth century the Great Plains (the United States from the ninety-eighth parallel to the Rocky Mountains, and from the Saskatchewan River basin to central Texas) had become home to some thirty different tribes from at least six different language groups, ranging from the Blackfoot, Assiniboine, Gros Ventre, Arikara, Crow, Mandan, Lakota, and Dakota in the north, to the Cheyenne, Arapaho, and Pawnee in the center, and the Kiowa, Apache, and Comanche to the south. They had been familiar with the horse for more

"A long time ago my father told me what his father had told him, that there was once a Lakota holy man, called 'Drinks Water,' who dreamed what was to be . . . He dreamed that the four-leggeds were going back to the Earth, and that a strange race would weave a web all around the Lakotas. He said, 'You shall live in square gray houses, in a barren land . . .' Sometimes dreams are wiser than waking." —Black Elk

THE
AMERICAN INDIAN
AUTHENTIC PORTRAITS OF 50 CELEBRATED
INDIAN CHIEFS
PUBLISHED BY
ALLEN & GINTER
RICHMOND
VIRGINIA.
MANUFACTURERS OF
RICHMOND STRAIGHT CUT No. 1
VIRGINIA BRIGHTS
& PET CIGARETTES

Sioux Indians, Seth Eastman

than 120 years and with firearms for nearly as long, and had become supremely proficient with both. By the 1830s, when Anglo-European settlers began to straggle out of the woodlands east of the Mississippi and fix an appraising eye on all that unreal estate to the west, a fully developed, equestrian-based Plains culture had reached its zenith.

It is ironic that Plains Indians, who in the greater context were a very brief phenomenon and whose culture derived in considerable part from a four-legged tool acquired from European invaders, should have become the stereotypic "Indian"—the war-bonneted emblem of noble savagery refusing to adapt to the sweeping tide of (heartless) civilization. As the historian James Wilson observes in his superb book *The Earth Shall Weep*, "It would be difficult, in fact, to find a native group which better exemplified cultural change and adaptation, or one that gave a less accurate image of pre-Columbian America." Nevertheless, Wilson explains:

Because it was the final military conflict in the long struggle for possession of North America, the war for the Plains, when it did come, has attained a unique place in the national mythology of the United States—and, since America so powerfully dominates the global imagination, in the mythology of the world. . . . In popular culture and the popular imagination, it came to represent the ultimate, archetypal encounter between the timeless, unchanging, elemental Savage and the dynamic, thrusting European. It was the defeat of the Plains tribes that seemed to consign the Indian irreversibly to history and finally put the stamp of "civilization" on the entire continent.[7]

The Plains tribes were not so easy to defeat as their horseless eastern and far western counterparts had been, but initially those Indians encountered by Lewis and Clark, and by the fur trappers who followed in their wake, were mostly friendly, eager to trade, and willing to share territory. They paid a huge price for their benevolence—first as a consequence of their susceptibility to European diseases, and second through their inability to imagine the magnitude of their adversary's perfidy and faithlessness, and the ferocity of his greed.

The group of tribes called "Sioux" was defined more by language than by cultural similarities. The Yankton and Santee, who lived in the woodlands of Minnesota and Iowa, used canoes on the area's many waterways. Their linguistic relatives, the Lakota, were the quintessential horse nomads usually associated with the name Sioux.

THE EMIGRANT INVASION

A few years more, and white men will be all around you. They have their eyes on this land. My son, never forget my dying words. This country holds your father's body. Never sell the bones of your father and your mother.

—Tuekakas (Chief Joseph's father), 1871

Years before the flood of emigrants began to move westward across Indian lands, their diseases had arrived to wreak havoc on the tribes of the Great Plains. Smallpox emerged on the upper Missouri in 1837 and ravaged the Blackfeet, Mandan, and Assiniboine, wiping out entire clans in a single season. In the early nineteenth century, the Pawnee, farther south, had numbered about ten thousand. Smallpox and cholera flared up in Pawnee territory around 1850 and quickly reduced the tribe to a scattered group of about six hundred survivors. Even the tribes who had had time to recover from the direct effects of the epidemic were able to do little about the onslaught of huge numbers of well-armed trespassers. All roads west led squarely through Indian lands. Emigrants who weren't settling permanently in these areas were passing through by the thousands, and the tribes coped in the only ways they knew. Some fought for their ancestral hunting grounds, but most, at least initially, tried to trade and otherwise accommodate the newcomers. By the 1870s the wild game was all but annihilated and tribes that had depended on these animals for food and clothing were in a desperate state.

Oregon Trail 1836
California Trail 1840
Bozeman Trail 1864
Mormon Trail 1846
Santa Fe Trail 1821
South Pass 1812

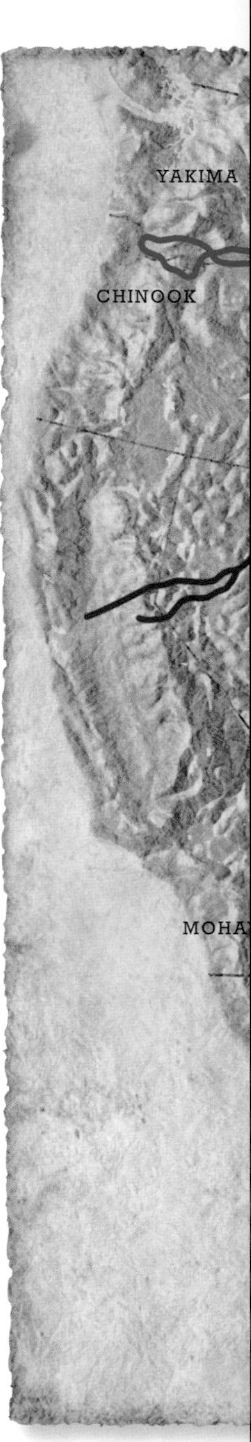

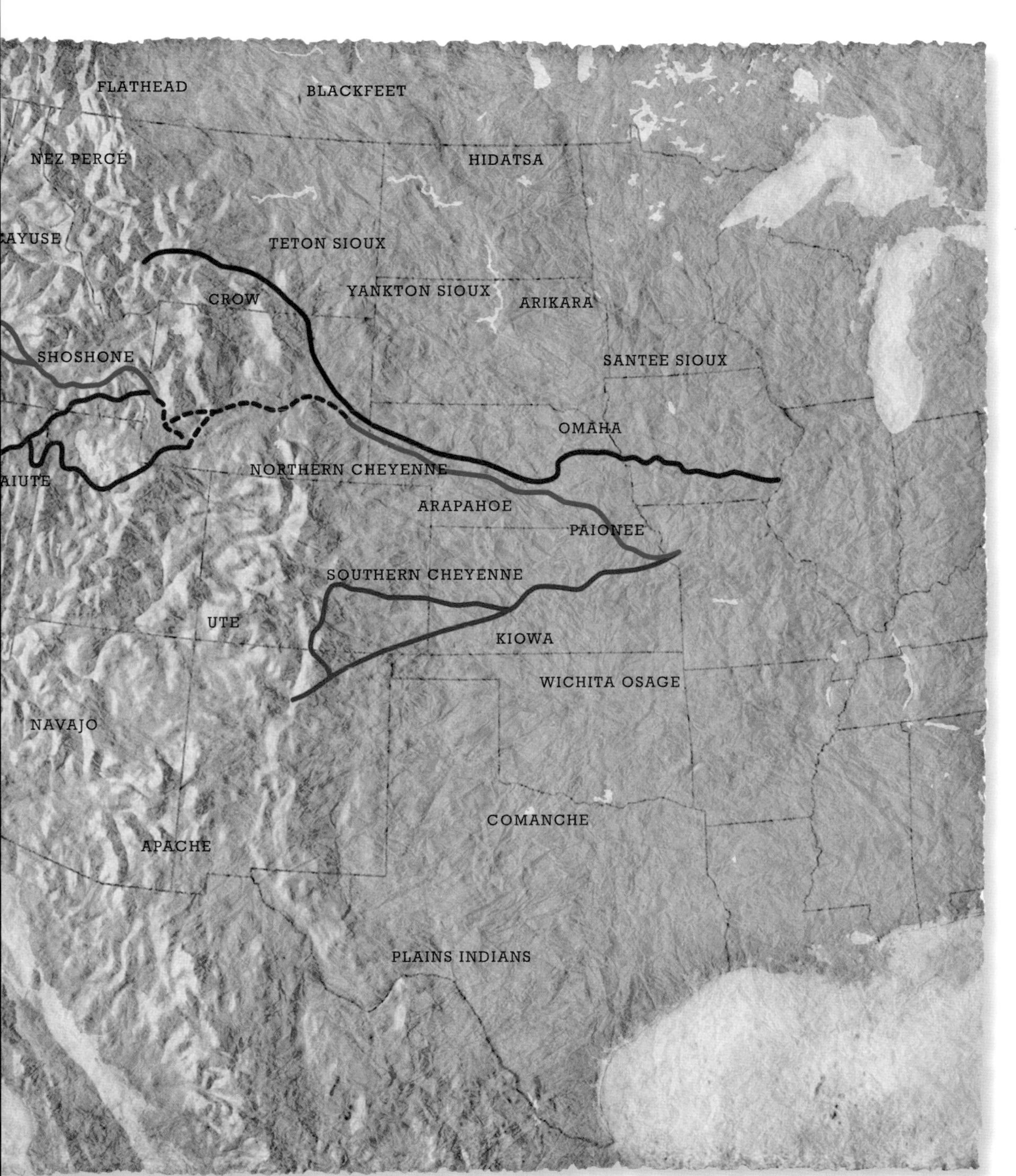
FLATHEAD
BLACKFEET
NEZ PERCÉ
HIDATSA
CAYUSE
TETON SIOUX
CROW
YANKTON SIOUX
ARIKARA
SHOSHONE
SANTEE SIOUX
OMAHA
NORTHERN CHEYENNE
PAIUTE
ARAPAHOE
PAIONEE
SOUTHERN CHEYENNE
UTE
KIOWA
WICHITA OSAGE
NAVAJO
COMANCHE
APACHE
PLAINS INDIANS

An illustration from a contemporary magazine, right, depicts the gruesome aftermath of an 1867 frontier fight. Cheyenne Indians had risen in opposition to construction of the Union Pacific Railroad in western Kansas. Lt. Lyman Kidder, with a patrol of ten soldiers and a Sioux guide, was carrying dispatches when a war party caught them and left their scalped, arrow-riddled bodies on the prairie.

It is hard to say which of these failures was more devastating. Between the beginning of the sixteenth century and the end of the nineteenth, there were approximately one hundred epidemics among Native American peoples, and according to the historical demographer Russell Thornton, "Without doubt the single most important factor in American Indian population decline was an increased death rate due to diseases introduced from the Eastern Hemisphere."[8] During the late 1820s and early 1830s, tribes in the Columbia River basin were all but destroyed by pestilence brought into the region by British and American fur-trapping parties; in 1837 a smallpox epidemic decimated a number of tribes along the Missouri and virtually eradicated the Mandan, among whom fewer than 150 survived; in 1849 smallpox and cholera killed one-fourth of the Pawnee living along the Platte River in Nebraska. These were the kinds of losses, as historian James Wilson points out, that are generally associated with events of overwhelming mass destruction—slate wipers during which a huge percentage of an entire population is suddenly *gone.*

But conquest by pandemic was an unintended consequence of contact between Native American tribes and the Europeans. The intended consequence features a less passive morphology—captivation, domination, subjugation, elimination—all of which, as we have seen, was

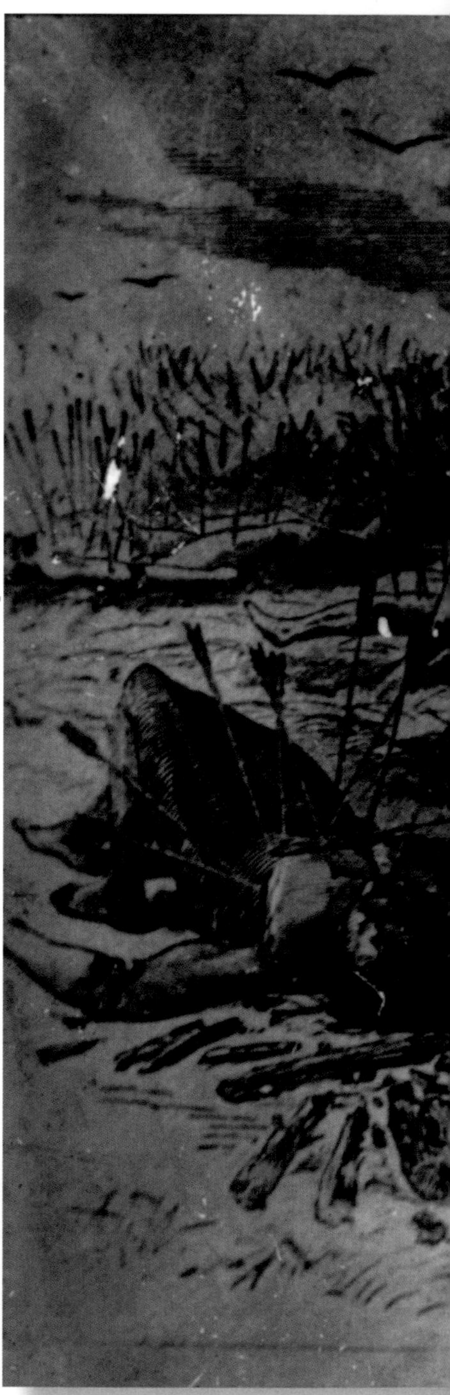

THE DAILY GRAPHIC

AN ILLUSTRATED EVENING NEWSPAPER.

39 & 41 PARK PLACE.

VOL. XI. | All the News. Four Editions Daily. | NEW YORK, WEDNESDAY, JULY 26, 1876. | $12 Per Year in Advance. Single Copies, Five Cents. | NO. 1050.

accomplished through *reductio ad absurdum* treaties, and ultimately, when the subjugated complained or fought back, a display of military might. The experience of the Cheyenne at Sand Creek during the nineteenth century is as good an example of this policy as any.

The influx of one hundred thousand gold miners across the plains and into the Rockies in 1859 created a large number of potential conflicts between Anglos and the northern tribes, particularly the Southern Cheyenne and Arapaho, whose growing irritability with incursions onto their treaty-sanctified lands led federal officials in February of 1861 to "encourage" them to abandon their claims to a large part of Colorado (guaranteed to them in 1851) and to agree to remove to a small reservation between the Arkansas River and Sand Creek in eastern Colorado. Two chiefs, Black Kettle and White Antelope, signed an agreement to this effect drawn up by Governor John Evans of Colorado, but other Cheyenne angrily rejected it and their warriors began a three-year campaign of raiding that affected mining camps, ranches, and stage lines throughout the territory.

This, of course, provided Governor Evans with justification to simply take the Indian lands by force. On June 24, 1864, he demanded that all marauding bands surrender at once to Fort Lyon or suffer extermination, and when that ultimatum was utterly ignored, he ordered the commander of the Colorado militia, a former minister and virulent Indian hater named Colonel John Chivington, to launch a series of raids against the Cheyenne. Black Kettle, attempting to avoid an all-out war, sought a negotiated peace through Major Edward Wynkoop, the federal commander at Fort Lyon, and at Wynkoop's request brought his band to an encampment at Sand Creek, some thirty miles from Fort Lyon, where he understood they would be safe.

Unfortunately, no Indian was safe from the psychopathic Colonel Chivington. At daybreak on November 29, 1864, he and his civilian militia of several hundred men, a good many of them drunk, swooped down on the Sand Creek village and

Our Common Humanity. Blest Be The Tie That Binds" The cover of The Daily Graphic, *a New York newspaper, far left, reflects national ambivalence to the Indian wars. This issue was published one month after the Battle of the Little Bighorn. Humanitarian groups in the East lobbied against war and in favor of what they considered the "civilizing" of Native Americans. They believed that through education and religious training, Indians would adopt white lifestyles, and peace would soon follow.*

The Medicine Man, Charles M. Russell

slaughtered 105 women and children and 28 men (the preponderance of Black Kettle's warriors were away on a hunt). Colorado's finest then distinguished themselves by a display of some of the most excessive and grotesque butchery ever committed against the weak, the helpless, and the dead. Lieutenant James Connor, reporting his findings on the day following the massacre, said, "I did not see a body of man, woman, or child but was scalped, and in many instances their bodies were mutilated in the most horrible manner . . . I heard one man say that he cut out a woman's private parts and had them for exhibition on a stick . . . I also heard of numerous instances in which men had cut out the private parts of females and stretched them over their saddle-bows and wore them over their hats while riding in the ranks."[9] In such a manner did "civilization" triumph once again over "savagery."

George Armstrong Custer, far right, remains a figure of controversy. Was he a brilliant but over-daring leader? Or was he, as Indian historian Vine Deloria Jr. calls him, "Eichmann of the Plains"?

Black Kettle and others from his band escaped Chivington's bloodbath and carried news of the treachery to tribes throughout the region. By 1865 the central plains were engulfed in a war of retaliation by the Sioux, Cheyenne, and Arapaho that left every settlement along the South Platte a smoking ruin, and consigned an entire detachment under the command of Captain William Fetterman to pushing up daisies on the plains outside Fort Philip Kearny, where they had been lured and dispatched by the Lakota war leader, Red Cloud.

Things simmered down a bit with the Fort Laramie treaty in 1868, which closed the Bozeman Trail and guaranteed the Sioux and Northern Cheyenne their old hunting grounds east of the Bighorn Mountains, but the relentless pressure of Anglo migration gradually rekindled the fires until things exploded again in 1874. Gold was discovered in the Black Hills of South Dakota, which just happened to be the spiritual center of the "Great Sioux Reservation"; and rather than try to deal with the frenzy of trespassing whites who were illegally invading the territory, the government decided, as usual, that it would be easier to remove the Indians.

However, these Indians, with leaders like Red Cloud, Sitting Bull, Crazy Horse, and Gall, did not remove very easily. General

THE DAILY GRAPHIC

George Crook, along with an army of thirteen hundred men, was sent in March of 1876 to round up the Sioux and Northern Cheyenne and move them onto reservations away from the Black Hills, but while Crook fought a terrific battle with a group of Cheyenne and Oglala Sioux under the war leader Crazy Horse, he went home empty-handed. In fact, he was forced to retreat. He tried once more in June and was again stopped by Crazy Horse at the battle of Rosebud Creek. A week later General George Armstrong Custer, in command of a six-hundred man strike force of the U.S. Seventh Cavalry, was informed of an Indian encampment down on the Little Bighorn and made the biggest mistake of his short, vainglorious life when he decided to attack it. Every schoolchild knows the result.

But winning battles does not win a war, and in the end it was a simple matter of statistics. Stung by various defeats, the federal government poured thousands of troops onto the Great Plains, and eventually there was nowhere for a red man to run, nowhere to hide, and not enough physical presence left to carry on a fight. Disease, starvation, and military conflict had taken their toll. Over a period of four hundred years the number of Native Americans had been reduced from as high as ten million souls to fewer than 250,000, and rectitude and determination notwithstanding, odds are still odds.

Volumes have been written on what has been called the trail of broken treaties, and on the myriad ways in which the government of the United States attempted to deal with its "Indian problem." The real problem, of course, was one of trying to make rampant racism and unalloyed cupidity appear to be bodiless abstractions, not U.S. domestic policy. Whether those policies were called extermination, removal, relocation, assimilation, or allotment, they all boiled down to the same thing: federal power crushing the powerless and confining the survivors on ever smaller and more distant pieces of undesirable land—and defining the action as the

An Indian hunter signals to his village that buffalo are in sight, far left. The massive animals, in their great migratory herds, were half of the equation that made nomadic plains life possible. The other half was horses. Brought to America by the Spanish, they gave buffalo-hunting people unprecedented mobility and speed.

Bodmer's painting of a Sioux encampment, right, details classic elements of plains life. The tepee coverings are made of buffalo hides. A woman prepares a fresh hide for tanning. Stick tripods hold drying meat beyond reach of camp dogs. Alfred Jacob Miller's watercolor, Shoshone Camp Fording River, *illustrates the mobility of Native life before their lands were taken from them.*

realization of an enlightened humanitarian generosity. One need only listen to the words of one old Hidatsa woman to understand that despair and nostalgia, not gratitude and illumination, was the only response left to those who had been uprooted from their traditional way of life and transplanted into what had become, by the end of the nineteenth century, a white man's world: *I am an old woman now. The buffaloes and black-tail deer are gone, and our Indian ways are almost gone. Sometimes I find it hard to believe that I ever lived them.*

My little son grew up in the white man's school. He can read books, and he owns cattle and has a farm. He is a leader among our Hidatsa people, helping teach them to follow the white man's road.

He is kind to me. We no longer live in an earth lodge, but in a house with chimneys; and my son's wife cooks by a stove.

But for me, I cannot forget our old ways. Often in summer I rise at daybreak and steal out to the cornfields; and as I hoe the corn I sing to it, as we did when I was young. No one cares for our corn songs now. Sometimes at evening I sit, looking out on the big Missouri. The sun sets, and dusk steals over the water. In the shadows I seem again to see our Indian village, with smoke curling upward from the earth lodges; and in the river's roar I hear the yells of the warriors, the laughter of little children as of old. It is but an old woman's dream. Again I see but shadows and hear only the roar of the river; and tears come into my eyes. Our Indian life, I know, is gone forever.[10]

Sioux Camp, Karl Bodmer

NATIVE AMERICANS OF THE WEST

Plains Indians were a favorite of artists drawn to their striking appearance. Feathers, paints, fur, and flamboyant hairstyles fascinated East-Coast and European audiences. George Catlin, whose painting *Sioux Encamped on the Upper Missouri Dressing Meat and Robes*, appears on the following page, vowed to document the scene. He wrote in 1841 that native people "may rise from the 'stain on a painter's palette,' and live once again upon canvass, and stand forth for centuries yet to come, the living monuments of a noble race."

Vig. XIII.

Imp. de Bougeard.

NDIANER INDIENS CORBEAUX.

CROW INDIANS

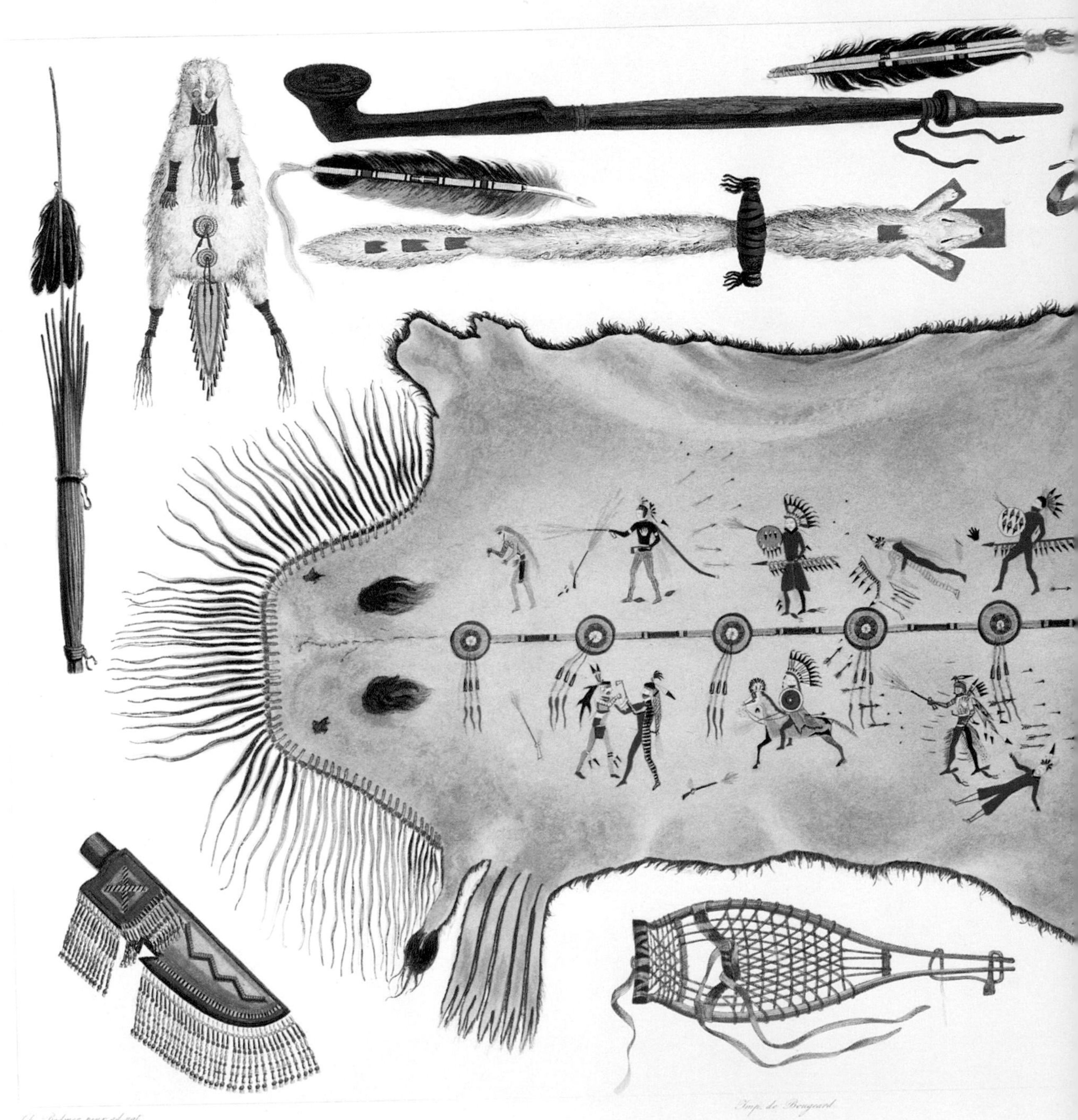

Ch. Bodmer pinx. ad nat.

Imp. de Bougeard.

INDIANISCHE GERÄTHSCHAFTEN UND WAFFEN. | USTENSIL

INDIAN UTENSILS AND ARMS.

Coblenz bei J. Hölscher.

London published by Ackermann & C° 96 Strand 1st of July 1840.

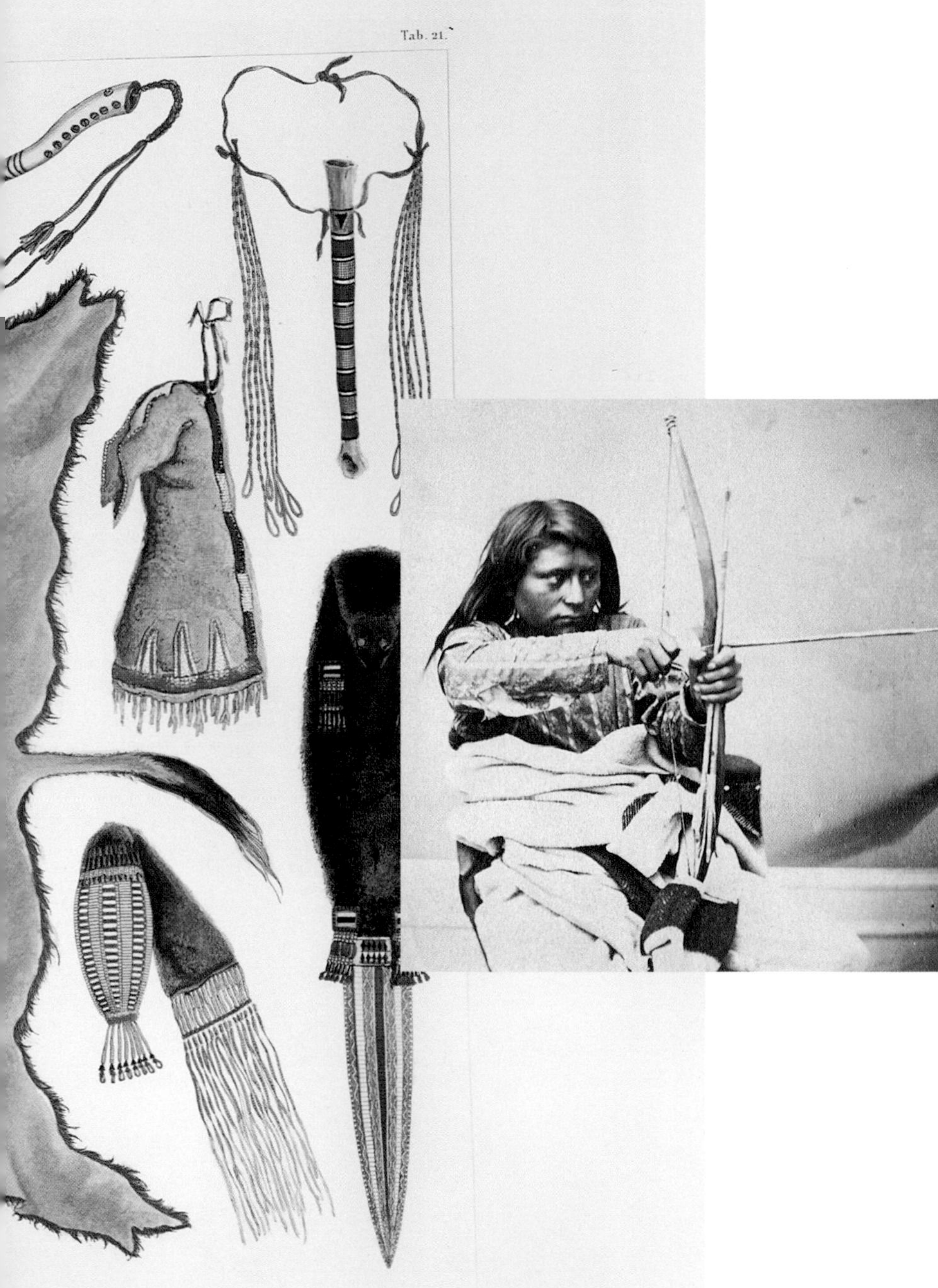

A. Zschokke & Hurlimann sc.

ARMES INDIENS.

Paris, Arthus Bertrand éditeur

Acquisition of horses made life easier, allowing more time for such cultural activities as craftsmanship and storytelling. Nothing was factory made. Every object, even the most utilitarian knife sheath or showshoe, was a work of art expressing its maker's individual taste. The painted buffalo skin in the center is an illustrated history of war events.

LIBBY McNEILL & LIBBY'S
Is valuable for Explorers & Travelers
COOKED
CORNED
BEEF

San Francisco has not a justice of the peace left.”

—Thomas Larkin, American consul in San Francisco, describing the gold rush in 1848

American Progress, John Cast

TO SEE THE ELEPHANT

[1849–1899]

My messenger sent to the mines, has returned with specimens of gold; he demonstrated in a sea of upturned faces. As he drew forth the yellow lumps from his pocket, and passed them around among the eager crowd, the doubts which had lingered till now, fled. All admitted they were gold, except one old man, who still persisted they were some Yankee invention, got up to reconcile the people to the change of flag. The excitement produced was intense; and many were soon busy in their hasty

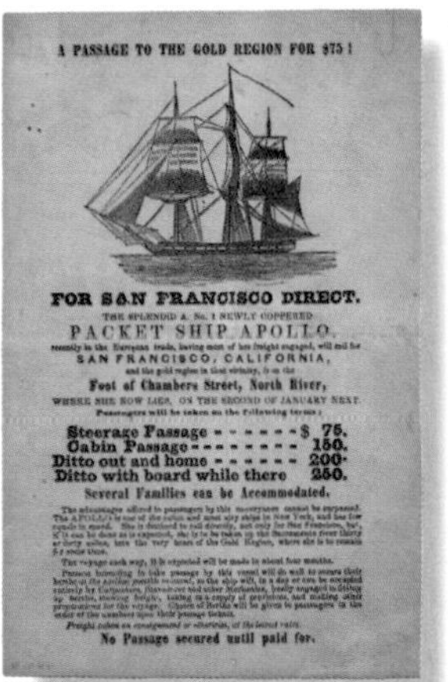

preparations for a departure to the mines. The family who had kept house for me caught the moving infection. Husband and wife were both packing up; the blacksmith dropped his hammer, the carpenter his plane, the mason his trowel, the farmer his sickle, the baker his loaf, and the tapster his bottle. All were off for the mines, some on horses, some on carts, and some on crutches, and one went in a litter. An American woman, who had recently established a boarding-house here, pulled up stakes, and was off before her lodgers had even time to pay their bills. Debtors ran, of course. I have only a community of women left, and a gang of prisoners, with here and there a soldier who will give his captain the slip first chance. I don't blame the fellow a whit; seven dollars a month, while others are making two or three hundred a day! That is too much for human nature to stand.[1]

—Walter Colton, mayor of Monterey, and publisher of the first newspaper in California

A Shining Dream

John Sutter, below, built his famous fort in a beautiful grassy meadow, right, near the confluence of the Sacramento, Feather, and American Rivers. The fort's eighteen-foot high adobe walls enclosed a quadrangle the size of a football field, but they could not defend Sutter's interests when gold fever struck California.

ON A RAINY afternoon in January of 1848, John August Sutter was sitting in his office at New Helvetia (commonly known as Sutter's Fort) when one of his employees, a millwright named James Marshall, was ushered in and asked to speak with him "in secret." Somewhat puzzled, Sutter took him to a room in a private part of the house, whereupon Marshall produced a vial from his pocket that contained about two ounces of a yellow metal he believed to be gold. He had found it, he said, in the tailrace he was in the process of widening at Sutter's gristmill on the American River near Coloma. Sutter tested the specimen with nitric acid, checked his conclusions against an article in the *Encyclopedia Americana,* and declared it, indeed, to be gold—in fact, twenty-three-carat gold, though how he arrived at such a degree of specificity remains unclear.

Marshall's insistence on secrecy was somewhat after the fact, since at least a dozen hands around the mill had already fondled his "discovery," and Sutter's attempt to silence his employees for a mere six weeks so that he could finish building a large flour mill at Brighton was equally fruitless. The story was local gossip within days, and by the time a Mormon storekeeper named Sam Brannon traveled to San Francisco and commenced running up and down the street waving a small bottle, yelling "Gold! Gold! Gold in the American River," he was doing little more than confirming the rumors that had already preceded him.

Not everyone was overjoyed by the discovery, least of all John August Sutter. He probably knew what was coming, though he could not have anticipated that it would constitute the fastest mass migration in American history. He would later write: "What a great misfortune was this sudden gold discovery for me! It has just broken up and ruined my hard, restless, and industrious labors, connected with many dangers of life, as I had many narrow escapes before I became properly established. From my mill buildings I reaped no benefit whatever, the mill stones even have been stolen and sold." His workers abandoned him. His tannery went vacant, as did his blacksmith and carpentry shops. His wheat crop rotted in the field, there being not even Indians left to harvest it. "Had I

John August Sutter

succeeded for a few years before the gold was discovered," he mourned, " I would have been the richest citizen on the Pacific shore; but it had to be different. Instead of being rich, I am ruined . . . "[2]

Although it would take at least six months for people on the East Coast to fully digest the import of James Marshall's find, no such lag time impeded the good citizens of California, and within weeks towns all up and down the coast began to empty out—Santa Cruz, Monterey, Sonoma, San Jose, San Francisco. The American consul in San Francisco, Thomas Larkin, wrote to the secretary of state in Washington that three-quarters of the houses in town had been deserted, "every blacksmith, carpenter and lawyer is leaving; brick-yards, saw-mills and ranches are left perfectly alone. A large part of the volunteers at San Francisco and

THE DONNER PARTY

Possibly the worst tragedy in the history of western migration befell a group of emigrants known as the Donner Party—eighty-seven men, women, and children who set out from Springfield, Illinois, in April of 1846 bound for California. The three organizers, Jacob and George Donner and James Reed, were all greenhorns, unfamiliar with conditions on the trail and prone to squandering time along the way through their general lack of organization and know-how. Nevertheless, they made it without major incident to Fort Laramie by late June, and only about a week behind schedule. There James Reed ran into an old friend from Illinois named James Clyman, a seasoned mountain man on his way back from California, and asked him about a shortcut he had heard of across the Utah and Nevada desert, the now-infamous Hastings Cutoff. Clyman sternly advised him not to try it.

Most of the company paid attention to that warning and, where the trail forked at the Little Sandy River, continued along the California/Oregon Trail toward Fort Hall. But the Reed and Donner families, along with eleven other wagons, branched south to Fort Bridger and tried to force their way through the incredibly tangled canyons of the Wasatch front. What they had thought would take them a week took a month of exhausting labor and left them worn-out, discouraged, and not on the banks of the Great Salt Lake until late August. They still had six hundred miles to go.

The eighty miles of pickled desert to the south and west of Salt Lake had nearly killed Jedediah Smith when he crossed it in 1827, and there were no Jedediah Smiths among the Donner Party. It took them six days and nights, and their water ran out on the third day. By the time they staggered up to the springs at Pilot Peak, thirty-six oxen had run off or died of thirst, many families had been forced to abandon their wagons, and even those who still had teams and rigs left miles of discarded baggage in their wake. Most of Nevada remained to be crossed, as well as the high peaks of the Sierra, and by now it was clear that they had insufficient food to see them through.

It took an entire month to reach Truckee (now Donner) Lake at the foot of the nine-thousand-foot pass over the crest of the mountains. "Digger" Indians had stolen or killed most of the travelers' stock, they were down to a dozen or so wagons, and they were nearly starving. They were bickering and fighting

amongst themselves, furtive, suspicious, and uncaring. On November 1 they attempted to cross the pass but were turned back by five feet of snow. They tried again on the third, abandoning the wagons and tying whatever they could onto the few oxen they had left, and failed again. Exhausted and demoralized, they camped for the night, and when they woke the next morning they found themselves covered by a heavy blanket of snow. Winter—one of the worst winters ever recorded in the Sierra Nevada—had arrived with a vengeance.

The rest is just gruesome detail—agonizing deaths, murders, cannibalism. A rescue party finally made it through on February 19 to find twelve dead strewn about on the snow. Forty-eight remained barely alive; the rescuers were able to carry out only twenty-three, not all of whom survived. Three subsequent relief parties were destined to make even more grisly discoveries. Jacob Donner's children were found "sitting upon a log, with their faces stained with blood, devouring the half roasted liver and heart of the[ir] father, unconscious of the approach of the men, of whom they took not the slightest notice even after they came up." James Reed reported that "among the cabins lay the fleshless bones and half-eaten bodies of the victims of the famine. There lay the limbs, the skulls, and the hair of the poor beings who had died from want and whose flesh preserved the lives of their surviving comrades who, shivering beneath their filthy rags and surrounded by the remains of their unholy feast, looked more like demons than human beings."[3]

Of the eighty-seven who had started off from Springfield a year earlier, eighty-two had made it as far as the Sierra, and thirty-five died at Truckee Lake. For many, the Hastings Cutoff proved to be nothing more than a shortcut to the grave. For a few, like Virginia Reed, California would become a new, if poignant, home. "It is a beautiful country," she wrote to her cousin back home. "It is mostly in vallies and mountains. It ought to be a beautiful country to pay us for our troubles in getting to it."

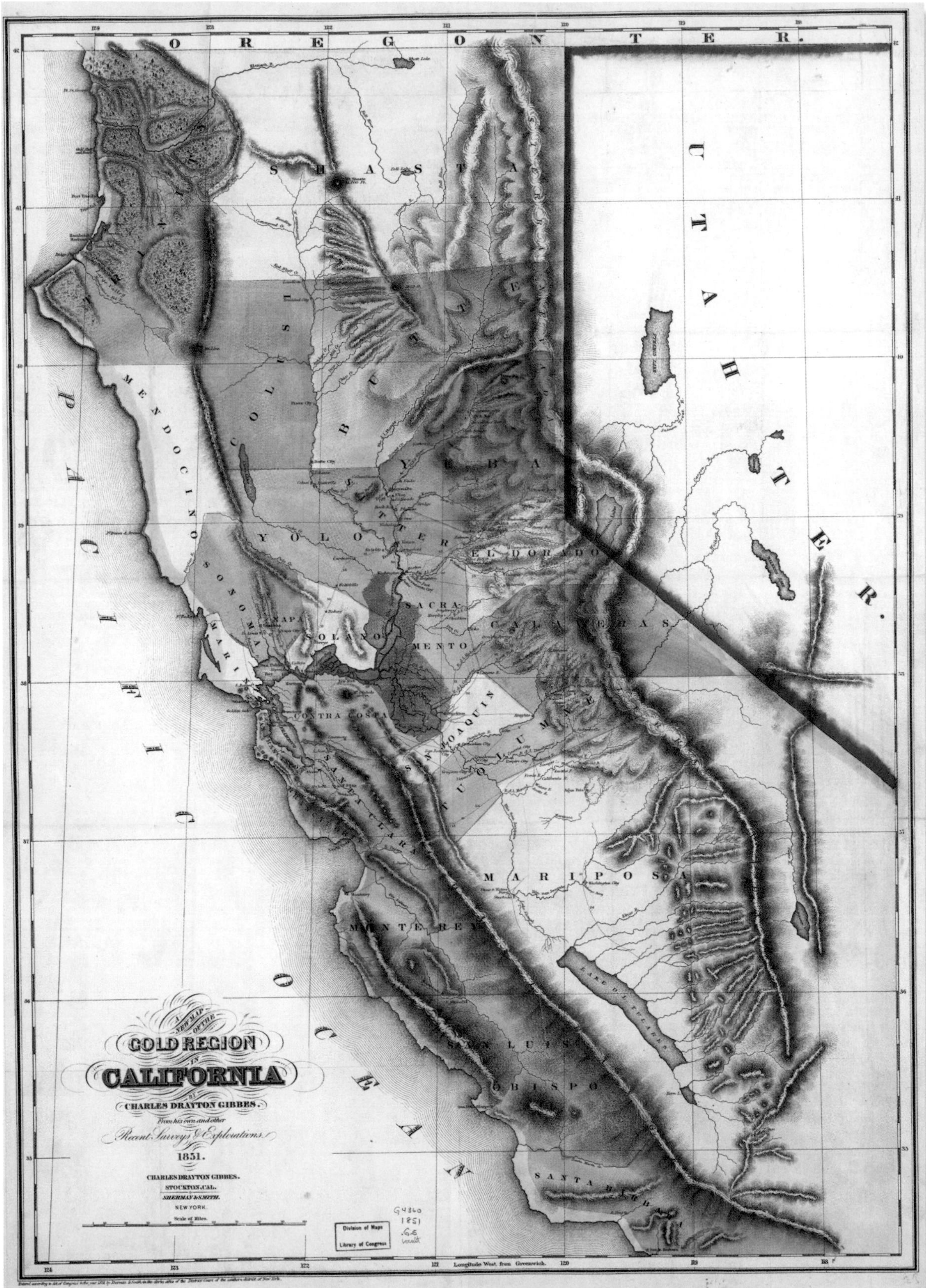
O R E G O N T E R.
U T A H T E R.
P A C I F I C O C E A N
SHASTA
BUTTE
YUBA
COLUSI
MENDOCINO
YOLO
SUTTER
EL DORADO
SONOMA
NAPA
SOLANO
MARIN
SACRAMENTO
CALAVERAS
CONTRA COSTA
SAN JOAQUIN
TUOLUMNE
SANTA CLARA
MARIPOSA
MONTEREY
LAKE DE TULARES
SAN LUIS OBISPO
SANTA BARBARA
A NEW MAP OF THE
GOLD REGION
IN
CALIFORNIA
BY
CHARLES DRAYTON GIBBES.
From his own and other
Recent Surveys & Explorations.
1851.
CHARLES DRAYTON GIBBES.
STOCKTON, CAL.
SHERMAN & SMITH.
NEW YORK.
Scale of Miles.
Longitude West from Greenwich.

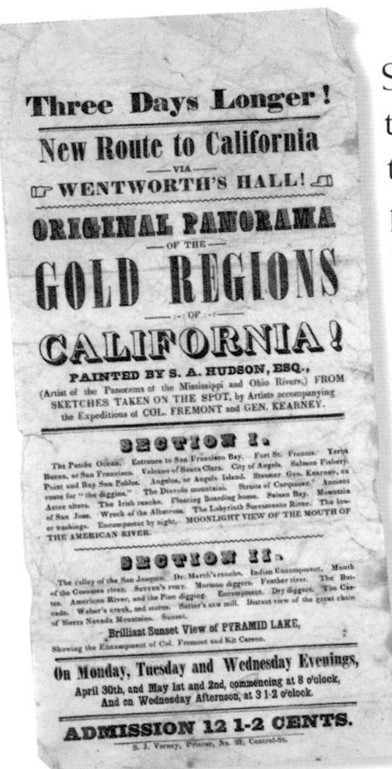

Sonoma have deserted . . . vessels are losing their crews . . . both our newspapers are discontinued. . . . San Francisco has not a justice of the peace left."[4] Even American naval ships were forced to put out to sea in order to prevent their sailors from deserting.

Every able-bodied male from Oregon to Mexico was obsessed with "striking it rich"—or, in the vernacular of the time, heading for the Mother Lode "to see the elephant." They called themselves Argonauts, recalling the Greek heroes who sailed with Jason in search of the Golden Fleece, and by the end of 1848 over five thousand of them had flooded into the foothills of the Sierra Nevada. A year later the number had grown to at least fifty thousand, though some historians believe that a more accurate figure might be closer to eighty thousand. They came by sea, "round the Horn" or through the Straits of Magellan (a five-month journey that could cost as much as one thousand dollars), or, debarking at Aspinwall, followed the Yankee strip across the Isthmus of Panama to the Pacific, and thence north to San Francisco (a bit shorter route, but just as expensive). They came overland in carts and wagons, on horseback and on foot, which was cheaper, but far more arduous. They came singly, in pairs, in small groups, and in large companies, and they were mostly young, and mostly men. The 1850 census affirmed that 92 percent of California's population was male, and 73 percent between the ages of twenty and forty.

The lure of gold called to them and they went—by the tens of thousands, prospectors swarmed over the mountains of the West. Although few ever struck riches, the search drove them to explore every nook and cranny.

"What a great misfortune was this sudden gold discovery for me! It has just broken up and ruined my hard, restless, and industrious labors . . ." —John A. Sutter

By the mid-1850s, at about the time when placer mining had nearly exhausted what surface gold could be gathered in a washing pan or a sluice box, there were three hundred thousand of these elephant seekers crawling around in every gorge and gulch of what would number, over time, 3,500 gold camps scattered the length and breadth of the new El Dorado.

The scene of a trading post at Bellevue, Nebraska, far right, is a romanticized vision of the commercial life of the West. In fact, a field of tree stumps usually accompanied wooden buildings, and an unspoiled landscape was not to be found anywhere near a boomtown, or a goldfield like the one pictured below.

Most of them, in the vernacular of our own time, would wind up eating the elephant. A great many would take leave of their mining careers in a state of disillusionment and disappointment, with nothing but broken dreams and sore backs to accompany them. One such case was a young emigrant named Bernard Reid, whose overland journal records what he came to define as "a long dreadful dream." The dreadful part began when he signed on with a transportation outfit called the Pioneer Line that promised for a fee of two hundred dollars to deliver him and his fellow travelers to California in sixty days or less, thereby saving him the trouble of trying to negotiate 2,200 miles of unfamiliar territory and unmentionable perils by himself. Unfortunately, the managers of the transportation company didn't know any more about western travel than Bernard did. As described by historian Patricia Limerick in her book *The Legacy of Conquest,* they were overloaded, undersupplied, and "floundering on every count." Their baggage had to be jettisoned. They eventually wound up walking. People began dying of cholera and, later, scurvy. "Like many overland diaries, Reid's became a litany of deaths recorded and of graves glimpsed along the way," Limerick wrote.[5]

Reid's life in the Mother Lode was every bit as dismal as his journey to reach it, though he was hardly isolated in his misery. Every prospector faced sickness, loneliness, malnutrition, backbreaking labor, accidents, violent neighbors (one estimate had it that in 1849, two out of every ten men in the camps would be dead within six months), and all for a wage of about eight to ten dollars a day. True, this was eight times more than an eastern coal miner was making,

but an eastern coal miner was paying four cents for the same loaf of bread that cost the western placer miner seventy-five cents. The western miner also had to cough up as much as three dollars for an egg and five dollars for one pound of coffee. "At the Stanislaus diggings," one Argonaut wrote, "a box of raisins sold also *weight for weight,* for about four thousand dollars in gold dust. Incredible as this may appear, it is a well known fact, and these raisins were eaten for the cure of scurvy, prevailing without remedy."[6]

Failure dogged poor Mr. Reid at every turn, and ultimately he sank under continuous poor health and a mountain of bad debt. "Oh! how bitterly do many curse the day they left home," he lamented. Leaving the golden fleece to adorn somebody else's girl, he eventually abandoned the mountains and took a teaching job in Santa Clara, where he was able to earn enough to pacify his creditors and procure a return passage to the tamer climes from whence he had come.

A more carefully planned, if no better informed, migration to California than Bernard Reid's was that of the Hartford Union and Mining Trading Company of Connecticut, whose 115 "investor-entrepreneur" partners set forth in 1849 and sailed around Cape Horn, arriving at San Francisco in September of that year and debarking immediately for the mountains. Well, not exactly debarking. As Kevin Starr describes it in his introduction to *Rooted in Barbarous Soil,* they were about to be divested of certain illusions they had maintained about the nature of their collective enterprise. They had thought they could sail to the goldfields and base their entire mining operation from the comfort of their five-hundred-ton ship. As Starr reports, "It was at Sacramento that the company, faced by the realities of California geography and the difficulties, at the time, of large-scale corporate mining, disbanded; and the men set off, singly, or in groups, into the Mother Lode."[7]

That was the high point. Twelve of the original company were dead before the end of the first year, and twenty-six more had given up and gone back to Connecticut, richer per man by a little less than thirteen hundred dollars.

Forty-niners who traveled by sea arrived in San Francisco after journeys of five months or longer. They landed with few possessions on an undeveloped shore, left, still a long distance from the diggings of their dreams. Here, new arrivals, ferried from ships in small boats, faced the next stage of their journeys.

THE PONY EXPRESS

The legend of the Pony Express is considerably more enduring than any actual impact it had on history. Founded in 1860 by Majors, Russell & Co. of Leavenworth, Missouri, it carried an insignificant amount of mail at a very fast pace—just eight days to go from St. Joseph, Missouri, and San Francisco, California—across 1,996 miles of territory often infested with hostile Indians. The Express rider was a romantic figure, to be sure, dashing across the country on horseback at an average of 250 miles a day, but he wasn't as dashing as the telegraph message, which moved at the speed of electricity." The Pony" was basically shut down when telegraph lines were completed to the Pacific by October of 1861.

Nevertheless, the legendary rider lives on, aided by such hyperbolic exposition as one finds in the pages of journals like *Hutchings' California Magazine* for July 1860:

The loud peals of thunder, and the fierce flashes of lightning, or even the fall of the drenching rain, detains him not. What though the storm-swollen banks of the streams are full to over-flowing, so that even the landmarks for crossing are altogether invisible, it deters him not, for in it he plunges and speeds along on his rapid course, undismayed.

Whether sun-dried or soaked, snow-covered or frozen, by day or by night, in starlight or darkness, be he lonely or merry, forward he hastens, until the thrice welcome station is just there, in sight, when he leaps from his saddle, and with full heart rejoices that his task for the present is fully accomplished.[8]

The Coming and Going of the Pony Express, Frederic Remington

Notice!

We the Undersigned claim this piece of Ground, formerly occupied as a Milk Ranch, and containing 400 feet, for mining purposes

Knickerbocker Flat May 7 1860

H. Lenz.
W. Naumann
Robert Lindsay
Giovanni Geofsdri

Those who remained, according to Starr, were "averaging some $1,239 per man in cumulative earnings. The general average of earned money for the surviving members was $1,116 each." If one deducts $350 per man for the cost of passage and equipment, the fortune accumulated by the Hartford Union Mining and Trading Company partners came to $766 each.

Perhaps the most poignant testimony to penury and pain, however, was composed in 1857 by John Marshall, the very man whose discovery at Sutter's Mill had started it all. In response to a request for a portrait of himself to accompany a story in *Hutchings' California Magazine*, he wrote the following declaration to the editor:

COLOMA, SEPT. 5TH, 1857

Dear Sir:—In reply to your note received three days ago, I wish to say that I feel it a duty I owe to myself to retain my likeness, as it is in fact all I have that I can call my own, and I feel like any other poor wretch—I want something for self. The sale of it may yet keep me from starving; or, it may buy me a dose of medicine in sickness; or pay for the funeral of a—dog—and such is all that I expect, judging from former kindnesses. I owe the country nothing. The enterprising energy of which the orators and editors of California's early golden days boasted so much, as belonging to Yankeedom, was not national but individual. Of the profits derived from the enterprise, it stands thus—

Yankeedom................................$600,000,000

Myself Individually........................$000,000,000

Ask the records of the country for the reason why; they will answer—I need not. Were I an Englishman, and had made my discovery on English soil, the case would have been different. I send you this in place of the other. Excuse my rudeness in answering you thus.

I remain, most respectfully,

J.W. Marshall[9]

Notice! We the undersigned claim this piece..." and so a group of prospectors register their hopes and warn others to stay away. If there was gold to be found, it demanded hard work. Nuggets rarely sat on the surface like fallen plums. Prospectors first had to find a likely, unclaimed spot; then dig through rocks and gravel, and sometimes ice, to discover if there was anything worth claiming. For most who tried, the answer was no.

"What a clover is to a steer, the sky to the lark, a mudhole to a hog, such are newer diggings to a miner."—DAILY OREGONIAN, JULY 12, 1862

Marshall ended his days, misanthropic and embittered, as a gardener in the town of Coloma, where he had originally found his gold. John Sutter, his employer, who had fled to Pennsylvania after his vast land holdings had been overrun by squatters and speculators, spent the rest of his life vainly seeking compensation for his losses. Restitution was denied on the grounds that the laws of military conquest invalidated the original grants that had been bestowed upon him by the now vanquished Mexican authorities.

Even those who made the occasional strike, or managed to pan an ounce a day out of the gravel bar of some icy Sierra stream (it took on average 160 buckets of washed gravel to yield an ounce of gold worth sixteen dollars), were not always fortunate enough to hang on to it. If it didn't go toward the purchase of exorbitantly inflated supplies, it was likely to be spent on recreational activities involving games of chance, accompanied by the serious consumption of alcoholic refreshments. The journal of one young miner heading back from the mountains to San Francisco offers the following account of a typical evening at Sutter's Fort:

Crossing the beautiful plain, that afternoon we reached Sutter's Fort, covered with dust from head to foot, and enjoying the novelty of fresh provisions and a table to eat at once more. That night, and the one following, we availed ourselves of the only opportunity while in California to rest in a bed. . . . A great row was also in progress every night among the miners and others tarrying at the fort. Drunkenness reigned supreme, and fighting followed of course. A poor Frenchman was nearly killed for saying sacre bleu; and bottles full of wine, and heads full of sap were broken without discrimination, and in the greatest confusion. Hundreds of dollars were often spent this way in a single night, and thousands on Sunday, when Pandemonium was in full blast. Gambling prevailed without limit or cessation; men often losing pounds of gold dust in a night, which they were months of dreadful hardship and toil in obtaining.

Theodore T. Johnson, 1849[10]

It should by no means be concluded that every account culled from narratives of California's gold rush participants is the parable of a loser. There were huge success stories as well, and many people did get fabulously rich, though the greatest wealth that was taken out of the Sierra occurred after the mad scramble of the first five or six years, once hydraulic and hard-rock mining had replaced the pan and cradle of the placer miner. The halcyon days when the fabled range of light was

With pick, shovel, and gold pan, far left, prospectors searched for placer gold—nuggets and flakes eroded from hard-rock veins and washed downstream with sand, gravel, and boulders. As placer deposits were depleted, miners dreamed of the "mother lode," where the flakes and nuggets were born.

The Winter of 1849, Francis Samuel Marryat

prospected by two or three old bewhiskered geezers with the front of their hat brims pinned flat were soon gone, replaced by an era of large companies whose serious capital investment was capable of amassing the equipment and technology required to extract minerals from deep underground, or of blasting away whole mountainsides with hydraulic hoses and processing the debris in giant crushers. In short order, mining became a large-scale industry, and the Argonaut a man who was working for wages.

A cartoon version of early San Francisco, left, illustrates ramshackle boomtown life. Shoddy buildings line a flooded street where rats, dogs, and people struggle for dry footing. One man tugs the coattails of a dandy trying to be gallant while another loses a boot in the mire and the butcher helps a man up through the window.

Most of the real tycoons who emerged during this flamboyant period were entrepreneurs who had perceived from the outset that "mining the miners" was a much more profitable business than digging up dirt clods in the foothills. George Hearst, father of William Randolph, was one of the few exceptions, though he did precious little digging once he had invested first in the Ophir Mine in Nevada, then the Anaconda in Montana, and the Homestake in South Dakota. But the "big four," as they are still known in California—Mark Hopkins, Leland Stanford, Collis P. Huntington, and Charles Crocker—all started out as shopkeepers in Sacramento.

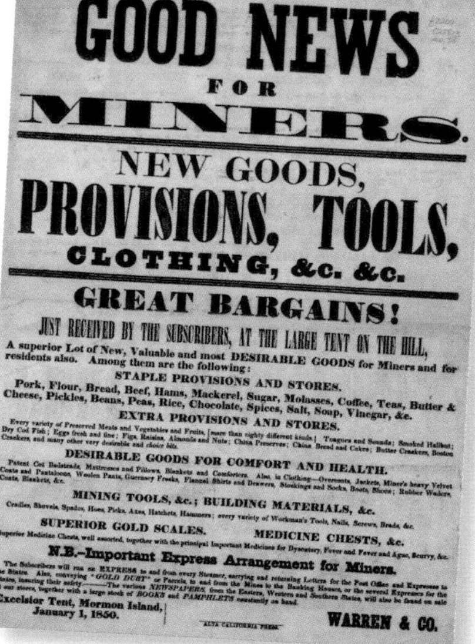

Crocker marketed dry goods, Hopkins and Huntington sold hardware, Stanford bartered groceries on the wholesale exchange, and all did exceedingly well even before their subsequent railroad and banking activities made them wealthy beyond imagination. Domenico Ghirardelli, the chocolate king, was a purveyor of general merchandise in Mariposa and Stockton before opening two confectionery stores and a factory in San Francisco that is still in operation today. John Studebaker built wheelbarrows in Placerville, selling them to miners in such quantity that his highly profitable company in time metamorphosed into a car manufacturing enterprise in Indiana. Levi Strauss opened a San Francisco branch of his family's firm, Jonas Strauss of New York, eventually entering into a fortuitous partnership with a Reno tailor named Jacob Davis, who was short the sixty-eight dollars he needed to patent his latest invention—the world's first pair of riveted pants.

Any man, rich or poor, could be a placer gold miner. It took only a shovel, a pan, some water, and hard work. Gold is denser than stone, and therefore heavier. By swirling water over a panload of sand, a miner washes out the debris in hopes of finding "color" at the bottom of the pan.

The gold rush, which so dramatically and abruptly populated the new commonwealth of California, brought a form of settlement that was for all intents and purposes nonsettlement, a boom-and-bust transience that left, in the words of the famous Dame Shirley, what "was to have been" cities all up and down the state—towns that never made it past the hamlet stage before being abandoned to the elements and the few ghosts who cared to hang around. Unlike the agriculturally inspired land rushes in the Midwest, the California gold rush drew few people with any intention of staying and putting down roots; they came to get rich and get out, not settle down and become part of a community. This is not surprising when one considers the community—a bunch of ramshackle shanties on muddy streets with minimal attention to sanitation; no health facilities; no civilizing influences like women, children, or a church; nothing to do but work and get drunk. Most of the camps were, at best, scabrous and foul.

"From my mill buildings I reaped no benefit whatever, the mill stones even have been stolen and sold."—John A. Sutter

THE MINER'S TEN COMMANDMENTS

A man spake these words, and said: I am a miner, wandering "from away down east," to sojourn in a strange land. And behold I've seen the elephant, yea, verily, I saw him, and bear witness, that from the key of his trunk to the end of his tail, his whole body hath passed before me; and I followed him until his huge feet stood before a clapboard shanty; then with his trunk extended he pointed to a candle-card tacked upon a shingle, as though he would say Read, and I read the

Miner's Ten Commandments

I.

Thou shalt have no other claim than one.

II.

Thou shalt not make unto thyself any false claim, nor any likeness to a mean man, by jumping one: for I, a miner, am a just one, and will visit the miners around about, and they will judge thee; and when they shall decide, thou shalt take thy pick, thy pan, thy shovel and thy blankets with all thou hast and shall depart seeking other good diggings, but thou shalt find none. Then when thou hast paid out all thy dust, worn out thy boots and garments so that there is nothing good about them but the pockets, and thy patience is like unto thy garments, then in sorrow shall thou return to find thy claim worked out, and yet thou hath no pile to hide in the ground, or in the old boot beneath thy bunk, or in buckskin or in bottle beneath thy cabin, and at last thou shalt hire thy body out to make thy board and save thy bacon.

III.

Thou shalt not go prospecting before thy claim gives out. Neither shalt thou take thy money, nor thy gold dust, nor thy good name, to the gaming table in vain; for monte, twenty-one, roulette, faro, lansquenet and poker, will prove to thee that the more thou puttest down the less thou shalt take up; and when thou thinkest of thy wife and children, thou shalt not hold thyself guiltless—but insane.

IV.

Thou shalt not remember what thy friends do at home on the Sabbath day, lest the remembrance may not compare favorably with what thou doest here. Six days thou mayst dig or pick; but the other day is Sunday; yet thou washest all thy dirty shirts, darnest all thy stockings, tap thy boots, mend thy clothing, chop the whole week's firewood, make up and bake thy bread, and boil thy pork and beans, that thou wait not when thou returnest from thy long-tom weary. For in six days' labor only though canst do it in six months; and though, and thy morals and thy conscience, be none the better for it; but reproach thee, shouldst thou ever return with thy worn-out body to thy mother's fireside.

V.

Thou shalt not think more of all thy gold, and how thou canst make it fastest, than how thou will enjoy it after thou hast ridden rough-shod over thy good old parents' precepts and examples,

THE MINER'S TEN COMMANDMENTS.

A man spake these words and said: I am a miner, who wandered "from away down east," and came to sojourn in a strange land and "see the elephant." And behold I saw him, and bear witness, that from the key of his trunk to the end of his tail, his whole body has passed before me; and I followed him until his huge feet stood still before a clapboard shanty; then, with his trunk extended, he pointed to a candle-card tacked upon a shingle, as though he would say read, and I read the

Miners' Ten Commandments.

I.

Thou shalt have no other claim than one.

II.

Thou shalt not make unto thyself any false claim, nor any likeness to a mean man, by jumping one: whatever thou findest on the top above, or on the rock beneath, or in a crevice underneath the rock — or I will visit the miners around to invite them on my side; and when they decide against thee, thou shalt take thy pick and thy pan, thy shovel, and thy blankets, with all that thou hast, and "go prospecting," to seek good diggings; but thou shalt find none. Then, when thou hast returned, in sorrow shalt thou find that thine old claim is worked out, and yet no pile made thee, to hide in the ground, or in an old boot beneath thy bunk, or in buckskin or bottle underneath thy cabin, but hast paid all that was in thy purse away, worn out thy boots and thy garments, so that there is nothing good about them but the pockets, and thy patience is likened unto thy garments; and at last thou shalt hire thy body out to make thy board and save thy bacon.

III.

Thou shalt not go prospecting before thy claim gives out. Neither shalt thou take thy money, nor thy gold dust, nor thy good name, to the gaming table in vain; for monte, twenty-one, roulette, faro, lansquenet and poker, will prove to thee that the more thou puttest down the less thou shalt take up; and when thou thinkest of thy wife and children, thou shalt not hold thyself guiltless, but—insane.

IV.

Thou shalt not remember what thy friends do at home on the Sabbath day, lest the remembrance may not compare favorably with what thou doest here. Six days thou mayest dig or pick all that thy body can stand under; but the other day is Sunday; yet thou washest all thy dirty shirts, darnest all thy stockings, tap thy boots, mend thy clothing, chop thy whole week's firewood, make up and bake thy bread and boil thy pork and beans, that thou wait not when thou returnest from thy long-tom, weary. For in six days' labor only thou canst not work enough to wear out thy body in two years; but if thou workest hard on Sunday also, thou canst do it in six months; and thou, and thy son, and thy daughter, thy male friend and thy female friend, thy morals and thy conscience, be none the better for it; but reproach thee, shouldst thou ever return with thy worn-out body to thy mother's fireside; and thou strive to justify thyself, because the trader and the blacksmith, the carpenter and the merchant, the tailors, Jews, and buccaneers, defy God and civilization, by keeping not the Sabbath day, nor wish for a day of rest, such as memory, youth and home, made hallowed.

V.

Thou shalt not think more of all thy gold, and how thou canst make it fastest, than how thou wilt enjoy it, after thou hast ridden, rough shod, over thy good old parent's precepts and examples, that thou mayest have nothing to reproach and sting thee, when thou art left ALONE in the land where thy father's blessing and thy mother's love hath sent thee.

VI.

Thou shalt not kill thy body by working in the rain, even though thou shalt make enough to buy physic and attendance with. Neither shalt thou kill thy neighbor's body in a duel; for, by "keeping cool," thou canst save his life and thy conscience. Neither shalt thou destroy thyself by getting "tight," nor "slewed," nor "high," nor "corned," nor "half-seas-over," nor "three sheets in the wind," by drinking smoothly down — "brandy-slings," "gin-cocktails," "whisky-punches," "rum-toddies," nor "egg-nogs." Neither shalt thou suck "mint-julips," nor "sherry-cobblers," through a straw, nor gurgle from a bottle the "raw material," nor "take it neat" from a decanter, for, while thou art swallowing down thy purse, and thy coat from off thy back, thou art burning the coat from off thy stomach; and, if thou couldst see the houses and lands, and gold dust, and home comforts already lying there—"a huge pile"—thou shouldst feel a choaking in thy throat; and when to that thou addest thy crooked walkings and hiccuping-talkings, of lodgings in the gutter, of broilings in the sun, of prospect-holes half full of water, and of shafts and ditches, from which thou hast emerged like a drowning rat, thou wilt feel disgusted with thyself, and inquire "Is thy servant a dog, that he doeth these things?" verily I will say, Farewell, old bottle, I will kiss thy gurgling lips no more. And thou, slings, cocktails, punches, smashes, cobblers, nogs, toddies, sangarees, and julips, forever farewell. Thy remembrance shames me, henceforth, I "cut thy acquaintance," and headaches, tremblings, heart burnings, blue-devils, and all the unholy catalogue of evils that follow in thy train. My wife's smiles and my children's merry-hearted laugh, shall charm and reward me for having the manly firmness and courage to say NO. I wish thee an eternal farewell.

VII.

Thou shall not grow discouraged, nor think of going home before thou hast made thy "pile," because thou hast not "struck a lead," nor found a "rich crevice," nor sunk a hole upon a "pocket," lest in going home thou shalt leave four dollars a day, and go to work, ashamed, at fifty cents, and serve thee right; for thou knowest by staying here, thou mightest strike a lead and fifty dollars a day, and keep thy manly self-respect, and then go home with enough to make thyself and others happy.

VIII.

Thou shalt not steal a pick, or a shovel, or a pan, from thy fellow miner; nor take away his tools without his leave; nor borrow those he cannot spare; nor return them broken, nor trouble him to fetch them back again; nor talk with him while his water rent is running on; nor remove his stake to enlarge thy claim, nor undermine his bank in following a lead, nor pan out gold from his "riffle-box," nor wash the "tailings" from his sluice's mouth. Neither shalt thou pick out specimens from the company's pan to put them in thy mouth, or in thy purse; nor cheat thy partner of his share; nor steal from thy cabin-mate his gold dust, to add to thine, for he will be sure to discover what thou hast done, and will straightway call his fellow miners together, and if the law hinder them not, they will hang thee, or give thee fifty lashes, or shave thy head and brand thee, like a horse thief, with R upon thy cheek, to be known and read of all men, Californians in particular.

IX.

Thou shalt not tell any false tales about "good diggings in the mountains" to thy neighbor, that thou mayest benefit a friend who hath mules, and provisions, and tools, and blankets, he cannot sell — lest in deceiving thy neighbor, when he returneth through the snow, with naught save his rifle, he present thee with the contents thereof, and like a dog, thou shalt fall down and die.

X.

Thou shalt not commit unsuitable matrimony, nor covet "single blessedness"; nor forget absent maidens; nor neglect thy "first love";—but thou shalt consider how faithfully and patiently she awaiteth thy return; yea, and covereth each epistle that thou sendest with kisses of kindly welcome—until she hath thyself. Neither shalt thou covet thy neighbor's wife, nor trifle with the affections of his daughter; yet, if thy heart be free, and thou love and covet each other, thou shalt "pop the question" like a man, lest another more manly than thou art, should step in before thee, and thou love her in vain, and in the anguish of thy heart's disappointment, thou shalt quote the language of the great, and say, "sich is life"; and thy future lot be that of a poor, lonely, despised and comfortless bachelor.

A new Commandment give I unto thee—if thou hast a wife and little ones, that thou lovest dearer than thy life—that thou keep them continually before thee, to cheer and urge thee onward until thou canst say, "I have enough—God bless them—I will return." Then as thou journiest towards thy much loved home, with open arms shall they come forth to welcome thee, and falling upon thy neck, weep tears of unuterable joy that thou art come; then in the fullness of thy heart's gratitude, thou shall kneel before thy Heavenly Father together, to thank Him for thy safe return. AMEN—So mote it be!

FORTY-NINE.

The Miner's Ten Commandments, Harrison Eastman (engraving)

that thou mayest have nothing to reproach thee, when left ALONE in the land where thy father's blessing and thy mother's love hath sent thee.

VI.

Thou shalt not kill; neither thy body by working in the rain, even though thou shalt make enough to buy physic and attendance with; nor thy neighbor's body in a duel, or in anger, for by "keeping cool," thou canst save his life and thy conscience. Neither shalt thou destroy thyself by getting "tight," nor "stewed," nor "high," nor "corned," nor "half-seas over," nor "three sheets in the wind," by drinking smoothing down—"brandy slings," "gin cocktails," "whiskey punches," "rum toddies," nor "egg-noggs." Neither shalt thou suck "mint juleps," nor "sherry-cobblers," through a straw, nor gurgle from a bottle the "raw material," nor take "it straight" from a decanter; for, while thou art swallowing down thy purse, and the coat from off thy back thou art burning the coat from off thy stomach; and if thou couldst see the houses and lands, and gold dust, and home comforts already lying there—"a huge pile"—thou shouldst feel a choking in thy throat; and when to that thou addest thy crooked walkings thou wilt feel disgusted with thyself, and inquire "Is thy servant a dog that he doeth these things!" Verily, thou shalt say, "Farewell, old bottle, I will kiss thy gurgling lips no more; slings, cocktails, punches, smashes, cobblers, nogs, toddies, sangarees and juleps, forever farewell. Thy remembrance shames one; henceforth, I cut thy acquaintance, and headaches, tremblings, heart-burnings, blue devils, and all the unholy catalogue of evils that follow in thy train. My wife's smiles and my children's merry-hearted laugh, shall charm and reward me for having the manly firmness and courage to say NO. I wish thee an eternal farewell."

VII.

Thou shalt not grow discouraged, nor think of going home before thou hast made thy "pile," because thou hast not "struck a lead," nor found a "rich crevice," nor sunk a hole upon a "pocket," lest in going home thou shalt leave four dollars a day, and going to work, ashamed, at fifty cents, and serve thee right; for thou knowest by staying here, thou mightst strike a lead and fifty dollars a day, and keep thy manly self respect, and then go home with enough to make thyself and others happy.

VIII.

Thou shalt not steal a pick, or a shovel, or a pan from thy fellow-miner; nor take away his tools without his leave; nor borrow those he cannot spare; nor return them broken, nor trouble him to fetch them back again, nor talk with him while his water rent is running on, nor remove his stake to enlarge thy claim, nor undermine his bank in following a lead, nor pan out gold from his "riffle box," nor wash the "tailings" from his sluice's mouth. Neither shalt thou pick out specimens from the company's pan to put them in thy mouth or pocket; nor cheat thy partner of his share; nor steal from thy cabin-mate his gold dust, to add to thine, for he will be sure to discover what thou hast done, and will straightaway call his fellow miners together, and if the law hinder them not, will hang thee, or give thee fifty lashes, or shave thy head and brand thee, like a horse thief, with "R" upon thy cheek, to be known and read of all men, Californians in particular.

IX.

Thou shalt not tell any false tales about "good diggings in the mountains," to thy neighbor that thou mayest benefit a friend who had mules, and provisions, and tools and blankets he cannot sell,—lest in deceiving thy neighbor, when he returneth through the snow, with naught save his rifle, he present thee with the contents thereof, and like a dog, thou shalt fall down and die.

X.

Thou shalt not commit unsuitable matrimony, nor covet "single blessedness;" nor forget absent maidens; nor neglect thy "first love;"—but thou shalt consider how faithfully and patiently she awaiteth thy return; yea and covereth each epistle that thou sendest with kisses of kindly welcome—until she hath thyself. Neither shalt thou cove thy neighbor's wife, nor trifle with the affections of his daughter; yet, if thy heart be free, and thou dost love and covet each other, thou shalt "pop the question" like a man.

A new Commandment give I unto thee—if thou has a wife and little ones, that thou lovest dearer than life,—that thou keep them continually before thee, to cheer and urge thee onward, until thou canst say, "I have enough—God bless them—I will return." Then from thy much-loved home, with open arms shall they come forth to welcome thee, with weeping tears of unutterable joy that thou art come; then in the fullness of thy heart's gratitude, thou shalt kneel together before thy Heavenly Father, to thank him for thy safe return. AMEN—So mote it be.

These "commandments" were actually written in 1853 by James M. Hutchings (1818–1902), and first published in the Placerville Herald *newspaper. This was the most popular of the hundreds of letter sheets published in the 1850–70 era, and was so profitable for Mr. Hutchings that he was able to publish the successful* Hutchings' California Magazine.

Mount Lyell, California, William Keith

FORTY-NINER ROUTES WEST

Neither the Crusades nor Alexander's expedition to India can equal this emigration to California.

—C. N. Ormsby, 1849

Fueled by the dream of instant, unearned wealth, gold-seekers flooded across the West toward California in 1849. They came from the East Coast, but also from the Azores, the Sandwich Islands, Europe, China, Chile, and Mexico. Those who made the two-month trip cross-country often made their way by rail to the Great Plains, then by stagecoach, wagon train, or, in the case of a few brave souls, by horseback through hostile territory. They died by the thousands en route, from cholera, scurvy, hunger and bad weather, accident and Indian attack, in landslides, floods and other accidents.

But a straight line was not the only route available. About forty thousand came by ship. Some sailed to Panama, hiking across the mosquito-infested isthmus to waiting ships on the Pacific side, which shunted them up the coast to San Francisco, five months after leaving the East Coast. There they were joined in San Francisco Bay by seafarers who had made the long and perilous eight-month journey around the Horn, through the icy, stormy Straits of Magellan at the southern tip of South America. At the height of the gold rush the harbor was clogged with abandoned ships, deserted by crew and passengers alike, all seeking their fortune in the muddy goldfields east of Sacramento.

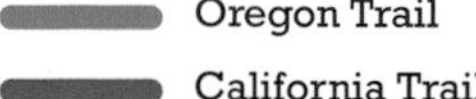

Oregon Trail

California Trail

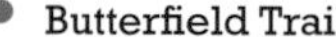

Butterfield Trail

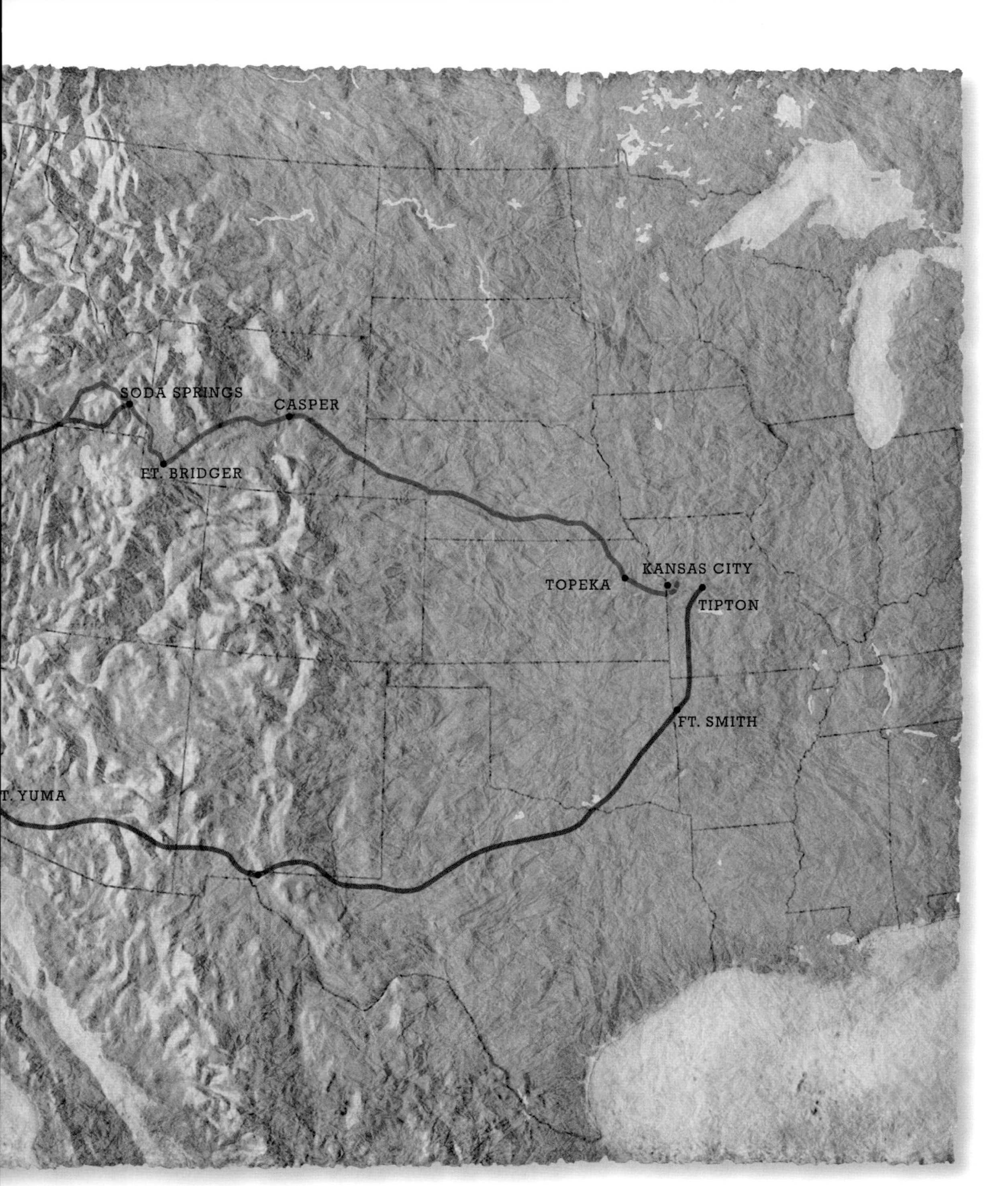
SODA SPRINGS
CASPER
FT. BRIDGER
KANSAS CITY
TOPEKA
TIPTON
FT. SMITH
T. YUMA

The forty-niners may have, indeed, admired the surrounding scenery, even as they were in the process of destroying it, but they gave not a nanosecond's thought to the long-term consequences of the environmental havoc they created. Hydraulic mining, with high-pressure hoses and nine-inch-diameter nozzles capable of discharging twenty-five million gallons of water a day, blasted away whole mountainsides and washed the choking debris down into the rivers. "Slickens," a composite of gravel, sand, and mud, surged down from the foothills and out onto agricultural lands in the central valley, flooding thousands of acres and destroying crops and cattle alike, strangling fisheries, and contaminating even the oyster beds in faraway San Francisco Bay.

More effective than a gold pan was a sluice-box—a wooden trough with a ridged bottom, far left. Miners shoveled gold-bearing sand and gravel into the trough, where flowing water washed away the lighter material. The gold, if there was any, stayed behind, trapped by the ridges.

Careless fires burned off entire forests, and what the fires missed, the miners scalped for lumber. Mercury, used for separating out gold particles, contaminated every stream and infected those few riparian corridors not already condemned to death by silt. Add to this over-hunting and a major depletion of fish and game, followed by overgrazing and the destruction of mountain meadows throughout the Sierra as native plants and grasses were wiped out by sheep ("a plague of locusts," John Muir would later call them), and foreign exotics took over in their place. "The hills have been cut and scalped," wrote one observer, "and every gorge and gulch and broad valley have been fairly torn to pieces and disemboweled . . ." It left, in fact, a legacy of destruction that is still being dealt with in California today.

Never has the root of all evil inspired quite so much in mimicry of its own base disposition. If moral insight may, on occasion, have been visited upon a few, what this slavish devotion to Mammon created in terms of environmental consciousness was a complete void. What it created in the way of a collective social consciousness was on the one hand a soupçon of happy male bonding, but on the other a denaturant of avarice, envy, distrust, rivalry, violence, and lawlessness. Worst of all, it produced, in one concentrated expression, a powerful display of the racial and ethnic prejudices prevalent throughout the nineteenth century—a virulent form of bigotry and intolerance that would continue to be the locus of social struggle in America for the next 153 years.

In California's mining country, resolutions were quickly passed in virtually every camp forbidding the presence of all foreigners. Moreover, the "other" races, those who were either indigenous or beginning to make a significant showing (blacks, Asians, Indians, Mexicans, and South Americans), were forbidden by statute to testify in court in cases involving whites. One need not explicate the obvious. Since whites could with impunity evict, restrict, exploit, brutalize, malign, debase, abuse, violate, and even murder anyone they found objectionable, except other whites, they did so with appalling frequency.

Chinese miners, far right, had the same hopes as everyone else—a chance at bettering their lives. The largest numbers came from Fujian, a mountainous, poverty-stricken province in south-eastern China whose people had a long history of traveling to find work. Most were men who planned to return home with their savings, but many of them stayed to help build railroads, above.

What this meant for the 25,000 Chinese who had arrived in the gold camps by 1852 was not only a constant pattern of physical abuse, but exclusion from any mining activity except in areas already picked over and abandoned by whites, and restrictions on employment except in lines of work that no self-respecting white would touch. They could be cooks, laundrymen, woodcutters, produce farmers, and later, track layers building a railroad over the Sierra Nevada, but if they moved into areas of the labor force that whites considered off-limits, it was at the peril of their lives.

Adding insult to injury, and placing an official stamp on the common policy of racial exile, the new California constitution in 1879 forbade Chinese from employment on public works projects and prohibited them from voting—"no native of China, no idiot, insane person, or person convicted of any infamous crime . . . shall ever exercise the privileges of an elector of this State." And in the interests of national unity Congress passed the Chinese Exclusion Act in 1882, forbidding further immigration of Chinese laborers into the United States for ten years—a piece of legislation that was renewed in 1892 and made permanent in 1902. Congress was silent on the subject of idiots, lunatics, and criminals.

"No native of China, no idiot, insane person, or person convicted of any infamous crime . . . shall ever exercise the privileges of an elector of this State."—From the California constitution of 1879

THE OVERLAND STAGE

Almost touching our knees, a perpendicular wall of mail matter rose up to the roof. There was a great pile of it strapped on top of the stage, and both the fore and hind boots were full.

We had twenty-seven hundred pounds of it aboard, the driver said—"a little for Brigham, and Carson, and 'Frisco, but the heft of it for the Injuns, which is powerful troublesome 'thout they get plenty of truck to read." But as he just then got up a fearful convulsion of his countenance which was suggestive of a wink being swallowed by an earthquake, we guessed that his remark was intended to be facetious, and to mean that we would unload the most of our mail matter somewhere on the Plains and leave it to the Indians, or whosoever wanted it.

We changed horses every ten miles, all day long, and fairly flew over the hard, level road. We jumped out and stretched our legs every time the coach stopped, and so the night found us still vivacious and unfatigued.

—MARK TWAIN, *ROUGHING IT*

Was stagecoach mail delivery really treated as cavalierly as the stage driver would have us believe? Probably not—at least not all the time. But then, the ride was not nearly as clean and comfortable as Mark Twain makes it sound, either. In 1865, a traveler named Demas Barnes made his way across the West in a stagecoach, and it was something to write home about: *The conditions of one man's running stages to make money, while another seeks to ride in them for pleasure, are not in harmony to produce comfort. Coaches will be overloaded, it will rain, the dust will drive, baggage will be left to the storm, passengers will get sick, a gentleman of gallantry will hold the baby, children will cry, nature demands sleep, passengers will get angry, the drivers will swear, the sensitive will shrink, rations will give out, potatoes become worth a gold*

Staging in California, Joseph Gutzon Borglum

dollar each, and not to be had at that, the water brackish, the whiskey abominable, and the dirt almost unendurable. I have just finished six days and nights of this thing; and I am free to say, until I forget a great many things now very visible to me, I shall not undertake it again.[11]

Of all the creatures involved in this ride, the horses may have had it best. Roads were little more than rutted tracks most of the way, stagecoach suspensions were harsh, and seat cushions nearly nonexistent. Even so, the Overland Stage was the first commercial passenger and mail transportation across the West, and served until the railroads were built to carry visitors and tourists who had no need for wagon trains and little interest in sitting all day in the saddle.

By its nature, placer mining involved destruction of streambeds. Loose gold, being relatively heavy, settled toward bedrock, and the most concentrated deposits were usually well buried. Hydraulic mining, right, introduced larger and faster devastation. Here, powerful jets dislodge alluvial deposits—the so-called overburden—into sluice boxes, which separate gold from debris.

Asians, Hispanics, and blacks were all treated with approximate equality when it came to contemptuous dismissal and dislike, and they were the impartial recipients of retaliation when they expressed dissatisfaction over unconscionable and barbarous treatment. But their lot was a cakewalk in comparison to the genocidal extermination of California's Native American population, a devastation generally exacted by white civilians who gave no more thought to murdering an Indian than they gave to taking a potshot at a jackrabbit or slapping off a mosquito.

In 1848 there were approximately 150,000 Indians still living in California. Twelve years later, according to Professor James Sandoz of the University of Redlands, they had been reduced to about thirty thousand. Some of the attrition was due to the spread of Anglo diseases, some to starvation, and some to natural causes. "But it was the unnatural factors, the systematic murders of Indians by whites, that seem to have been the greatest single cause of death after 1848," Sandoz wrote.[12] Newspapers like the *Chico Courant* called for their annihilation: "It is a mercy to the red devils to exterminate them, and a saving of many white lives . . . there is only one kind of treaty that is effective—cold lead." Politicians joined the fray. ". . . there is no place within the territory of the United States in which to locate them," said State Senator J. J. Warner, "better, far better, to drive them at once into the ocean, or bury them in the land of their birth."

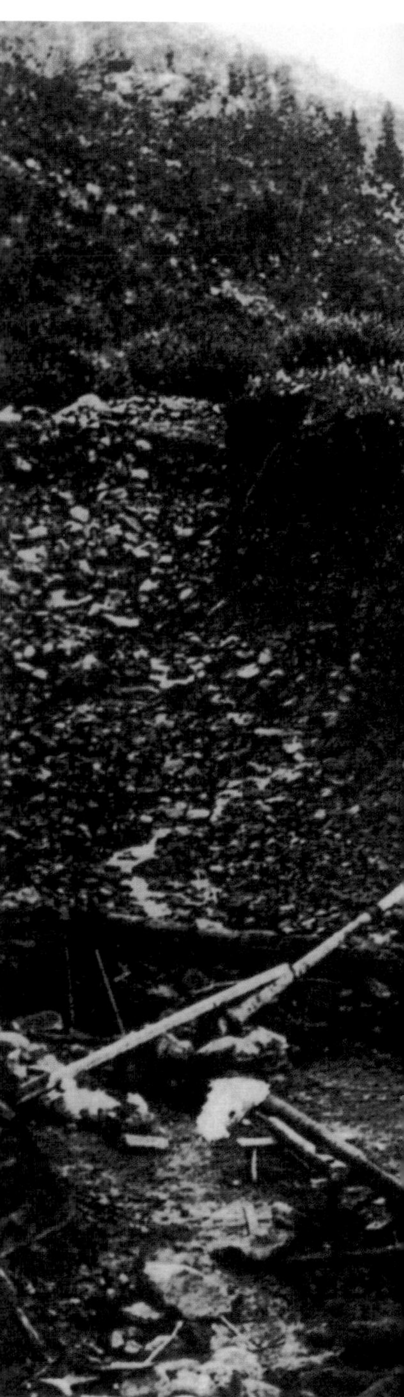

The capturing and enslaving of California's Indian population hardly began with the arrival of the Americans, and its continuance provided an easy way of procuring indentured servants to do the back-breaking work of placer mining and of providing a labor force for California's ranches and farms. However, killing Indians out of pure racial hatred, or in retaliation for occasional Indian stock raiding, was an Anglo escalation of historical practices that went far beyond their Spanish antecedents. And there were plenty of whites who hunted Indians just for the pure fun of it, wiping out whole tribes just as they might extirpate any form of pestilence that irked them. The Yanas of far northern California, for example, were systematically hunted down and shot until their numbers (about two thousand in 1849) had been reduced in less than two decades to fewer than fifty. "When whites ambushed a remnant group and killed 45 of them in 1867," Sandoz noted, "not enough Yana survived to bury the dead."[13] The last sad survivor of the Yahi, a subgroup of the Yana, appeared naked and starving and quite literally alone in Oroville in 1911. He was taken to San Francisco to be studied by the anthropologist Alfred Kroeber, who gave him the name "Ishi"—man.

A contemporary illustration, far left, portrays brutal Indians overwhelming white men. In fact it was the natives of California who were overwhelmed in savagery and genocide. Their tribal names are nearly forgotten: Modoc, near left, Yana, Patwin, Costano, Pomo, Miwok, Yuki, Nomlaki, Salinan, Chumash, Konkow, Maidu, Yahi, Chimariko, Esselen, Wintun, and many others.

Just as the fur trade had been the precipitant force behind the leap of fledgling civilization over the Great Plains to the Rockies, and from the Rockies over the Great Basin to the Pacific coast, the discovery of gold in California was the spontaneous combustion that turned fledgling into flock. Now Americans could start filling in the blanks, continuing to heed Horace Greeley's advice to "go west" by going east, by backtracking toward new mining discoveries in Nevada,

The placer rush had faded when, in 1859, the Comstock Lode was discovered on the eastern slope of the Sierra in what would become Nevada five years later. Virginia City, right, leaped into existence in 1861. Its mines were underground, hard-rock mines whose development required large financial investments, mills, smelters, and many employees.

Arizona, Utah, western Montana, Idaho, and the Dakotas. As the *Daily Oregonian* for July 12, 1862, observed, "What a clover is to a steer, the sky to the lark, a mudhole to a hog, such are newer diggings to a miner."[14] Wherever there was metal to be found, be it in Virginia City, Coeur d'Alene, Helena, the Black Hills, Leadville, Tombstone, Cripple Creek, or Tucson, former California Argonauts would be there, though they had the company of thousands of greenhorns still rushing from points east to join them in the hunt.

Until 1869 migrants had no choice but to do their rushing in the old-fashioned way—with horses, mules, oxen, covered wagons, handcarts, and shank's mare—in short, no choice but to earn it. Riverboats could get a man only as far as Great Falls on the Missouri, or maybe one thousand miles up the Red River and the Arkansas. So it wasn't until the decades-old dream of a transcontinental railroad was finally realized that the sheer amount of goods and services necessary to facilitate major settlement in the interior West would really begin to transform the American landscape and link it from "sea to shining sea."

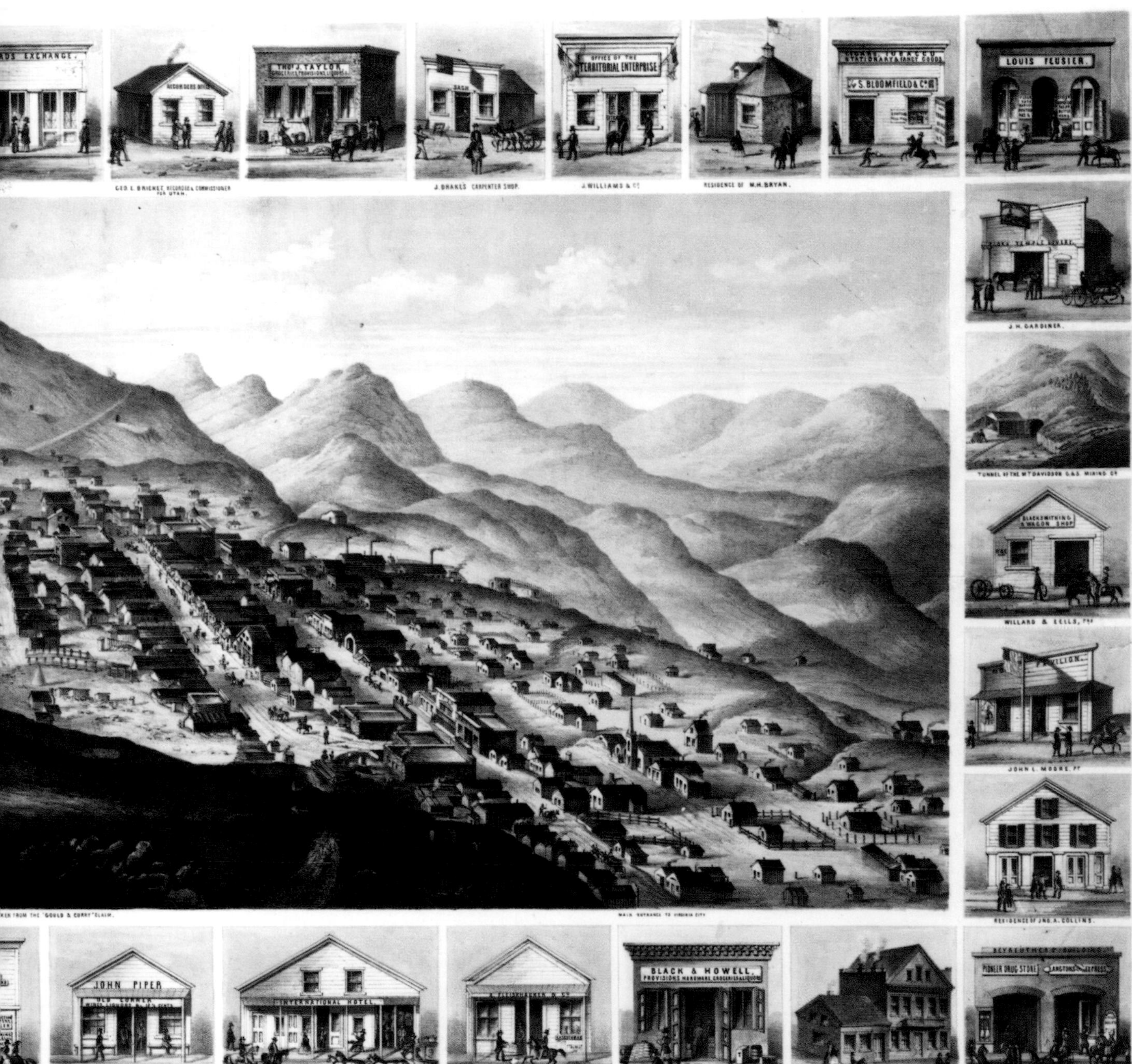
LOUIS FEUSIER
S. BLOOMFIELD & Co.
OFFICE OF THE TERRITORIAL ENTERPRISE
THOS. J. TAYLOR
GEO. L. BRIGHT, RECORDER & COMMISSIONER FOR UTAH.
J. DRAKES CARPENTER SHOP.
J. WILLIAMS & Co.
RESIDENCE OF M.H. BRYAN.
J. H. GARDINER.
TUNNEL OF THE Mt. DAVIDSON G.& S. MINING Co.
BLACKSMITHING & WAGON SHOP
WILLARD & EELLS, Prs.
JOHN L. MOORE, Pr.
RESIDENCE OF JNO. A. COLLINS.
MAIN ENTRANCE TO VIRGINIA CITY
JOHN PIPER
INTERNATIONAL HOTEL
PAUL & BATEMAN, PROPRIETORS.
A. FLEISHHACKER & Co.
BLACK & HOWELL,
PROVISIONS HARDWARE, GROCERIES & LIQUORS
L. HERMANN.
G. MALDONADA.
PIONEER DRUG STORE
LANGTONS EXPRESS
Dr. E. SMITH.
NELSON W. WINTON, AGENT.
BRITTON & Co. PRINT.
C.C. KUCHEL LITH. 174 CLAY ST S. FRANCISCO, CAL.

A railroad that would connect the East Coast with the Pacific had been discussed for many years before the discovery of gold in California made it almost politically de rigueur, and Congress, which had been debating potential routes throughout the 1850s, had happily authorized a series of U.S. Army surveys to come up with the most economical and practical options. Those surveys produced a lavishly illustrated, twelve-volume report full of wonderfully engraved representations of flora, fauna, and scenic vistas along the way, but oddly failed to give elevations, grades, or estimates of costs.

At the same time the Army was conducting its review, a group of California businessmen were proposing to build a short line railroad from Sacramento to the base of the mining camps, and they hired a young civil engineer from Bridgeport, Connecticut, named Theodore Judah to plan and oversee its construction. Judah completed the job in one year; he then stayed on in California to pursue his *real* dream, which was to explore a feasible route over the Sierra and across Nevada and Utah—thereby generating a major link in what he knew would eventually become a transcontinental system. It took Judah four years of obsessive proselytizing (indeed, he became known as "Crazy Judah") before he was able to convince a group of local entrepreneurs, the most conspicuous of whom were Leland Stanford, Mark Hopkins, Collis Huntington, and Charles Crocker, that not only did his plan have merit, but they would profit enormously from its success. Judah's coalition incorporated as the Central Pacific Rail Road of California on June 28, 1861, only a few months after the Union and Confederate states had clashed at Fort Sumter. Civil war was about to put Manifest Destiny on hold—but not the Central Pacific Rail Road.

War meant that the issue previously dividing Congress over the specific route of a transcontinental railroad (slave states vs. antislave states) was moot. It also meant that the government was no longer in any immediate position to fund or build such a project. Judah and his associates, however, were ready, and they argued that if the government would just be so kind as to assist with some thirty-year bond loans at 6 percent interest, grant a right-of-way over federal lands, and for every mile of track laid cede to the company alternate sections of the public's turf (at 6,400 acres per section), work could begin almost immediately. The government responded in the affirmative, and for good measure added a charter for a second company, the Union Pacific Railroad (charged with building west from Nebraska Territory). President Lincoln signed the act into law on July 1, 1862.

Theodore Judah, sadly, would not be around to witness what his imagination had created. His partners, better remembered for their rapacious greed than their kindly dispositions, squeezed him out long before track laying had progressed more than a few miles into the Sierra foothills, though Judah continued to maintain the illusion that he would eventually be able to buy them out and regain control.

By the 1870s, Virginia City, far left, had mushroomed around its tailings, piles, and smelters to an unofficially estimated population of more than thirty thousand. Wealth from the Comstock Lode had a major impact on the nation's finances. It built railroads (the transcontinental railroad was completed in 1869, below), mansions, and a number of great fortunes. Virginia City, however, became a ghost town.

THE CELESTIALS

When Charles Crocker, the general superintendent of the Central Pacific Railroad, told his Irish work boss, James Strobridge, to hire Chinese workers to build the roadbed for the transcontinental railway, Strobridge fumed, "I will not boss Chinese. I will not be responsible for work done on the road by Chinese labor. From what I've seen of them, they're not fit laborers anyway. I don't think they can build a railroad."[15] Crocker, of course, prevailed, though the fifty enforced hires that Strobridge acceded to were initially given menial jobs because they were clearly considered too small and delicate to do the work of real men. Denigrated as "Celestial monkeys" and "heathens," they were held in abject contempt by Europeans, and even the governor of California, Leland Stanford, dismissed them as "the dregs of Asia."

Most came from Kwangtung Province on the Canton delta, and from a country with a long history of building roads in extreme locations. It wasn't long before their engineering skills and work ethic dispelled any lingering concerns about their "frailty," but they continued to be despised for an even stranger reason—they built their roadbeds faster and straighter than their white counterparts, who refused to work on the same crews, and they did it without complaint no matter how adverse the conditions. Two weeks before the Central Pacific met the Union Pacific at Promontory Point in Utah, Charles Crocker is said to have made a bet that his "coolies" could lay ten miles of track in one day—which is to say some 3,520 lengths of rail, spiked to 28,000 ties. Crocker won. They exceeded his estimate by some fifty-six feet.

The completion of a transcontinental rail line was only the beginning. Chinese labor accounted for a large part of most of the railroads built in the West during the latter half of the 1800s, including the Southern Pacific, the Northern Pacific, and the Canadian Pacific. What is remarkable is that in spite of their obvious skill and dedication, in spite of their sacrifice (thousands of them died, unrecorded, in the process), the Chinese workers continued to be vilified and were never afforded the credit they were due. Not even in the famous photograph taken at Promontory Point to celebrate the meeting of the Union and Central Pacific is there a single Asian face to be seen among the crowd.

Transportation was critical to binding the nation together. Before railroads, overland choices were limited to the speed of a horse. It took months to cross the continent, or to make the long trip by sea. As railroads proved their value in the east, entrepreneurs rushed to extend their reach. In 1856, the Mississippi was bridged, and planners turned their eyes toward the coast.

Express Train, Currier & Ives

Perhaps he could have raised the needed capital through his contacts in the East, but it will never be known. Returning to New York via Panama in October of 1863, he contracted yellow fever at the Isthmus and died soon after his arrival in New York—four months short of his thirty-eighth birthday.

Over the six and a half years between January 8, 1863, and May 10, 1869, some 650 miles of track was laid between Sacramento, California, and Promontory, Utah, the eventual meeting point of the Union and Central Pacific railroads, and another 950 miles between Omaha, Nebraska, and Promontory. There have been dozens of books written on the staggering difficulties of building by hand labor alone a roadbed over the mountains and across the plains and deserts—blasting, tunneling, constructing giant trestles over abysmal canyons, and coping with freezing temperatures in winter, blast-furnace heat in summer, hostile Indians, and financial crises. Suffice it to say it was a Herculean task.

And they got it done in record time. On that great day in the spring of 1869 when the two lines were finally joined in northern Utah there was a celebratory contingency of some five hundred people in attendance, with Chinese and Irish laborers, train crews, teamsters, and workers mingling with distinguished officials and illustrious guests. Leland Stanford and Mark Hopkins exchanged formalities with UP executive Thomas C. Durant. Photographer A. J. Russell snapped his famous picture of the two locomotives, the Jupiter and No. 119, about to kiss cowcatchers. Telegraph operators stood by ready to transmit to a breathless

Just sixty-three years after Lewis and Clark returned to St. Louis, the first transcontinental railroad was completed. Others, including the Central Pacific, below, in the Nevada desert, followed in short order. The illustration at right shows the cross-country march of white civilization while native Americans, on the wrong side of the tracks, get a blast of smoke and cinders.

nation the news that (paraphrasing Hubert Howe Bancroft) the royal marriage had been consummated. In fact, a telegraph line had been attached to the golden spike itself so that the sound of Leland Stanford's silver hammer might ring across the country when he drove that final clinch pin into the last laurel-wood tie, itself beautifully finished and inlayed with a silver plaque, symbolically uniting East with West. Stanford raised his hammer, took aim . . . and missed the spike. The percipient telegraph operator simulated the anticipated impact with his sending key; manifest destiny's finest hour was duly transmitted, and America cheered.

There would soon be other transcontinental railroads built. The Atcheson, Topeka, and Santa Fe would reach the Pacific coast by 1883; the Northern Pacific would arrive in Portland that same year; the Great Northern would connect Seattle with Duluth in 1893. The journey across the country that had taken the Argonauts and their predecessors and immediate successors four to five months could now be done in a few weeks or less, and it could be done with all of one's equipment and belongings in tow. But while the railroads would alter the ease and manner of travel, and radically alter the patterns of migration, one thing they could not change was a people's motivation. Call it materialism, avidity, pipe dreaming, perennial dissatisfaction, or merely the prospect of cheap land and the chance to make a better life, "heading west" would keep Americans on the move long after corporeal gains had stopped being measured in ounces and appraised by the carat.

Across the Continent, F. F. Palmer (Currier & Ives)

ETERNAL LANDSCAPES

Between the Sierra and the Rockies lies a huge, challenging expanse called the Great Basin. Occupying most of Nevada and parts of neighboring states, the basin is a desert studded with small but imposing mountain ranges. Rivers run down from their snow-laden summits, but no water flows out. Instead, it pools in isolated depressions such as Pyramid Lake in western Nevada, right, or the Great Salt Lake in Utah. There was gold and silver to be found in this difficult region but only by the most determined of prospectors. Those who could manage the rugged conditions discovered a beautiful but strange landscape sporting such oddities as Hot Springs Geyser in the Black Rock Desert, inset. The house on the next page is among remnants of Bodie, California, a boomtown so famously lawless that a girl whose family was moving there wrote in her diary, "Good-bye God, I'm going to Bodie."

Mining fortunes laid the foundations of cities including Denver and San Francisco. Wagon trails built to haul ore and other supplies became the highways and railroads of today. Ranches, bakeries, sawmills, hotels, churches, and saloons got their start serving mines and miners, and found ways to survive when the ore ran out. But where there was no reason to stick around, as in the Nevada boomtowns of Palmetto, left, and Austin, inset, people vanished like ghosts.

just a plain bowlegged human who smelled very

horsey, slept in his underwear and was subject to boils and dispepsia."

—Jo Mora, cowboy and historian, 1901

The Herd Quitter (detail), Charles M. Russell

THE STRENUOUS LIFE

[1870–1899]

They had very little grub and they usually run out of that and lived on straight beef; they had only three or four horses to the man, mostly with sore backs, because the old time saddle ate both ways, the horse's back and the cowboy's pistol pocket; they had no tents, no tarps, and damn few slickers. They never kicked, because those boys was raised under just the same conditions as there was on the trail—corn meal and bacon for grub, dirt floors in the houses, and no luxuries. . . . They used to brag they could go any place a cow could and stand anything a horse could. It was their life. . . .

In person the cowboys were mostly medium-sized men, as a heavy man was hard on horses, quick and wiry, and as a rule very good natured; in fact it did not pay to be anything else. In character there like never was or will be again. They were intensely loyal to the outfit they were working for and would fight to the death for it. They would follow their wagon boss through hell and never complain. I have seen them ride into camp after two days and nights on herd, lay down on their saddle blankets in the rain, and sleep like dead men, then get up laughing and joking about some good time they had had in Ogallala or Dodge City. Living that kind of a life, they were bound to be wild and brave. In fact there was only two things the old-time cowpuncher was afraid of, a decent woman and being set afoot.[1]

—E. C. "Teddy Blue" Abbott, Cowboy

The Open Range

Most of the year cattle roamed the range, scattering to wherever they could find grazing. Unlike sheep, they weren't kept in a bunch, watched over and protected by a cowboy until the roundup before a cattle drive. Trail drives were often punctuated by a stampede, either because the herd was spooked by lightning, far right, or because they smelled water after several days of walking over a parched landscape.

IT WAS PERFECTLY clear to those early explorers who first ventured out onto the Great Plains that the region was unsuitable for human habitation. And since the focus of their interest was primarily on the distant Rocky Mountains and the even more distant Pacific, they were predisposed to regard it primarily as an uninspiring obstacle to westward migration and dismiss it. Zebulon Pike acknowledged a possibility for population as far as the ninety-eighth parallel, though he advised potential inhabitants to plan on living in adobe mud houses (for lack of wood) and limit their agricultural activities to "the multiplication of cattle, horses, sheep, and goats . . ." As for the country beyond the ninety-eighth parallel, he judged that it might prove useful to the United States in one particular respect, "viz: The restriction of our population to some certain limits, and thereby a continuation of the union."[2]

If the usually upbeat Mr. Pike always tended to see a glass that was half full, Major Stephen Long was inclined to see it half empty. In the only account that remains of his 1819–20 expedition to find the sources of the Red River, his botanist/geologist, Dr. Edwin James, opined: "In regard to this extensive section of country, I do not hesitate in giving my opinion, that it is almost wholly unfit for cultivation and of course uninhabitable by people depending upon agriculture for their subsistence."[3] Like Pike he felt that its greatest importance was as a barrier against American overextension into the West, and as a buffer against possible aggression from Spain and Great Britain.

There is a geographical band of demarcation through the middle of America where eastern mixed forest stops and tall-grass prairie begins to shade gently upward into short-grass plains, and where precipitation declines from more than twenty annual inches to as few as ten. It is not a precise boundary that can be drawn with a straightedge, but it can be traced generally downward from Canada (using a palsied hand) through the eastern half of the Dakotas, central Nebraska, and western Kansas, Oklahoma, and

The Stampede by Lightning, Frederic Remington

Texas. And it extends, with some notable islands of exception (the Rockies, the Sierra, western Washington and Oregon), all the way to the Pacific slope. Its principal geophysical features, in order of importance, are aridity, treelessness, and a comparatively level surface.

The land's psychological features are less prosaic. The painter John Noble remarked, "You look on, on, on, out into space, out almost beyond time itself. You see nothing but the rise and swell of land and

THE HAT THAT WON THE WEST

When the era of the big cattle drives began in the 1860s, hats worn up to that time by frontiersmen weren't up to the job. The cheap wool brims quickly collapsed under the wear and tear of rain, wind, and sun, and cowboys who wore them often found it necessary to pin the front of the brim to the crown to keep it out of their eyes. The first Stetson hat, the "Boss of the Plains," was a practical, durable, and stylish hat that would last through years of grueling work on the prairie. But the West is a big place; the needs of the men varied and so did the styles of their hats.

Desert drifters preferred a hat with a flat-topped crown and wide brim to reflect sun and provide as much shade as possible. The southwestern cowboys wanted a wide-brimmed hat with a high crown to keep their heads cooler. Men from the windy northern plains liked a smaller brim for more stability in the wind.

A hat's individual style, though, came from the hatband, originally added to provide more stability to the base of the crown, and from the crease added to the top. And the way a man wore his hat often signaled his mood. A hat tilted back on the head indicated the wearer was relaxed. If it was pulled down in front, he was in a serious mood. And cocked to the side meant the man may be shifty. The hat afforded shade as well as individuality. In a pinch it was a fan to help start a fire, a water container to put one out or to water a horse with, even a goad to get a mount moving in a hurry.

Cavalry-style slouch hat with a slope crease

Carlsbad crease and snap brim

Well-worn cowpuncher's hat with a rolled brim

Flat brim with a Canadian crease

High crown with a Carlsbad crease and ranch brim

"Boss of the Plains" with an open crown

Carlsbad crease with a rolled brim

In his 1866 painting, The Lost Greenhorn, right, Alfred Jacob Miller portrays the disorienting effects of the vast, nearly featureless sea of grass that was the Great Plains before fences and roads and power lines cut it into smaller patches. A confused rider could see a long distance and find nothing familiar in all that space.

grass, and then more grass—the monotonous, endless prairie! A stranger traveling on the prairie would get his hopes up, expecting to see something different on making the next rise. To him the disappointment and monotony were terrible. 'He's got loneliness,' we would say of such a man."[4]

Its most common comparative is the ocean, which to the viewer appears measureless and empty, its rolling horizon of grass like swells on a storm-tossed sea:

Like an ocean in its vast extent, in its monotony, and in its danger, it is like the ocean in its romance, in its opportunities for heroism, and in the fascination it exerts on all those who come fairly within its influence. The first experience of the plains, like the first sail with a 'cap' full of wind, is apt to be sickening. This once overcome, the nerves stiffen, the senses expand, and man begins to realize the magnificence of being.[5]

Viewed through a Victorian lens, the Great Plains seemed essentially a hurdle to be vaulted on the way to the mountains, to the beaver streams and goldfields, and it wasn't until the middle of the nineteenth century that Europeans were able to find a rightful purpose for all that great empty space. Of course, for the Apache, Kiowa, Arapaho, Teton-Dakota, Cheyenne, Comanche, and some twenty-five other tribes, it was home, as it had been at least twenty-five thousand years earlier, when the first "paleo-Indian" hunters arrived in the Southwest. And for the Spanish, once the conquistadors had concluded there was nothing there to exploit and the friars found nobody to convert who would stay converted, it was a miserable wilderness to be avoided, and avoided it was.

The Lost Greenhorn, Alfred Jacob Miller

CATTLE DRIVE TRAILS

Look out for the cows' feet and the horses' backs and let the cowhands and cook take care of themselves.

—TRAIL BOSSES' SLOGAN

In the years between the Mexican War and the Civil War, Texas cattlemen drove their longhorns up the Shawnee Trail from southern Texas through Missouri to St Louis and to railheads farther north, where they were loaded onto trains bound for the slaughterhouses of Chicago. But during the 1850s, Missouri cattle began to die by the thousands from a mysterious illness that was soon connected to the ticks carried north by hardy Texas longhorns. Missouri lawmakers banned Texas cattle from entering the state in 1858. Vigilantes turned back herds at the state line, and, after a hiatus in cattle drives caused by the Civil War, cattlemen began to follow a new route to market known as the Chisholm Trail, which terminated at Ellsworth and Abilene, Kansas.

The Colorado gold rush created a new western market, and the Goodnight-Loving Trail to Denver became wildly profitable, but not just to feed hungry emigrants. Army posts in former Indian lands had to feed the captive and starving Plains Indian tribes as well as themselves, and the government paid premium prices for beef and brood stock, and Goodnight-Loving, as well as the Western Trail after about 1885, became longhorn thoroughfares northward.

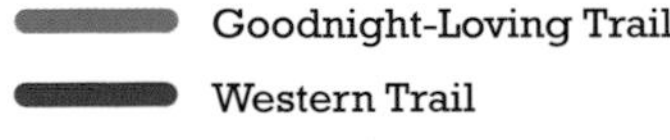

Goodnight-Loving Trail
Western Trail
Chisholm Trail

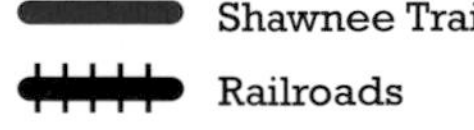

Shawnee Trail
Railroads

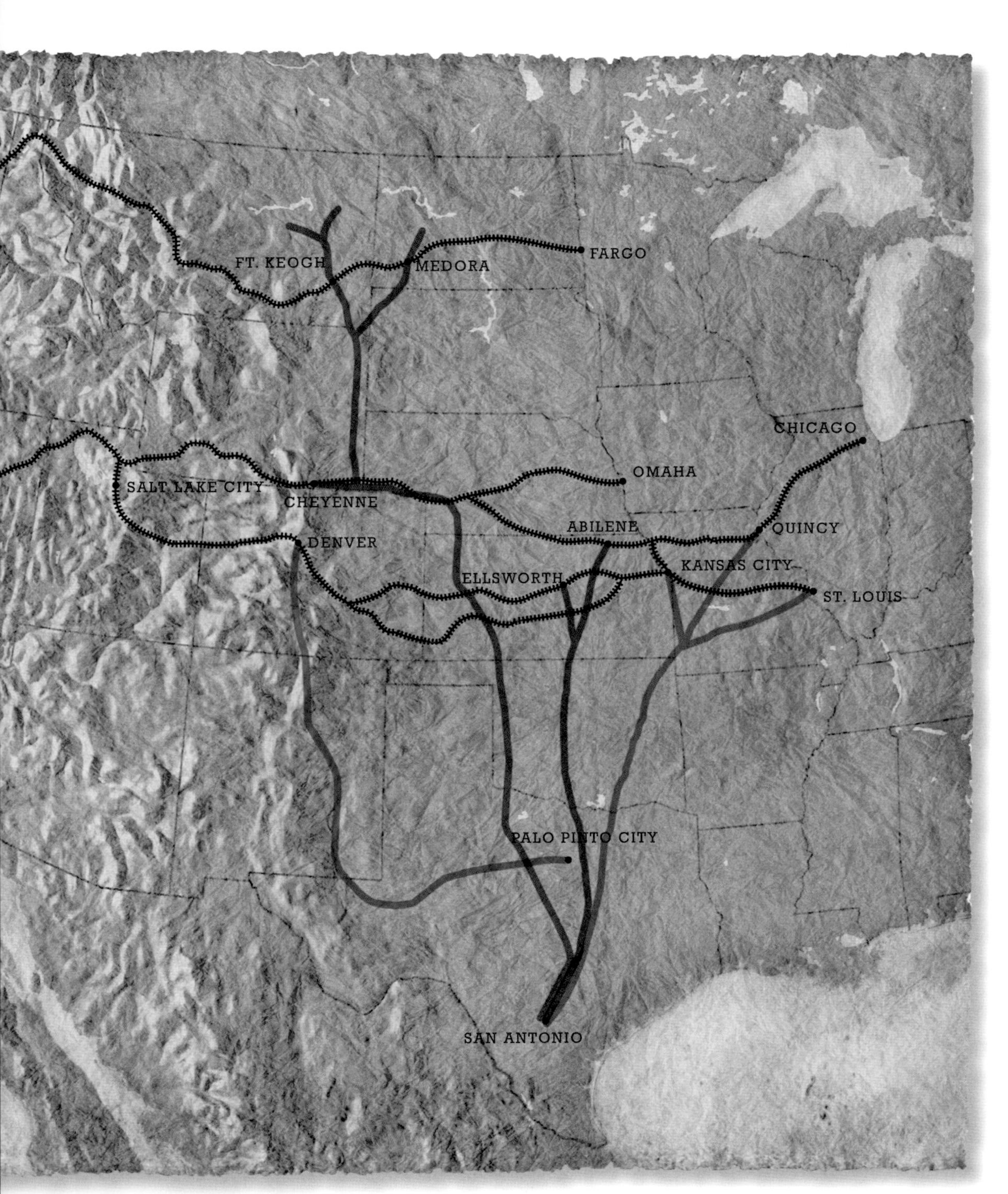
FT. KEOGH
MEDORA
FARGO
CHICAGO
OMAHA
SALT LAKE CITY
CHEYENNE
ABILENE
QUINCY
DENVER
KANSAS CITY
ELLSWORTH
ST. LOUIS
PALO PINTO CITY
SAN ANTONIO

With the exception of Santa Fe and San Antonio, they made only feeble efforts at colonization and established only a few missions (the mission system was abandoned on Spain's northern frontier in 1772); otherwise they left the land to its rightful inhabitants, the Comanche and Apache.

Throughout the first half of the nineteenth century the plains were, for Americans, little more than a highway to the Pacific. The frontier stopped where the woodlands stopped, some three hundred miles west of the Mississippi, and then jumped two thousand miles to Oregon country and California, where emigrants found themselves in a geophysical environment they could understand—one that may have taken them a great effort to reach, but that required very little in the way of adaptation once they got there. Even migration into Texas during the 1820s was concentrated in the eastern half of the territory, where the land was well watered and well timbered. But repeated traversing of that broad subhumid expanse of prairie, whether by the Oregon Trail through the northern plains or the Santa Fe Trail across the southwest, familiarized a great many people with its true characteristics and revealed that it was not, as the textbooks continued to portray right up through the 1850s, a Sahara Desert of howling winds and sand fit for neither man nor beast. In fact it sustained beasts in great plenty—buffalo, for one, and in the Nueces and Rio Grande Valley, wild cattle.

The plains of the north, being better watered than those of the south, offered the best grass. A gentle drainage in Wind Cave National Park near South Dakota's Black Hills, left, represents the lush and diverse grasslands that once supported millions of buffalo and fueled the dreams of early cattlemen.

To understand the origins of the cattle "kingdom" on the Great Plains one needs to start in Mexico, where in the sparse environment of the Sierra Maestra ranching dates back to the mid-sixteenth century. Over a period of 150 years, livestock raising gradually spread northward into the present states of Coahuila, Chihuahua, and Tamaulipas, until in 1690 a Spaniard named Alonso de León drove the first herd into east Texas to the Spanish mission at San Francisco de los Tejas. Within a couple of decades cattle had wandered as far as the Neches and Trinity Rivers, and had become ubiquitous throughout an area that extended from present-day Houston to Nacogdoches. Other herds were pushed north out of Nuevo Leon into the valleys of the Nueces and Rio Grande to supply the missions along the San Antonio River, and when these outposts were abandoned because of persistent problems with the Indians, the cattle stayed behind. By the time Anglos began arriving in Texas during the early nineteenth century, thousands of cattle were roaming wild throughout the eastern and southern part of the territory.

It was one thing to grow cattle on the Great Plains, but quite another to get them to market. One of the main jobs of a cowboy was to help round up the cattle each year and drive the ones chosen for sale, far right, to the nearest railhead, which could be hundreds of miles away.

These cattle were that bovine star of the silver screen, the Texas longhorn, a breed that evolved from the first cattle ever to set foot on North American soil and one that over time became uniquely adapted to the primitive brush-country range of Mexico and the southwestern United States. The longhorn was tough and aggressive, and it acquired over a period of three centuries the ability to eat almost anything it could find on its sparse, arid range—buffalo grass, of course, but also such delicacies as mesquite, yucca, willow, and acacia. The brute had a longevity of over twenty years, and was highly resistant to both parasites and tick fever. Moreover, because its uterine canal was wide and the birth weight of its calves low, its fertility and survival rate was a

"The coffee has the dropsy,
the tea the grippe.

The butter was consumptive, the flapjacks they had fits.

The beef was strong and jubilant, it walked upon the floor.

The spuds lost all their dignity and rolled right out the door.

The pudding had the jimjams, the pie was in disguise.

The beans came to the table with five hundred thousand flies . . ."

—Part of a poem written by the patrons of one western boardinghouse

PEACEKEEPERS OF DODGE CITY

Dodge City, located five miles from Fort Dodge on the old Santa Fe Trail, began as a trading post for buffalo hunters and then became a shipping point for Texas cattle once the Santa Fe Railroad arrived in 1872. Like most cow towns, it sported an ample supply of saloons, dance halls, gambling houses, and brothels, and since most of its tourist trade tended to be thirsty drovers in a mood to "paint the town (any town) red" it had a high incidence of drunken comportment and generalized antisocial behavior that required the full attention of some pretty stiff-necked, competent lawmen.

"Doc" Holliday

For the first year of its unincorporated life Dodge had no government or law enforcement at all, but it had fifteen killings, and this level of disorderliness led to the formation of a vigilance committee. Unfortunately, the vigilantes soon became the problem rather than the solution, and they undermined their own civic support when two of them, for no apparent reason, shot and killed the servant of Colonel Richard Dodge, commanding officer of Fort Dodge. Colonel Dodge went ballistic and called in the troops to deal with the vigilantes. That same day Charlie Bassett was appointed sheriff of Ford County, serving two terms from 1873 to 1877, then being replaced by one of the most famous lawmen of all time, William "Bat" Masterson.

William "Bat" Masterson

The first marshal of Dodge City, Lawrence Deger, was completely overwhelmed trying to deal with the dozens of libidinous, binge-drinking waddies who shepherded over 200,000 cattle into Dodge every year, and was said to be greatly relieved when, in 1876, the city's mayor hired Wyatt Earp to give him a hand. Earp, who was given full control to institute policy and handpick his own assistants, created a "deadline" at the edge of town, beyond which any cowboy carrying a gun would be arrested. "Each officer carried two six-guns," he

Wyatt Earp

once said in an interview, "and I placed shotguns at convenient points, as I had in Wichita, but killing was to be our last resort . . . I figured that if the cowboys were manhandled and heaved into the calaboose every time they showed in town with guns on, or cut loose in forbidden territory, they'd come to time quicker than if we kept them primed for gunplay. Hoover had hired me to cut down the killings in Dodge, not to increase them."[6]

1873 Colt Single Action Peacemaker

phenomenal 99 percent. No wonder that by the end of the Civil War there were an estimated five million longhorn strolling around Texas.

Like the longhorn, the occupation of cattle herder was imported from Latin America; the cowboy was preceded (and paralleled) in time by the Argentinean *gaucho*, the Venezuelan *llanero*, the Chilean *huaso*, and the Mexican *vaquero*. When Americans began moving into Texas and learning to adapt to an environment that was unlike anything they had previously experienced, one of the more exotic aspects of their education was learning to do everything while bouncing along on the back of an equine, be it chasing adversaries (both Mexicans and Indians were highly accomplished equestrians), hunting wild game, visiting neighbors, or managing a herd of cattle. In this latter regard, the man on foot was utterly without influence over the Texas longhorn.

One weakness of western ranching was, and remains, limited water. The West, on average, is a desert that becomes parched and dusty during summer. Mountains serve as natural reservoirs, trapping abundant winter snow and releasing moisture gradually. Moisture trapped by the Sierra never makes its was east to the deserts, left, leaving vast tracts of land too arid to support cattle.

Colonel Theodore A. Dodge, in his 1877 book *The Hunting Grounds of the Great West*, had a few observations to make about the nasty disposition of "domesticated" Texas beef: "A footman is never safe when a herd is in his vicinity; and every sportsman who has hunted quail in Texas will have experienced the uneasiness natural to any man around whom a crowd of long-horned beasts are pawing the earth and tossing their heads in anger at his appearance."[7] The tame Texas cow, said Mr. Dodge, was "fifty times more dangerous to footmen than the fiercest buffalo."[8]

An 1880 report on the livestock industry in the Southwest prior to the Civil War reveals that there was considerable activity on the open range before the big northern drives began in 1865, but that it was sporadic and insignificant in comparison to what was to come:

There wasn't much leisure time for cowboys on the trail. The usual workday was dawn to dusk, plus time spent on night watch. In the photo at far right, the man on the left wears cowhide chaps, leg coverings that button up the side and protect his legs. The rope-twirler's are made of angora goatskin, valued for its supple fit.

In 1837 and 1838, the "cowboys" gathered herds of from three hundred to a thousand head of the wild unbranded cattle of the Nueces and Rio Grande country, and drove them for sale to cities of the interior. In 1842 the driving of cattle to New Orleans began. The first shipment from Texas was by a Morgan steamer in 1848, but up to 1849 there were very few outlets for the stock, which had increased enormously since 1830. . . . In 1850 drives began to California. The first drive to Chicago was in 1856. From the beginning of the northern drives in 1846 until the war of the rebellion there was always some movement of cattle out of Texas, but it was irregular. A large proportion of the cattle driven was sold on the plains.[9]

There was not much value to five million cows confined in a small area south of the Nueces River and along the eastern border with Louisiana. According to that same 1880 livestock report, they would have been worth between three and four dollars a head if a local market for them had existed—which it didn't. But markets did exist in the North and East, where those same cows would fetch ten times as much, the only problem being how to get them there in a condition where they were still fit to eat. Trailing them through the difficult timbered country of Arkansas to the railhead at St. Louis left them emaciated, their meat stringy and tough, and southern Missouri and southeastern Kansas were a viper's nest of rustlers, bandits, and killers.

Enter Joseph McCoy, an Illinois livestock shipper and the prototype "Real McCoy." McCoy figured out that he could make a fair piece of change if he could establish a safe point to which drovers could trail

"Have not got the Blues but am in Hel of a fix . . . My back is Blistered badly . . . Flies worse than I ever saw them . . . One man down with the Boils & one with Ague . . . Found a Human skeleton on the Prairie today."—COWBOY GEORGE DEFFIELD ON A CATTLE DRIVE IN 1866

VIGILANTES

Prior to the formation of a formally constituted government and the establishment of a legally chartered system for law enforcement, many frontier communities had vigilance committees that tried to keep some semblance of order. In the mining camps, which tended to attract an unusually large number of lowlife miscreants in search of easy marks, the vigilance committee would be formed by a few leading citizens. Membership would gradually increase until there was a large and determined enough force to challenge the lawless element that had taken over. Then two or three of the most unsavory desperadoes would be identified, hunted down, tried on the spot, and immediately hanged from the nearest tree, which had the effect of discouraging further malfeasance on the part of other operatives still remaining in town.

The most notorious vigilante action took place in 1862 in Bannock County, Idaho Territory, near the overcrowded goldfields around Lewiston. Truth and innuendo have become so intermingled that it is difficult to tell precisely who was guilty of what, but what is not open for speculation is the fact that a vigilante committee organized by a young lawyer named Wilbur Sanders decided that Sheriff Henry Plummer was leading a double life as both a law officer and the head of a gang of murdering bandits. For openers, the vigilantes hanged two of Plummer's alleged accomplices, one of whom supposedly confirmed Plummer's guilt just before he died; then they dragged the sheriff and two of his deputies from their homes, and after the merest whiff of a trial hanged them as well. The only Hispanic in Bannock, a man referred to as "the greaser," was next to swing, though he had nothing to do with Plummer; his only obvious crime was being Mexican. Five more suspects "stretched the hemp" on January 14, and the grand total for February was nine.

Eventually it became clear to the civilized denizens of eastern Idaho and western Montana that the Bannock County vigilantes were little better than the alleged criminals they were so enthusiastically stringing up, and support for their conduct dissipated. One angry citizen group even threatened to hang five vigilantes for every future outlaw executed without the benefit of a trial by law. Unfortunately for Sheriff Plummer, of whose guilt there was no hard evidence, civil revulsion came a little too late.

J. C. Kuhn, Photographer.

their herds north across the plains and intersect with a railroad, and he set about to implement that vision. He negotiated a shipping contract with the Kansas Pacific Railroad and another with the Hannibal and St. Joe; then he checked out suitable points along the line that might be receptive to his idea. Eventually he settled on Abilene, one of the few that was. In his famous book *Historic Sketches of the Cattle Trade of the West and Southwest*, McCoy describes Abilene as "a very small, dead place, consisting of about one dozen log huts, low, small, rude affairs, four fifths of which were covered with dirt for roofing."[10] He chose it, he says, "because the country was entirely unsettled, well watered, excellent grass, and nearly the entire area of country was adapted to holding cattle."[11]

The year was 1867, and the United States had its first "cow town." There would be others like Ellsworth, Ogallala, Cheyenne, Wichita, and Dodge City, but none quite so romantically mythologized. Wickedness was not invented in Abilene, but in its saloons and whorehouses the base and sinful were free to revel, and it was well known throughout the cattle kingdom as the best place for a cowboy to "paint the town red." Dodge gave it a run, but Dodge had Wyatt Earp, "Bat" Masterson, "Doc" Holliday, Charles Bassett, and "Shotgun" Collins as its marshals (Abilene had only "Wild Bill" Hickok), and these gentlemen had a reputation for keeping the lid on. In Andy Adams's *Log of a Cowboy* an old drover tells him, "Dodge is one town where the average bad man of the West not only finds his equal, but find himself badly handicapped. . . .

Mixed bloodlines are evident in this group of cattle, left. The first western cattle were Spanish longhorns, toughened to hard conditions in the southwest and strong enough to survive long trail drives. As transportation improved, ranchers switched to less hardy but fast-growing shorthorn breeds—Devon, Hereford, Angus and others.

Don't ever get the impression that you can ride your horses into a saloon, or shoot out the lights in Dodge; it may go somewhere else, but it don't go there. . . . Most cowboys think it's an infringement on their rights to give up shooting in town, and if it is, it stands, for your six-shooters are no match for Winchesters and buckshot; and Dodge's officers are as game a set of men as ever faced danger."[12]

To fling a lariat over the horns of a running, 800-pound steer was to grab the tail of a tiger. A cowboy could get pulled off his horse and dragged. If his hand got caught between the rope and the saddle horn, he could lose fingers. Having to do it in timber, right, just increased the hazards.

Between 1867 and 1871, just under one and a half million cattle passed through Abilene's stockyards and loading chutes. The typical drive began in the spring, plodding its way north in a long, winding line at a pace of about twelve to fourteen miles a day. A herd of two thousand cows might have a crew of seven or eight drovers, a cook, a horse wrangler to look after fifty to sixty horses, and a trail boss to hold it all together. There was a hierarchy, of course: top hands (pointers) were at the head of the herd, followed by the swing men, the flankers, and finally the drag men, whose dust-swollen eyes betrayed their lowly status to any who bothered to notice.

It was some eight hundred miles from the Nueces valley to Abilene, which meant about two months of hardship and danger on the trail, all for a wage of from twenty-five to forty dollars a month. A man could drown fording a river, get thrown and dragged, get swallowed up in a stampede, and wind up as carrion; he could get rained on, snowed on, dried out, and poached by the blistering sun. "The real cowhand's typical day," writes Ramon Adams, "was anything but romantic. There was no romance in getting up at four o'clock in the morning, eating dust behind a trail herd, swimming muddy and turbulent rivers, nor in doctoring screw worms, pulling stupid cows from bog holes, sweating in the heat of summer, and freezing in the cold of winter."[13]

There was no romance in a stampede either, even though stampedes make for great action shots in a Hollywood production, not to mention canonize the pointers who heroically turn the herd. In the first weeks of a drive almost anything could provoke spooky cattle into bolting—lightning, thunder, or any sudden, unexpected noise—and sometimes they'd freak out for no apparent reason at all except, perhaps, genetic memories of Ponce de León or Hernán Cortés and the Sierra Maestra. The famous Texas cattleman Charles Goodnight described the process of trying to stop the flight of a herd of stampeding cattle:

Hell in the Timber, B. Gollings

BLACK COWBOYS

Black slaves were brought into Texas during the 1830s and 1840s by Anglo settlers migrating west out of the South (an estimated 35,000 of them by the time of statehood in 1845), and because many of them had already acquired herding skills on southern "cattle plantations" in South Carolina, Georgia, Alabama, Mississippi, and Louisiana they were readily absorbed into the fledgling ranch culture of south Texas. Over time many escaped into northern Mexico, where they encountered the Mexican vaqueros (referred to as "greasers" by the racially sensitive white folks who lived on the right side of the Rio Grande) and learned their horsemanship and roping skills from the Latino cowboy.

In the aftermath of the Civil War, thousands of now "emancipated" blacks worked on ranches in the southeastern part of the state (estimates vary from five to nine thousand), and during the heyday of big cattle drives to the railheads in Kansas nearly one out of every four drovers was an African-American. Many were considered top hands, and for the most part their pay and job assignments were equivalent to those of their white counterparts, though few, if any, ever achieved the rank of "trail boss." Indeed, on at least one trail drive the entire crew was said to be black except the trail boss. However, social equality was a separate matter from occupational parity, and while African-Americans fared better than Hispanics, there was no less discrimination on the frontier than anywhere else in nineteenth-century America.

A few black cowboys went on to enjoy their fifteen minutes of fame, if not fortune—men like Bose Ikard, who rode with Charles Goodnight and Oliver Loving on the Goodnight-Loving Trail and later with John Chisum, or Jim Perry of the XIT ranch, or Bill Picket, a famous cow puncher turned bulldogger whom Richard Slatta identifies in *Cowboys of the Americas* as being known for wrestling a steer by grabbing its horns, biting its upper lip, then dropping his hands to his sides and bringing the animal down with his teeth. "He died," says Slatta, "as a result of kicks from a horse in 1932. . . ."

Twice a year, in spring and again in fall, cowboys would round up the herds. New calves were branded and young males castrated. These men are handling an adult animal stretched by two ropes, one to the horns and one to the hind legs. Their horses have been trained to pull back and keep the ropes taut while the cowboys do their work.

The task of the men was to gain control of the herd and gradually turn the cattle until they were moving in a circle. Then, although they might break each other's horns off and crush one another badly, the great danger was past. A well-trained night-horse needed but little guidance, and knew that if the herd came his way, all that he had to do was to lead. The speed of the herd was terrific, but the position at the head of the stampede was what the trail man desired, for there he was in position to start the herd turning. . . .[14]

If, however, that night-horse stepped in a gopher hole and threw his rider, or for any one of a number of reasons couldn't keep ahead of the herd, then the consequences were likely to be catastrophic—as happened during an Idaho stampede in 1889 when some 341 cattle were killed as well as several horses, and one cowboy "was literally mangled to sausage meat."

Had Hector St. John Crevecoeur been born a hundred years later than he was, he might well have changed his famous query to read, "Who then is the *cowboy*, this new man?" instead of "Who then is the American . . ." The cowboy is our most enduring cultural myth. He embodies our Walter Mitty dreams of freedom and irresponsibility, self-reliance, and toughness. We imagine him uncompromising, a little

prone to violence, tender when it comes to horseflesh, and wary, though polite, around women. He is rootless, unhampered by the workday trappings of family and community; his home is "where the buffalo roam" out on the "lone prairie," where "the lonesome cattle feed on the lowly jimsonweed."

But who was he really. One view is expressed by Wallace Stegner in his essay "The Twilight of Self-Reliance": "The cowboy, so mythically free in books and movies, was a hired man on horseback, a slave to cows and the deadliest enemy of the range he used to ride." Another is expressed by Joseph McCoy, the man who established Abilene as a cattle-shipping point:

He lives hard, works hard, has but few comforts and fewer necessities. He has but little, if any, taste for reading. He enjoys a coarse practical joke or smutty story; loves danger but abhors labor of the common kind; never tires riding, never wants to walk, no matter how short the distance he desires to go. He would rather fight with pistols than pray; loves tobacco, liquor and women better than any other trinity. His life borders nearly upon that of an Indian. If he reads anything, it is in most cases a blood and thunder story of a sensational style. He enjoys his pipe, and relishes a practical joke on comrades, or a corrupt tale, wherein abounds much vulgarity and animal propensity.[15]

Smoke of a .45, Charles M. Russell

FEED STABLE
LICENSED GAMBLING
$1000 REWARD

A horse, as any number of greenhorns and dudes have learned, does not a cowboy make. Yet what sort of man is a cowboy without a horse? It doesn't matter if he's a good roper, or can spit tobacco juice twenty-five feet, a horseless cowboy is a mere pedestrian, and not a cowboy at all.

It's hard to understand how working one hundred hours a week in the wake of an "ugly, clumsy, stupid, bawling, stinking, fly-covered, shit-smeared, disease-spreading" herd of cows (the characterization is Edward Abbey's), living on a diet of coffee, beef, and chewing tobacco, and entertaining one's self by binge drinking, puking on one's boots, and having an occasional poke with a pox-ridden whore could translate into a heroic figure. But there's no point in arguing about it. The cowboy is always going to be our most enduring myth, and only an incurable crank would insist on a realistic appraisal.

In the 1870s, a man looking to start ranching on the northern plains had only to find a site with good grass and good water, and build himself a house of some sort and a few corrals and holding pens. The range was open, and his "ranch" consisted of all the land his cows could graze on. He didn't actually have legal title to anything, but "range rights" were understood by all, and his neighbors (who might be thirty or forty miles away) respected them because they expected him to respect theirs. Cattle, of course, didn't know one owner from another and mingled freely, but brand markings identified each ranch, and whatever couldn't be kept separated by line riders "drifting" cattle back toward their own ranges got sorted out during the spring and fall roundups.

The roundup might cover an area of four or five thousand square miles and involve several hundred men from as many as twelve to twenty different outfits, with a remuda of two or three thousand horses, wranglers, chuck wagons, and cooks. Roundup districts were divided into ranges, generally using rivers and tributary creeks to mark boundaries, and as the cowboys fanned out across each range they drove everything "with hair and horns" forward in an ever-tightening semicircle until several thousand head might wind up bunched together at the center of the range. Men on cutting horses began the difficult job of separating the cattle according to brands, then moved on to the next range and repeated the process.

The Cowboy, Frederic Remington

At roundup on the open range, neighboring ranchers brought all the animals to one place, then separated them by brand. Ownership of new calves was determined by their mothers. The cow bawling loudly when a calf was roped must be the mother. Her brand went on its flank. If male, he was also castrated and became a steer.

This kind of reciprocal altruism between ranchers operated very well up until the early 1880s. Then came the great boom that distinguished the first half of the decade from the bust of its second half. For a variety of complicated reasons, the price of cattle rose by about one-third between 1879 and 1881. Demand for western beef was at its pinnacle, which led to a diminishing supply, which led to even higher prices. By 1882 they had risen to three times above their 1879 level. The same fever that had affected the nation when gold was discovered at Sutter's Mill struck again and was exacerbated by newspapers and magazines that began frantically boosting the lucrative joys of cattle raising. *The Breeder's Gazette*, for example, offered the novitiate the following assurance:

A good-sized steer when it is fit for the butcher market will bring from $45.00 to $60.00. The same animal at its birth was worth but $5.00. He has run on the plains and cropped grass from the public domain for four or five years, and now, with scarcely any expense to its owner, is worth forty dollars more than when he started on his pilgrimage. A thousand of these animals are kept nearly as cheaply as a single one, so with a thousand as a starter and an investment of but $5,000 in the start, in four years the stock raiser had made from $40,000 to $45,000.[16]

As Walter Prescott Webb put it, "the whole world . . . stampeded to the Great Plains to get a ranch while ranches were to be had. Easterners, Englishmen, Scotchmen, Canadians, and even Australians flocked to the Plains to become ranchers, to the amusement of the cowboys and to the disgust of the ranchmen . . ."[17]

There was very little, actually, for anybody to be amused about, including the cowboys. Speculation in large herds by business syndicates who knew very little about what they were doing, combined with all the Toms, Dicks, and Harrys who fancied themselves wearing a Stetson hat and spurs, led to a disastrous overstocking and overgrazing of the range, deterioration of its riparian corridors, and serious friction between the real cattlemen and the crowd of Johnny-come-lately imitators. Barbed wire, which was invented in 1874 but had been used sparingly in the West up to this point, began to be strung throughout the plains by those ranchers who had the money, the firepower, and the willingness to back up their newly imagined isolationism.

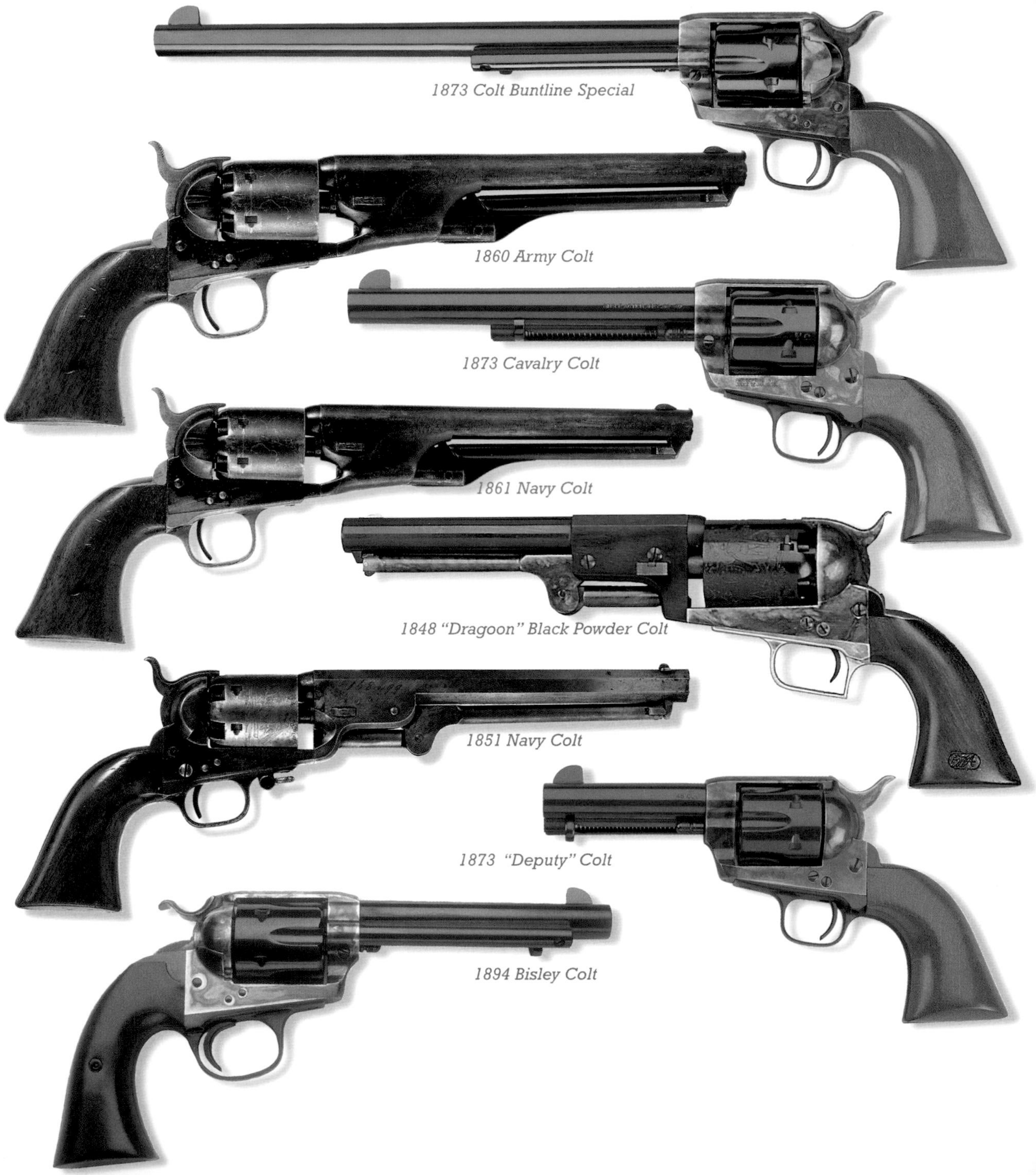

1873 Colt Buntline Special

1860 Army Colt

1873 Cavalry Colt

1861 Navy Colt

1848 "Dragoon" Black Powder Colt

1851 Navy Colt

1873 "Deputy" Colt

1894 Bisley Colt

THE COLT REVOLVER

Until the 1830s all handguns were basically single-shot weapons of the flintlock or percussion-cap variety, although there were some odd variations with two barrels, and one multi-firing revolver-type gizmo called a "pepperbox." Then, in 1836, Colonel Samuel Colt of Hartford, Connecticut, invented and patented a revolving-breech pistol that considerably augmented an individual's ability to wreak havoc on his fellow man. Some have argued that it revolutionized the West.

Colt's first revolver was a six-shooter of .34 caliber with a four-and-a-half-inch barrel and an unguarded trigger that dropped down when its handler cocked the gun. While there was no stampede on the part of the northeastern public to acquire this firearm, a number of these guns found their way into Texas and into the hands of the newly formed Texas Rangers, who found them better adapted for fighting on horseback than any of the alternatives. Still, the Colt .34 was a flawed implement—too lightweight and fragile, for one thing, and for reloading it had to be broken down into three pieces and the empty cylinder exchanged for a full one. This was hard to do from the back of one's trusty steed while riding across the prarie at full speed before a pursuing crowd of choleric Comanche. If you dropped one of the pieces, it was "Streets of Laredo" time.

Eventually a collaboration ensued between a Ranger named Samuel Walker and the innovative Mr. Colt. Walker explained the weapon's limitations, and the result was a new model, not surprisingly named the Walker Colt. It was heavier, with a visible trigger, a trigger guard, and a bigger and better-shaped grip that made it easier and steadier to hold, and it could be reloaded without removing and exchanging the cylinder. The bore was increased to .44 caliber, which made a bigger hole in the beneficiary of its projectile, but since shooting someone wasn't the answer to every problem, its increased length and weight made it doubly useful as a shillelagh—Texas style.

Samuel Colt

Night in Old Wyoming, F. T. Johnson

But by 1885, with prices plummeting and the land in such wretched shape that it was vulnerable to any variation in temperature and precipitation, not even the panicked departure of the speculators and the cowboy capitalists could save matters. The impact barbed wire had on closing the range is obvious, but it was adverse economics, combined with a murderous winter in 1885–86, followed by a summer drought, that would effectively finish off the open-range cattle industry.

That winter was among the worst ever recorded. By late November, snow lay so deep across the heavily overstocked northern plains that animals could not paw their way down to whatever grass was still available. In January a blizzard that blew from Canada all the way to Texas brought with it temperatures as low as sixty-eight degrees below zero, and cattle that normally could survive a heavy storm by drifting in front of it and holing up in sheltering ravines and draws were stacked into these sub-arctic refuges like sardines in a can—where they froze and died by the hundreds of thousands. The Clark & Plumb EG herd, for example, numbered eighteen thousand cows at the beginning of the winter and under two thousand come spring. What was left on display once the snows had melted was sorry testimony to the

E. *T. Johnson's* Night in Old Wyoming, *far left, is the cowboy myth at its strongest. A lone man and his horse amble through a classic western landscape on a still, moonlit night. The day's work is done, the air is turning cool, and the only sounds are hoofbeats echoing on canyon walls.*

"Deer Sur, We have brand 800 calves this roundup we have made sum hay potatoes is a fare crop. That Inglishman yu lef in charge at the other camp got to fresh and we had to kill the son of a bitch. Nothing much has happened sense you lef. Yurs truly, Jim."

—LETTER FROM A FOREMAN TO AN ABSENTEE EASTERN RANCH OWNER

cupidity and stupidity of a lot of stockmen for whom basic concepts of land stewardship and animal husbandry had never been an issue. It should have been. As one Texas cattleman named Dudley Snyder said, "I do not think I ever saw a business that was as prosperous as the cattle business up to 1884 and 1885 that went down as quick and fast, with no confidence left in it at all."[18]

Cowboys on the Matador Ranch, Texas, in 1908, right, try to persuade a horse to see life their way. Rabbits in California's San Joaquin Valley were given stronger medicine. Viewed as pests and competitors for limited forage, they were occasionally rounded up and killed, as in this 1898 rabbit drive, below.

For the few ranchers who survived—and they tended to run the smaller operations—new lessons had to be learned. After the winter of 1885–86 it was clear that cattle would have to be provided winter feed, and that herd sizes would have to be kept within sustainable limits, which meant that hay would have to be grown and a lot more fencing would have to go in so that pastures could be rotated. What's more, Cowboy Bob was going to have to climb down off his horse and trade his spurs for a post-hole digger and a pitchfork—implements with which he was unfamiliar and a form of work he was not temperamentally adjusted to do—and as a consequence a lot of cowboys retired or left their employers to homestead a small ranch of their own. Times were definitely changing.

Worsening matters, in many areas sheep began to make an increased appearance where only cattle had once roamed. And in the shepherds' wake came farmers, those poor, dreary, unimaginative followers of the plow, with their pedestrian notions of enterprise, hard work, and social responsibility. Taken together these sad samples of the bootless and unhorsed were enough to give any bronco-busting, gun-toting, cow-punching sociopath the trots. They inspired the contempt of such ranching advocates as the *Denver Republican*:

The physical and mental differences between the cowboy and the sheep herder are as great as those of their respective callings. From the very nature of his occupation the cowboy is a wild, free being.

He breaks the savage and almost untamable ponies to the saddle, and then rides them. His work is swift and vigorous, and his charges are the great, strong, free bulls and cows that have never known the touch of the human hand. He lives and endures hardships with others of his kind, and his pleasures are as fierce as his work. His is the strenuous life.

The sheep herder, on the other hand, pusues his solitary occupation afoot, his only companion being a dog and the thousands of stupid sheep, which have no individuality, and are maddeningly, monotonously alike. The very loneliness of his occupation has made the herder either a morose and sullen brute or a poetic dreamer, with all the fight worn out of him.[19]

In Lincoln County, New Mexico, the local stock growers' association would issue a sheepman a single warning, and if he failed to get the message they would slaughter his flock. In western Nevada, the owners of a large cattle ranch forbade the presence of sheep anywhere in the vicinity and shot two Mormon shepherds who decided to ignore their ordinance. And in Oregon, an organization called the Crook County Sheep Shooters Association was formed to deal with "the problem."

But violence was visited not only on farmers and sheepherders. Large ranchers were equally threatened by small ranchers, many of whom were former cowboys who had started a modest spread of their own, and who found wire cutters most useful in coping with large fenced-off sections of the preempted public domain.

F M. Brewster, far left, a Montana cowboy, poses with his rope and his horse. His work clothing is simple and practical—a broad-brimmed hat to keep the sun out of his eyes and the rain off the back of his neck. His bandanna serves double duty as shirt collar and dust-mask. Behind his saddle rides a rolled-up slicker.

"The horse's ribs was scraped bare of hide, and all the rest of the horse and man was mashed into the ground as flat as a pancake. The only thing you could recognize was the handle of his six-shooter." —COWBOY TEDDY BLUE ABBOTT DESCRIBING A MAN KILLED IN A CATTLE STAMPEDE

A Desperate Stand, Charles M. Russell

Sitting as if he is much more at home in the saddle than in a chair, an 1875 cowboy, below, seems to have been roped off the range and into the photo studio. He wears a pistol, most likely for varmints, not bad guys. The movie image of the cowboy as quick-tempered gunfighter is a fabrication.

The most famous of the resulting range wars occurred in Johnson County, Wyoming, and was ostensibly an attempt on the part of big cattlemen to put an end to rustling, by which they meant the practice of small ranchers branding mavericks (unmarked calves found on the range without their mothers) and adding them to their own herds. The Wyoming Stockgrowers Association lynched a homesteader named James Avrell and a whore named Cattle Kate who took her fee in purloined beef, then hired a trainload of Texas gunmen to come in and clean out the rest of the riffraff. A small army of forty-nine armed men managed to shoot two "rustlers" before riding off to Johnson County, where they were besieged by several hundred local settlers. In a standoff that lasted three days and wasted a lot of lead, there was but a single casualty. One of the Texans shot himself in his private parts and paid full price for his faux pas.

Whether the cattle industry liked it or not, agrarian expansion onto the Great Plains was on its way and picking up steam. An expanded use of windmills to pump water from the ground followed the use of barbed wire, and both disseminated farther and farther to the west. Railroads, eager for future customers, relentlessly promoted settlement on their land-grant properties, promising prospective emigrants cheap homesteads with fertile soil, close proximity to towns, and markets for their agricultural produce. The sodbuster was about to demand equal footing with the rancher, and the cowboy was soon to take a long ride into the sunset.

Cattle Drive #1, James Walker

THE ENDLESS COUNTRY

Buffalo country for thousands of years, the Great Plains became cattle country when the nation moved west following the Civil War. Broadly defined, the plains stretch from northern Texas, right, to southern Canada; from the Rocky Mountains to the 100th meridian of longitude—a line that slices through the middle of the Dakotas, Nebraska, and Kansas. The meridian is a moisture divide. To the east, rainfall averages more than twenty inches per year. To the west there's less. Settlers east of the line could plow the prairie and grow corn and raise dairy cattle. West of the line, unless they had irrigation, it was best to run cattle, feeding them on the rich, native shortgrass. For similar reasons, the Intermountain West also became cattle country, next page. Although mountains get ample moisture, the adjacent valleys are often too dry for general agriculture, but good for cattle.

Small wonder that cowboys are said to ride into the sunset. In a landscape where the sky makes up most of the view, people pay attention to what happens overhead. It's not only a matter of beauty but of survival. The plains are notorious for extreme weather: violent thunderstorms, hailstorms, dust storms, tornadoes, and blizzards. Summers are scorching, while winter sees deep cold sliding down from the Arctic and sticking well below zero for days or weeks without a break. In that setting, a quiet sunset is a treasure.

not make it out in the faint starlight. There was nothing

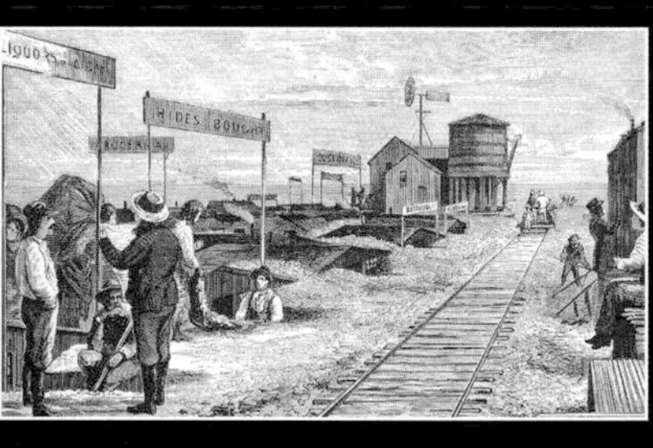

but land: not a country at all, but the material out of which countries are made."

Wagons on Their Way to the West, Artist Unknown

THE BORDER OF UTTER DARKNESS

[1840–1899]

Land of Milk and Honey

During the last two years more than six hundred thousand sturdy immigrants have landed upon our shores, and there is no ebb to the flowing tide. Our land is ringing with the din of her internal improvements; cottages are springing up far away to the west upon sunny acres where but yesterday roamed the Indian and the buffalo. Grand lines of railroad are stretching out across the continent—iron monsters resting upon either ocean, swallowing the values of one hemisphere to void them upon the other—revealing what our first Great Emigrant, Columbus, vainly sought to manifest in the gloom of earlier ages—that the shortest way to the Indies was via America. . . . We want yet more people to wake our sleeping wealth . . . to "tickle our prairies with a hoe that they may laugh with a harvest. . . ."

If past experience be worth any thing—if we may judge from the rapid settlement and appreciation in value of the lands of Ohio, Illinois and Indiana—surely the lands of the newer States and Territories, with their genial climate, great fertility, and vast mineral wealth—under the added stimulus of the great railroads opening up to the products the markets of the West as well as the East, and a larger national immigration than ever before—can not idly linger in their advancement. On the contrary, all reasonable inference tells us that they will as far outstrip the older States of the West in rapidity of development, as the emigrant of to-day upon the iron horse outrides the pioneers of those States moving slowly on the lumbering wagons of the past.[1]

—Frederick R. Goddard, 1869

WITH ASSURANCES LIKE Mr. Goddard's immensely popular disquisition, *Where to Emigrate and Why: Homes and Fortunes in the Boundless West and Sunny South,* and with pipe dreams of "tickling" the prairie with a hoe and laughing gaily all the way to the harvest, who could resist the urge to homestead on the Great Plains? The public domain, as Goddard cheerfully misinformed his readers, with its "healthful climate" and "mildly alternating seasons, which seem to compel exertion only to reward it," was virtually unlimited. And thanks to the Homestead Law, which he erroneously called "one of the most beneficent enactments of any age," there was a farm out there just waiting for any man or woman with ten bucks and the land office fees to come and settle it. And with additional thanks to the accommodating railroads, millions of aspiring sodbusters thronging west would now have quick and easy access to their latest little homes on the prairie, and there would be towns and cities, and rail lines would connect them to distant markets for the transportation of all the bountiful products of their labors.

Where to Emigrate and Why revealed that in spite of a few patches of drift sand, western Nebraska was a garden of earthly delights, and the plains of Wyoming were "as ready for the plow and spade as the fertile prairies of Illinois." Never mind, as Mark Reisner observed in his book *Cadillac Desert,* that "the Laramie Plains are five thousand feet higher than Illinois; the growing season is at least fifty days shorter; there is about a third as much rain." And as for western Nebraska, "by drift sand, Goddard may have meant the Sand Hills,

Promoters of western lands understood the importance of transport. So did residents of El Paso, Texas, right, whose city stood at a continental crossroads. During Spanish times, "The Pass" stood on the north-south road between Old Mexico and New. After American conquest, the same pass served east-west traffic. The result is a blend of cultures in one of America's first international cities.

Westward immigrants imagined a boundless land where hard work was richly rewarded. Farmers near San Jose, California, right, found the abundance they dreamed of. Others found a harsh land of extreme temperatures and weather. The Midwest, below, was subject to tornadoes, violent thunderstorms, severe winters, and drought. Immigrants coped with whatever they found. Some built farms and ranches; others established the towns and businesses that served them, lower right.

Harvesting Near San Jose, California, John Ross Key

a fifteen-thousand-square-mile expanse of thirsty dunes which, to this day, remains mostly uninhabited and unfarmed."[2]

It was one of the greatest advertising campaigns ever undertaken. Steamship companies looking for passenger revenue festooned Europe with posters and handbills promising transport to the land of milk and honey (and sometimes free return passage if an immigrant revisiting the auld sod would undertake a bit of missionary work during his sojourn and convince others to make the journey). Bureaus of Immigration were maintained in the East and in Europe by almost all the western states, with agents whose responsibility it was to persuade the farmers (and wannabe farmers) along the Atlantic states and in Great Britain, Scandinavia, Germany, and Holland that easy street was just a boat and/or a train ride away. Land was available in western America; in New England and Europe it was not.

And of course the principal advocates, promoters, and all-around boosters of western colonization were the railroads, recipients of 183 million acres of the public domain and therefore in the real estate business as much as they were in the transportation business (alternate sections on each side of a track were deeded by the federal government for every mile laid). Moreover, to quote James J. Hill, builder of the Northern Pacific, "You can lay track through the Garden of Eden . . . but why bother if the only inhabitants are Adam and Eve?" The railroads needed revenue from land sales to pay off huge federal loans; then they needed customers to keep them profitable.

And so the ad men worked the crowds with lavish depictions of golden wheat fields, acres of ripening corn, melons on the vine, berries in the patch, contented cows munching through pastures of sweet clover, yeoman farmers plowing their soil into rich, black furrows.

SOD HOUSES

To the first settlers who pushed out onto the Great Plains the most conspicuous feature of the landscape was the absence of trees, and, hence, the absence of familiar materials with which to build a house. But the prairie did provide. That same soil the farmer found so difficult to plow because of the thick, entangled root systems of the native grasses could be cut into sod squares. The sod held together perfectly, bound by a tough, flexible webbing of fibrous filament, and made excellent "bricks" with which to construct both the walls and roof of a dwelling. A few boards for rafters and a door frame was all the lumber that was needed.

Properly constructed, a sod house was warmer in winter and cooler in summer than a timber-framed structure, and if whitewashed inside could look less like a woodchuck's hole than when left *au naturel*. But it also provided habitat for a variety of unappetizing arthropods, arachnids, and nematodes that tended to make the lady of the house snappish. And when it rained, both roof and homesteader became sodden and started to leak. Generally speaking, as soon as he could afford it (if he could ever afford it), our hearty pioneer put in his order for some lumber and a few sheets of tin.

Rain, they assured those concerned with the apparent aridity of the plains, not only followed the plow, it always fell during planting season when it was needed. This astonishing bit of sophistry was bolstered by a University of Nebraska professor named Samuel Aughey, who explained in his book *Sketches of the Physical Geography and Geology of Nebraska* that the problem on uncultivated western lands was that rain hit the hard-packed ground and ran off into the rivers, hence the aridity. But when a farmer plowed the land, breaking up the soil and enabling water to soak in, subsequent evaporation returned moisture to the air, which became saturated, and bingo, more rainfall occurred. It was an endless cycle.

Boosters like the Honorable William Gilpin, territorial governor of Colorado, thundered their agreement. Heretofore imaginary hindrances to settlement had been resolved, Gilpin said, for not only did rain follow the plow, there were artesian waters underlying the whole of the western plains. It wasn't arid at all. Crops could be irrigated from underground. There were no woodlands to be cleared (an obvious boon to farming),

The Great Plains were a land of big skies and big weather. Constant winds drove people mad. Winter brought relentless subzero cold and killing blizzards that came so fast, people caught in the open might not find their way home. Summer brought parching heat, violent thunderstorms, crop-destroying hail, and tornadoes.

"August 16. Came 10 miles. Wind blew very hard this afternoon, consequently dust bad. The weather is comfortable. The nights are cold. Dust not as bad as I expected, but . . . let one come not prepared to endure hardships and he will find enough of them." —FROM THE DIARY OF MRS. JULIA NEWTON WOOD, 1853

Boomtowns grew fast but experienced different fates. The fortunes of Leadville, Colorado, below, dependent on mining, suffered cycles of boom and bust typical of mining towns. Paris, Texas, right, on a market day in 1888, began as a cattle and farming center. After the Civil War several railroads arrived, and from then on, its growth was slow but steady.

and there was certainly no need for them; the presence of Indian tribes provided ample testimony to the fact that the climate was so salubrious not even houses were needed. Firewood could be found abundantly in the hearty root system of the native vegetation and simply dug up out of the ground. It was all so unutterably wonderful, Mr. Gilpin might have added, that it caused a man to deny the evidence of his senses.

A few Americans, particularly those who had already tried homesteading in Minnesota, Iowa, Missouri, and Arkansas, and therefore knew something of the terrain west of the Mississippi, might have brought to this entire fantasy a measure of skepticism, though not necessarily enough to deter them from the confidence that there was always something better to be had. Europeans, to whom the sales pitch was equally directed, brought nothing but their own experience of forest, hedgerow, and meadow. "They had no more real idea of Montana than they had of the dark side of the moon," the British writer Jonathan Raban observed, "but they were devout believers and imaginers. The authors of the railroad pamphlets were able to reach out to an audience of ideal readers of the kind that novelists dream about, usually in vain."[3]

In Nebraska alone the Burlington and Union Pacific railroads spent a million dollars each trolling for settlers, their agents assuring anybody who cared to believe it that an acre of wheat could yield "over thirty bushels of grain . . . and many fields of corn over seventy." There was something there for the ladies, too. Women were so outnumbered by men in the West that, should they be inclined to emigrate, the only time they might likely venture a return to the East would be during their "bridal tour." In the region serviced by the Northern Pacific Railroad, spokesmen for James J. Hill attested that if

health issues were on anyone's list of particulars, it was a well-known fact that illness was unheard of in the robust and invigorating climate of Dakota Territory, and farther west in Montana the only infirmity ever recorded was a case of gluttonous indigestion.

Settlement on the Great Plains between 1870 and 1890 was undertaken by millions of American farmers for essentially the same reasons that initially impelled men westward out of the colonies and into the valley of the Mississippi during the late eighteenth and early nineteenth centuries, and into Texas and Oregon country during the 1830s and 1840s, namely: the illusion of better prospects, the promise of cheap land, and the dream of great (or at least greater) wealth. Escape was an equally motivating factor—escape from the economic deprivation of plebeian life in filthy industrial cities, escape from small, hierarchically dominated eastern farms, escape from crowding, escape from prior failures. The grass always seems a little greener over the fence, or in the next county, or the next state, and a sense of diminished possibilities where settlement had already occurred created a receptive audience for the reckless nonsense of the Gilpins, Goddards, and Samuel Augheys.

The story of U.S. land disposition policy goes back to 1790, a year after the Constitution was signed, when Congress asked Alexander Hamilton to come up with a general plan for dealing with the public domain (the public domain at this time being all the land owned by the United States except for the thirteen colonies). Hamilton's plan, which stressed two fundamental principles—that federal turf

Pioneers built homes with materials at hand. On the treeless prairie, that meant sod. Turned up by a plow and cut into bricks about three feet long and several inches thick, sod could be stacked like bricks of clay. For the roof, brush was laid on willow poles or imported rafters followed by a layer of cut grass, and finally shingles of sod. Judging by the size of the buildings and number of windows, this family was relatively prosperous.

Covered wagons were the moving vans and mobile homes of western settlement. This 1886 portrait, right, was made in Nebraska of a family on their way to claim a homestead. The wagon not only carried them and their gear, it housed them until they could build a shelter. Some wagons were later dismantled and made into furniture.

should be used to fill federal coffers, and at the same time provide settlers with homesteads—was never adopted, but it became the model for all future attempts and revisions over the next seventy-two years.

Major land policy legislation prior to the 1862 Homestead Act was passed in 1796, 1800, 1804, 1820, and 1832, and in each instance halved the minimum size of a plot that a buyer was required to purchase, from 640 acres in 1796 to just 40 acres under the preemption law of 1832. The price per acre was eventually reduced from $2 per acre to $1.25. The problem was that in the humid East, where settlement prior to the Civil War was largely confined, a section (640 acres) was a great deal more land than a single farmer could handle. He couldn't clear that much, nor cultivate it, nor pay for it. The same was true of 320 acres, and 160 acres, and even 80 acres. The preemption law of 1832, which basically granted title to a *fait accompli* (the settler having already appropriated as much land as he could use), acknowledged 40 acres as the suitable minimum.

By the early 1860s, however, the frontier had almost reached the plains and was about to burst out into a region that

few people understood anything about at all. In 1862, responding to a growing clamor for *free* land, and perceiving that in the long run the federal coffers might better be served by settlement than sales, Congress passed the Homestead Act, which offered 160 acres or less to "any person who is the head of a family, or who has arrived at the age of twenty-one years, and is a citizen of the United States, or who shall have filed his declaration of intention to become such . . ." The filing fee was ten dollars, and the prospective settler promised to live on the land for five years (and prove that he had done so by presenting two credible witnesses), after which time he or she would receive title.

The difficulties that had unfolded over the first seventy-two years of land disposition acts now reversed themselves. One hundred sixty acres of *free* land might have suited a farmer in Illinois, Iowa, or Arkansas just fine; if it was free, he could cultivate what he wanted and leave the rest fallow. But 160 acres wasn't enough on the Great Plains. Neither would 320 acres have been adequate, nor 640. An equivalent amount of land in the arid West would have to be 2,560 acres to equal the humid regions in productivity, and even so, farming methods and suitable crops would have to be entirely different. Benjamin Hibbard, in his book on the history of public land policies, sums this up:

The great weakness of the Homestead Act was, and is, its utter inadaptability to the parts of the country for which it was not designed. The idea of the farm small in acres within the semi-arid regions was tenacious, but untenable. It was even vicious in its operation. Congress was converted to the homestead principle in the large, and instructed in detail, by the people on the Missouri River frontier, backed up by the experience of the whole country, not essentially different, between Ohio and Missouri. The frontiersmen on the plains were too few in numbers, and too unlike the early frontiersmen to the east of them, to compel the working out of desirable modification of the land laws . . .[4]

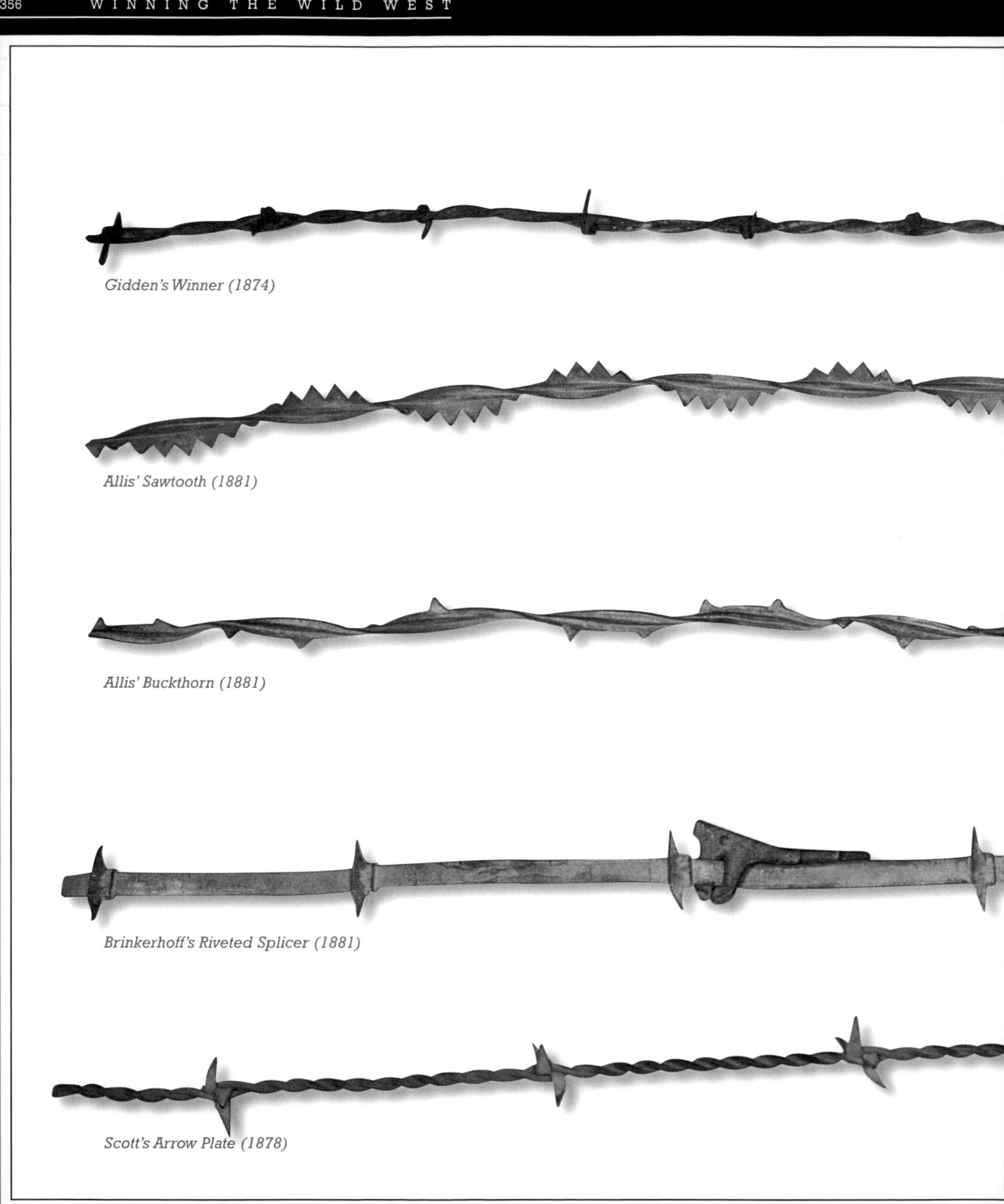

Gidden's Winner (1874)

Allis' Sawtooth (1881)

Allis' Buckthorn (1881)

Brinkerhoff's Riveted Splicer (1881)

Scott's Arrow Plate (1878)

BARBED WIRE

Joseph Glidden got the credit for inventing barbed wire, but he really just won the competition for the patent. Perhaps the fact that a number of men had applied for it proves it was an idea whose time had come. To the prosperous cattle ranchers who had claimed vast tracts of land in the West, barbed wire would allow selectively bred stock like Herefords, shorthorns, and polled Angus to remain protected from lascivious stray bulls wandering in from who knew where. Glidden's patent winner, called Winner, was only the first and most successful of many competing designs, including the Brotherton Barb, Oval, Buckthorn, Arrow Plate, and eight or nine hundred others that combined, by 1880, to sell 120 million pounds a year.

The wire had many advantages. It was light, easier and faster to set up than wood fencing, and would withstand prairie fires, floods, and high winds. But not everyone was in love with the stuff. Fence-cutting was rampant, practiced by men who still believed in the ideal of the open range, which included open grazing and watering rights. Violence sparked by fence-cutting incidents in Texas in the early 1880s led to wire-cutting being declared a felony, and Texas Rangers were dispatched to restore order. After things settled down, the wire began in earnest to transform the once-limitless prairie wilderness into a patchwork of farms and pastureland.

GLIDDEN PATENT STEEL BARBED WIRE POSSESSES THESE CLAIMS:

It is the strongest, cheapest and most durable of fence materials, as will appear from the universal testimony of those who have used it, as well as from the facts we are to present in the following pages.

The three leading kinds of Barbed Wire are the

Glidden Patent Two Point Barbed Wire.
Glidden Patent Thickset Barbed Wire.
Glidden Patent Four Point Barbed Wire.

The Glidden Patent Two Point has for several reasons led the market as the best and most popular Barbed Wire known from its Strength, Lightness, adaptability to all uses in Fencing and its imperishable character when once in place.

The Glidden Patent Thickset is an advanced form of last named in which increased protection is furnished by barbs more closely set. It is in great favor with all who have used it. It will turn hogs. Especially adapted to sheep husbandry as a protection against dogs.

The Glidden Patent Four Point has been rapidly adopted by very many who see great advantage in the increased number of points presented in the barbs.

In each of these the Glidden principle is preserved one and the same; a sharply pricking barb strongly attached to one of the wires of the fence strand, upon which the other wire is strongly twisted, holding the barb firmly in place. The barb is at right angles to the wire and does not form a hook but a straight, short, sharp steel thorn.

To farmers from the eastern woodlands, the prairies must have been both appealing and frightening. There were no trees to clear, no stumps to pull, and a man with a good team could plow a field in short order. That also meant no wood for buildings and fences, and a scary lack of shelter.

If Congress couldn't figure any of this out without the advantage of hindsight, it is perhaps not surprising that neither could homesteaders being lured west by settlement propaganda and inspirational books like Campbell's *Soil Culture Manual* and Charles Wagner's *The Simple Life*. They came mostly from the wet and wooded environments east of the Mississippi, or from a similar northern European climate, and were blinded by the great American dream of independence, opportunity, and something for nothing.

All the states on the eastern shore of the Mississippi, with the exception of Minnesota and Arkansas, lost population, with commensurate increases in Kansas, Nebraska, Wyoming, Montana, the Dakota Territory, and finally Oklahoma. And the numbers were even greater from abroad—Ireland, Germany, and especially Scandinavia, from which 10,000 immigrants set forth for America in 1865, with the numbers increasing steadily every year until they reached a peak in 1882 of 105,362. As Jonathan Raban described it: "In school atlases the [Great Plains] area was still called the Great American Desert—an imaginary vacancy, either without any flora and fauna or with all the wrong flora and fauna. The railroad writers and illustrators were assigned to replace that vacancy with a picture of free, rich farmland; a picture so vivid, so fully furnished with attractive details, that readers would commit their families and their life savings, sight unseen, to a landscape in a book."[5]

Driven from their homes in Illinois, the Mormons undertook perhaps the most ambitious migration in American history. They won, thanks to religious zeal and the organizational skill of their leaders. Still several hundred miles from Salt Lake City, a group of Mormon pioneers, right, gathers for a portrait near the Continental Divide in what would become Wyoming.

It is a pity that none of these early settlers had the benefit of a viewpoint less frenzied than the hyperbolic and holophrastic bromides of immigration bureau eulogists and railroad pamphleteers. In his 1891 book *Main-Travelled Roads,* the now largely forgotten son of the middle border Hamlin Garland, offered up a terse and realistic image of the northern Great Plains that has been echoed by almost every writer who has passed judgment on the region since. While the northern and southern plains were different in many respects, in others they were very much the same.

"The farther I got from Chicago," Garland said, "the more depressing the landscape became. . . . The houses, bare as boxes, dropped on the treeless plains, the barbed-wire fences running at right angles, and the towns mere assemblages of flimsy wooden sheds with painted-pine battlement, produced on me the effect of an almost helpless and sterile poverty."[6]

If *Main-Travelled Roads* had been written thirty years earlier, a good many people with itchy feet might have thought better about the palliative of

starting all over in the West. And if Garland's imagery failed to make an impression, one feels confident that Ole Rolvaag would have stopped the settlers in their tracks with his popular novel *Giants in the Earth,* a tale of four Norwegian families who leave Minnesota to homestead in Dakota Territory and are eventually done in by loneliness, poverty, backbreaking labor, and an unimaginably hostile land. Rolvaag's chapter titles alone—"On the Border of Utter Darkness," "Facing the Great Desolation," "The Great Plain Drinks the Blood of Christian Men and Is Satisfied"—define the hopelessness with which he viewed his characters' chances for survival in such a grim and malevolent domain. Unfortunately, *Giants in the Earth* didn't come out until 1927.

Other twentieth-century writers like Willa Cather, Laura Ingalls Wilder, Ernest Haycox, Frederick Manfred, Holger Cahill, Lois Phillips Hudson, Wallace Stegner, Ian Frazier, and Kathleen Norris may have found beauty in the drama of a prairie sky, the quality of its light, or the movement of wind through winter wheat, but all confirm the reality of a land

At first glance, the prairie of South Dakota, far right, looks like a slightly undulating sea of sameness. It never was, nor is it today. Buffalo and antelope are mostly gone, but many other creatures remain, from rodents to hawks, meadowlarks, coyotes, frogs, cranes, and so many more.

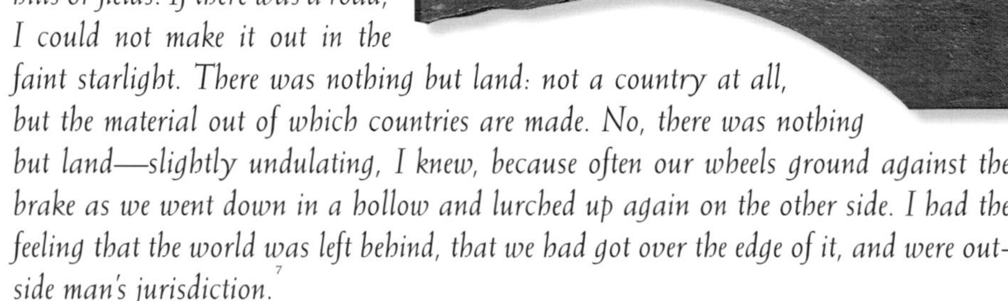

of pitiless extremes, a land that could force even the most industrious and self-reliant to their knees. As Cather described it in her book *My Antonia*:

There seemed to be nothing to see; no fences, no creeks or trees, no hills or fields. If there was a road, I could not make it out in the faint starlight. There was nothing but land: not a country at all, but the material out of which countries are made. No, there was nothing but land—slightly undulating, I knew, because often our wheels ground against the brake as we went down in a hollow and lurched up again on the other side. I had the feeling that the world was left behind, that we had got over the edge of it, and were out-side man's jurisdiction.[7]

The American farmer, as conceived by Crevecoeur and Thomas Jefferson, needed more than perseverance and hard work to prosper in an environment that holds the Western Hemisphere's record for absolute temperature range (a 181-degree variation in one year at a single location in North Dakota) and provides its citizenry with a methodical rhythm of drought, blizzard, prairie fire, windstorm, hailstorm, and crop-devouring grasshoppers. When Jonathan Raban conducted research there in the 1990s, he could have been traveling at any time in history:

The prairie made all my received ideas about landscape seem cramped and stultified. There were no vistas in it. It blew the picture frame apart, and taking a camera to it (or at least my taking a camera to it) was about as much use as trying to capture it in a Claude Glass. In Seattle, I collected my prints from the processors' and laid them out on the dining-room table. My wife made polite noises, but I could see what she was seeing: a hundred perfectly exposed snapshots of a badly maintained golf course.[8]

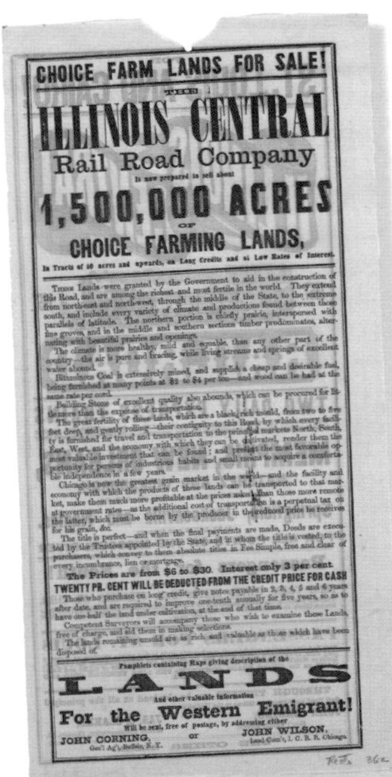

The reality that confronted homesteaders on the farmer's frontier was a bleak and empty plain stretching to infinitude, grassland to be sure, but in the north covered

A muskrat trapper strides through a Nebraska wetland. Moisture is an important factor in determining where trees can grow but not the only one. Summer heat stresses trees more than it does grass and can prevent them from growing in marginal conditions. Historically, fire played a part. But trees can survive, as proved by farmer-planted windbreaks that shelter modern prairie homesteads.

with thick, deep, heavily rooted western wheat grass, blue gramma, green needle, and prairie June grass that seemed almost impervious to the plow. Reality was that rain did not follow that plow, or any other discernible strategy known to man. Reality was an essentially treeless, arid environment that recommended houses made of sod, with a dirt floor and willow poles to hold up the roof—unless one lived near enough to a railroad that a few building materials could be procured for a tarpaper shack. The sod house was structurally sturdy enough, but attractive only to all manner of vermin, and it was hell on a marriage during the long, cold winters.

Evidence from the literature about homesteading on the plains suggests that it was particularly hard on women, though there is an occasional flash of humor in the midst of what is otherwise a ubiquitous dirge. "There was running water in our sod house," said one Nebraska lady. "It ran through the roof." The desolation, isolation, loneliness, and great distances between neighbors was all but intolerable. Living in a covered hole in the ground with a minimum of crudely fashioned furnishings, no pictures on the walls, no books, no music but the wind and the thump of grasshoppers on the roof, and nobody to talk to, it's a wonder they didn't all go stark, raving mad. Some did.

Halt on the Prairie, William Tylee Ranney

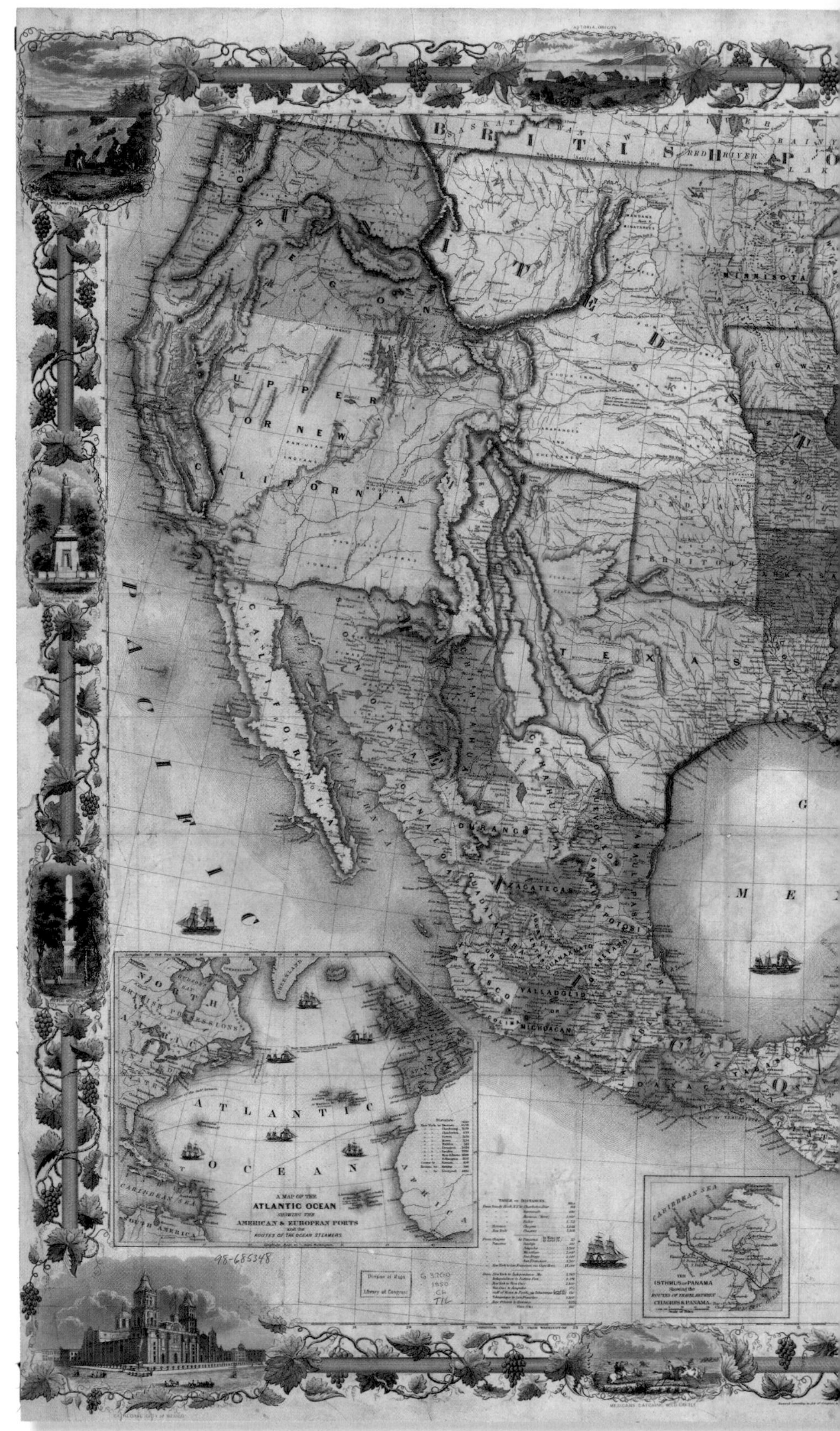

This 1850 map of the United States not only shows the states of Louisiana, Arkansas, Missouri, and Iowa in more or less final shape, it hints at the flood of emigration soon to surge westward. Note the concentration of cities, with their teeming populace, east of the Mississippi River basin. Note, too, the exaggerated size of the South Pass in the center of the mountain barrier, offering seemingly effortless access to the riches of California.

MAP OF THE
UNITED STATES
OF
AMERICA,
The British Provinces, Mexico, the West Indies and
Central America, with part of New Granada and Venezuela.
NEW YORK.
PUBLISHED BY J.H. COLTON
No. 86 Cedar St.
1850.
ATLANTIC
OCEAN
BAHAMA ISLANDS
WEST INDIES
CARIBBEAN SEA
LIBRARY AND ARCHIVES

Free lodging, reimbursed train fare, $5-per-acre land, reasonable terms, and an appealing photo entice buyers of railroad land, near right. The illustration opposite portrays travel across the plains. Emigrants to California crossed the Rockies at gentle South Pass, with the vast plains and deserts of the Great Basin beyond. The deserts would test their strength, and beyond that rose the formidable barrier of the Sierra Nevada. Overland immigrants to California earned whatever paradise they found.

And the ultimate reality was that all the hard work, planning, and resourcefulness in the world amounted to nothing without a continuous measure of good luck, because luck alone determined who would be spared from drought, blizzard, fire, a random cloud of locusts, a cyclone, or the irrational eccentricities of a hail storm. Those for whom luck was just another four-letter word would find life on the family farm far worse than bleak, as the following letter from one William Shadwell clearly indicates. Shadwell was appealing to his state government for relief:

I have been trying to live on my place and with sickness and bad luck in crops have well nigh run out of everything—I have been sick for months and my wife is not well from exposure and hunger and I thought that there was no other way than to ask you to help me—If you can let me have $25 and some close [sic] for my wife and daughter and myself as we have not close to cover our backs or heads—And if I can't get the money I shall lose my place after livin' from hand to mouth for three years on the frontier.[9]

Had prospective homesteaders looking anywhere west of the ninety-eighth meridian read and believed John Wesley Powell's 1878 *Report on the Lands of the Arid Region of the United States*, an enormous amount of human suffering (not to mention land abuse) could have been avoided. Powell's report conveyed his understanding, based on empirical evidence, that two-fifths of the country is so deficient in rainfall that it is useless for agriculture unless it is irrigated, and that because of limited streams and rivers, on only a fraction of that two-fifths is irrigation even a possibility. Powell went on to classify western lands into three

"The seven hundred miles I have travelled have been literally lined with the bones and carcasses of domestic animals . . ."—Demas Barnes, on the Overland Stage, 1865

HUTCHINGS' PANORAMIC SCENES.—CROSSING THE PLAINS.
CALIFORNIA
PIKE Co Mo
EMIGRANT TRAIN PASSING WIND RIVER MOUNTAINS
SIOUX INDIANS
INDIANS CHASING BUFFALOES, SCOTT'S BLUFFS
STUCK FAST
COURT-HOUSE ROCK
FIRST NIGHT ON THE PLAINS
MOUTH of ASH HOLLOW
CHIMNEY ROCK
DEVIL'S GATE
LARAMIE PEAK
SCENE ON THE DESERT
CASTLE ROCK
DRIVING STOCK ACROSS THE PLAINS
[Views drawn from Nature in 1853, by George H. Baker.
Published by J. M. HUTCHINGS, Placerville. Copyright secured.]
(SUN PRINT.)

View of Harmony, Karl Bodmer

basic types—irrigable, timbered, and pasturage—and offered a series of recommendations and proposed laws for their useful disposition.

What all this boiled down to was his insistence that the size of the land unit provided for in the Homestead Act (160 acres) was totally nonsensical in most, if not all, parts of the West. It was either too large if the land was irrigated (given the equipment available in 1870, a single farmer could barely work eighty acres), or too small if it was not—too small, according to Powell, by about 2,400 acres. In the well-watered East, a cow might survive nicely on an acre or two; in many parts of the West it was slim pickings on forty or fifty.

What Powell proposed was that the homestead unit for irrigated farms be 80 acres, and for pasturage farms be increased to 2,560 acres. Even this much, he argued, was worthless unless it contained some form of water, so each pasturage farm should contain at least 20 acres of irrigable ground within its boundaries. In order to accomplish this, the traditional method of surveying sections in a rectangular grid pattern would have to be abandoned and property lines would be determined by topographic basins no matter how weirdly configured. In this way everybody would receive an adequate portion of a stream. He also suggested water storage projects as a hedge against drought years, and federal involvement in their construction, as neither individuals nor groups (except the Mormons) had the requisite capital or skills.

Alas, it was all too much for a Congress whose mindset had been Gilpinized, and who had no clearer idea about the realities of a dry climate than they had about canals on Mars. Beside, they were not in a mood to hear about realities, so bedazzled were they by their notions of imperial expansion. They had the testimony of western politicians for whom the term "arid" referred to the prevailing weather in Gujarat, not the American plains. They had the assurances of railroad fat cats, immigration bureaus, land speculators, and windbag prophets. And they had the yowling *lumpen* chomping at their heels. As Wallace Stegner said in his biography of Powell, "Apparently he underestimated the capacity of the plains dirt farmer to continue to believe in myths even while his nose was being rubbed in unpleasant fact."

The land held true prosperity for those who settled on the eastern side of the Great Plains. Such was Harmony, Minnesota, left, as painted by Karl Bodmer in the 1830s. The country offered no better farmland and no better crop-growing climate than the deep soil of the northern Mississippi Valley.

There was one exercise in settlement that must be acknowledged as a major exception to the typical plains experience. When the Mormons descended into the Salt Lake Valley in 1847–49, they encountered a desert environment that appeared, on the face of it, to be utterly uncultivable. But the attitudes and ideals that had been metabolized by the Mormon faithful and formally incorporated in their theocratic institutions were completely different from those of other emigrants. As Brother Brigham put it: "No man can ever buy land here, for no one has any land to sell. But every man shall have his land measured out to him, which he must cultivate in order to keep it. Besides, there shall be no private ownership of the streams that come out of the canyons, nor the timber that grows on the hills. These belong to the people: all the people."[10]

What would have proved impossible for pioneers imbued with notions of private property and unaccustomed to the pooling of resources and labor was, at this point in their history, second nature to the Latter-day Saints. They brought with them the lessons learned from their earlier attempts at settlement in Nauvoo, Far West, Independence, and Kirtland, and they understood clearly from years

The reapers portrayed in the advertisement, right, may not have been the vanguard of the Western expansion, but they did represent one of the final pieces of the empire-building puzzle. The native way of life had long since given way first to cattlemen and then to farmers as the vast prairie landscape was subdivided into neat parcels that were not nearly as fertile as the romantic illustration implies.

of repeated banishment and persecution that all for one and one for all was the only way to survive.

Within days of their arrival they began the construction of an irrigation system that would insure equitable division of the water supply for farms, gardens, and municipal use—canals, ditches, and "laterals" that were all community controlled by an appointed "watermaster." Everybody contributed labor; everybody shared in the benefits. It was this same practice applied to every aspect of settlement that enabled them to make the desert "blossom as the rose, and the earth to yield abundantly of its diverse fruits." As the historian Leonard Arrington observed in his book *Great Basin Kingdom*:

It may yet be conceded that the well-publicized conflicts and differences between the Mormons and other Westerners and Americans were not so much a matter of plural marriage and other reprehensible peculiarities and superstitions as of the conflicting economic patterns of two generations of Americans, one of which was fashioned after the communitarian concepts of the age of Jackson, and the other of which was shaped by the dream of bonanza and the individualistic sentiments of the age of laissez-faire.[11]

Myths about the effortlessness of imperial expansion may have died hard, but for thousands of homesteaders they *would* eventually die. Consider the old dilapidated wagon seen heading back eastward with a painted sign hanging off the back that read: "In God We Trusted, In Kansas We Busted."

URSE OF EMPIRE TAKES ITS WAY" WITH McCORMICK REAPERS IN THE VAN.

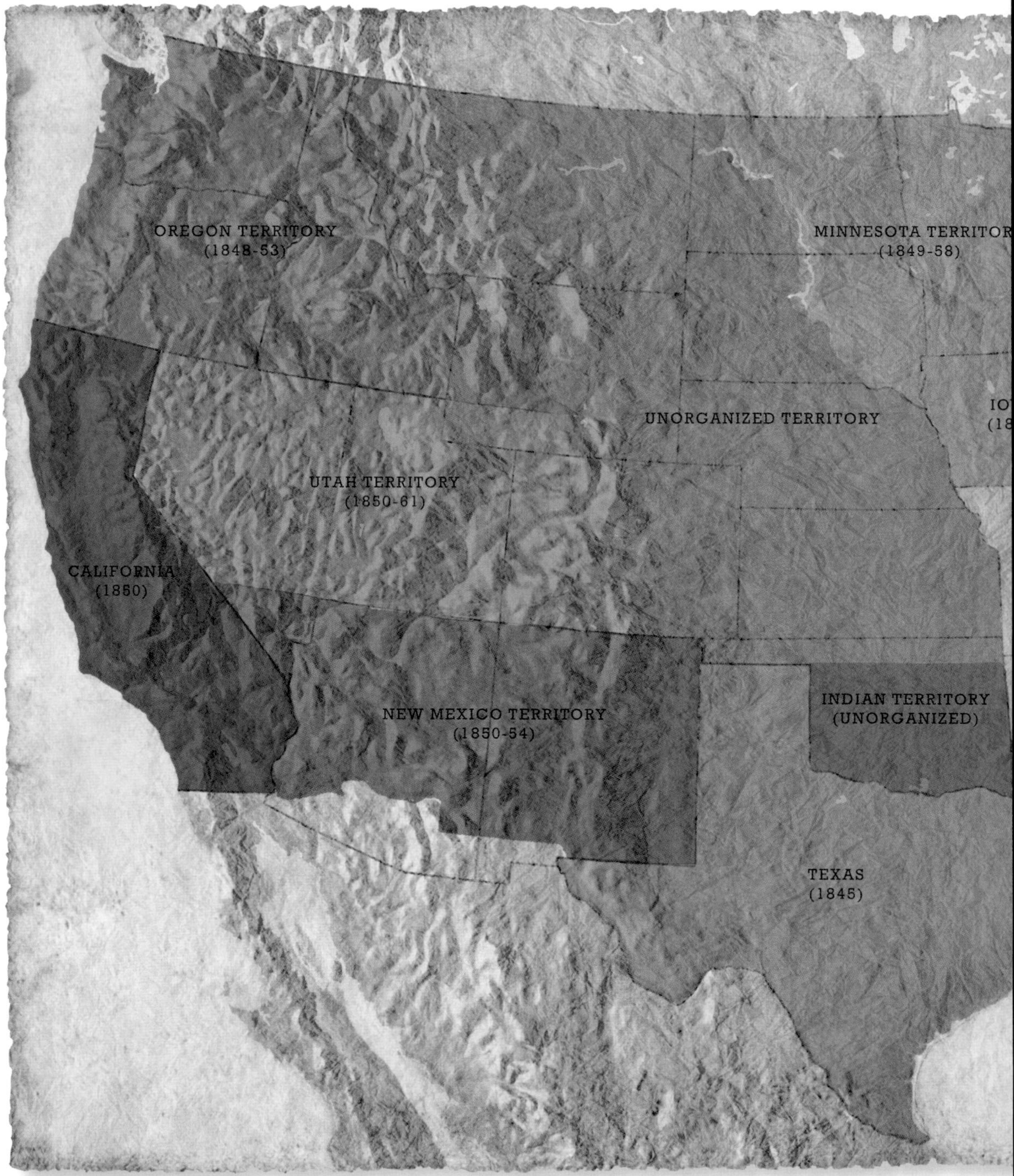
OREGON TERRITORY
(1848-53)
MINNESOTA TERRITOR
(1849-58)
UNORGANIZED TERRITORY
IO
(18
UTAH TERRITORY
(1850-61)
CALIFORNIA
(1850)
INDIAN TERRITORY
(UNORGANIZED)
NEW MEXICO TERRITORY
(1850-54)
TEXAS
(1845)

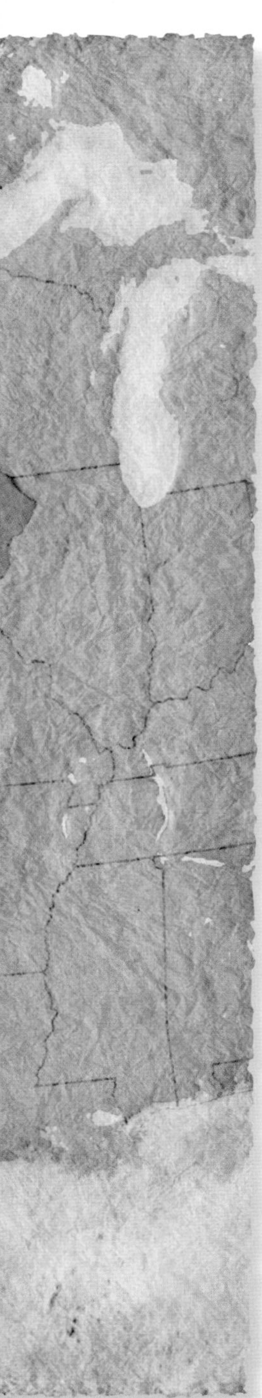

SETTLED TERRITORIES

Eastward I go only by force; but westward I go free.

—Henry David Thoreau

The modern look of the United States had taken shape by midcentury. Texas was annexed in 1845; the Oregon Territory was established in 1846. Following the Mexican War, the former Mexican territory, shown here as California, Utah Territory, and New Mexico Territory was ceded to the United States in 1848. The far southern area of present-day Arizona and New Mexico was acquired by the Gadsden Purchase in 1853, and the present-day border with Mexico was established. In the half-century after the United States had doubled its size with the Louisiana Purchase, it had absorbed an even larger parcel of land and had expanded across the width of the continent from ocean to ocean.

The first great emigrations had skipped over the Great Plains, crossing the mountains in search of land in Oregon and gold in California. The second wave settled the plains first with cattlemen, then with farmers. The domain of the Plains Indians was disappearing. Limited to a few southwestern and northern reservations and "Indian Territory" in the two decades after the Civil War, it was soon to be eliminated almost entirely by the Oklahoma land rushes that marked the end of the western expansion.

"49"
CUT PLUG
SMOKING
P. Lorillard
& Co.
JERSEY CITY, N.J.

Or the daughter of Laura Ingalls Wilder (author of *The Little House on the Prairie*) remembering her own family's exodus from the northern plains: *It was a saying in the Dakotas that the Government bet a quarter section against fifteen dollars and five years' hard work that the land would starve a man out in less than five years. My father won the bet. It took successive years of complete crop failure, with work, weather and sickness that wrecked his health permanently, and interest rates of 36 percent on money borrowed to buy food, to dislodge us from that land.*[12]

Had Powell been believed, settlers throughout the plains states might have avoided a good measure of the misery that was dealt them, and in eastern Montana and the Dakotas in particular might have been spared their inevitable collapse. Some of the worst climatic disasters occurred during the early twentieth century and are technically beyond the specific considerations of this book, but the data are relevant because they illustrate the consequences of fifty years of bad science (Powell excepted), bungled legislation, and an unwillingness to change one's patterns.

From 1916 to 1920 rainfall on the northern plains did not exceed twelve and a half inches, and was climaxed by a wickedly cold winter in 1919.

Advertising made it look so neat and possible. A California gold-rusher, far left, stands beside his tidy, flower-decked cabin. His clothes are clean; his tools stand neatly by the door. Gentle gold-laced hills roll in the background. The 1889 land-rushers who lined up outside the Guthrie, Oklahoma, land office, near left, imagined themselves in similar scenes.

"We first saw a glittering cloud high in the sky, and all sparkling in the sun, from which they fell one or two at a time. At first they came down so slowly that the fowls could clear them up, but presently they began to fall in earnest, and then nothing could check them."

—Percy G. Ebbutt, on a plague of grasshoppers in Kansas in the 1870s

Five years of drought coupled with temperatures that dropped into the minus 50- and 60-degree range spelled the end for a first wave of homesteaders. Dazed and broke, they moved on west into the Rockies, following the northern spur of the Milwaukee Railroad that had brought them into the territory in the first place, or they fled eastward from whence they had originally come.

The second massive evacuation took place during the 1930s when a wet cycle that had lasted about four years came to an abrupt halt, followed by great dust storms that sent most of the agricultural land between the Mississippi River and the Rocky Mountains airborne—at times as much a 150,000 tons of it suspended above the earth in a single square mile. The Dust Bowl, of course, encompassed the entire heartland of America, and ultimately three and a half million people were driven from their farms during the decade between 1930 and 1940. Not all were "dusted out," to be sure, but most were definitely busted.

On the northern plains the exodus began after the "great storm" of May 10, 1934. Like their 1920s predecessors, the "exodusters" migrated farther west into the mountains of Montana and Idaho, and many eventually found their way to the Columbia valley and from there to Seattle. There were, of course, those who stuck, and continue to stick to this day, though the reason was less a consequence

Claiming that Native Americans weren't using the land they had been given for "as long as the grass shall grow," and then forced to move onto, the government opened huge areas of Indian Territory to the general public. On April 22, 1889, an estimated sixty thousand land claimers rushed for the spoils. Towns like Guthrie, below, appeared virtually overnight.

Clouds Coming Over the Plains, Albert Bierstadt

THE CHEROKEE STRIP

In 1838–39, when President Andrew Jackson ordered the Cherokee Nation forcefully removed from their southeastern homelands during a period of Anglo settlement that many scholars have called among the blackest and most doleful in American history, they were given six and a half million acres of north-central Oklahoma on which to relocate. Unfortunately, the same rapacious greed that forced their initial expulsion was repeated during the 1880s and 1890s, as land-hungry whites again clamored for homesteads on the one remaining area west of the ninety-eighth meridian that was still good for farming—a 58-mile-wide by 226-mile-long tract known as the Cherokee Strip. That this was set aside in perpetuity for the Cherokee seemed to impress nobody except the Indians, who unquestionably knew that, once again, the time line on their traditional way of life was running out.

In 1885 Congress yielded to pressure from immigrants who were already illegally settling in the region and agreed to "negotiate" with the Indians. Enter the Allotment Act of 1887 (or Dawes Act, as it was often called), which dissolved Indian tribes as legal entities, divided their lands into160-acre plots that were to be given, one each, to every nuclear Indian family, and declared everything left over to be surplus and therefore open to white settlement. While this ultimately fleeced Native Americans of 82 million acres of their property, in Oklahoma it provided Anglo sodbusters with a bonanza that instantly provoked a land rush. Sixty thousand of them stampeded into the Oklahoma District on one day—April 22, 1889. And four years later,

on September 16, 1893, the Cherokee Strip was opened. There were only 42,000 claims to be had. Under the watchful eyes of federal troopers, one hundred thousand prospective settlers lined up at the border like sprinters crouching in the blocks for the hundred-yard dash, and at the stroke

of noon a pistol was fired in the air. A blacksmith by the name of Jim Fenlon set his anvil down square in the middle of the Old Freighters' Trail from Caldwell to El Reno on the site of what is now Enid, Oklahoma. Soon, others followed suit, and by noon on the twenty-second, the brand new town had a population of four. Three hours later, about twelve thousand people had settled there, and, in a frenzy of hammering, a number of buildings, including a hotel, were erected by midnight. This scene was repeated all across the strip, as one hundred thousand people settled the area in one day.

D 1653

of indomitable spirit and resolute character than it was of post–Dust Bowl government aid programs.

It has been argued that the frontier, and with it the incipient epoch in our national narrative, came to an end in 1890. In effect, this happened because Frederick Jackson Turner said it did. In his famous address at the 1893 meeting of the American Historical Association in Chicago, he insisted that the "existence of an area of free land, its continuous recession, and the advance of American settlement westward, explain American development;" then went on to proclaim, "now, four centuries from the discovery of America, at the end of a hundred years of life under the Constitution, the frontier has gone, and with its going has closed the first period of American history."[13]

That this inspired a plethora of controversy, rebuttal, debate, riposte, and rejoinder need not concern us here. Neither does the rest of his thesis, much of which, in the light of more than a century of historical research, even he might concede didn't pan out quite as he had imagined. Still, if we focus solely on the *agrarian* frontier, as Turner pretty much did, looking at it wholly through European eyes and from an east-to-west perspective, and as a process rather than a place—well, then, the argument makes some sense. (Seen through Native American, Mexican, or Asian eyes it has no relevance whatsoever.) Regarded strictly as a farming frontier, and as a time during which the apparently endless, westering band of free, unbroken, uncultivated land ceased to exist, 1890 might seem a rational date at which to proclaim the end of an era.

There was as much hope as dirt in this sod dugout—hope to establish a farm, to rise out of the earth, to build a proper house. One good or decent growing year could fuel hopes through a decade of disaster. For many, the only proper house lay somewhere else than a dry-land farm.

It took roughly three centuries to settle America from the colonies to the Mississippi. Thomas Jefferson thought it would take another two thousand years to fill it in all the way to the Pacific, though, as we have seen, it took only about eighty. Between the return of Lewis and Clark in 1806 and the 1890 Census Bureau report, the continent was crossed and recrossed, and its contours fully revealed. The four great government surveys conducted by Clarence King, Ferdinand

Hayden, Lieutenant Wheeler, and Major Powell were all completed by 1879 and their voluminous reports issued. By 1887 the open-range cattle industry had come and gone; America was becoming home to the barbed-wire fence.

And in 1890 the Native American population, whose military defeat had already been effected, were subjected to one final outrage at Wounded Knee when three hundred unarmed Sioux were pointlessly massacred by George Custer's old unit, the Seventh Cavalry, and dumped into a common grave. As James Wilson has written, "For Anglo-Americans, the massacre at Wounded Knee, with its desolate images of twisted Indian corpses frozen into the snow, has become a deeply significant moment. It poignantly represents the end of the frontier, the three-century process of continuous expansion that had carried their country from a few tiny trading posts to potentially the most powerful nation on earth."[14]

The Colorado Rockies near Denver, far right, gained national attention for a gold rush that began in 1859 and continued, with stops and starts, into the early 1900s. Mining, by its nature, ran itself out of business and encouraged short-term thinking. Ranching, farming, and forestry proved more sustainable, if the land permitted and was not abused.

So when the U.S. Census Bureau bulletin in 1890 announced that so many people had filled in the blank areas of the West that the term "frontier line" was no longer meaningful, they were, in fact, reporting something important. True, there might still be some 380 million acres of land available for dry-farmed or irrigable cultivation, but by 1890 the outline of America had been thoroughly stippled in. If that did not signal the "end of an era," it pointed, at the very least, to a significant milestone.

Yet the frontier persisted as the concept became woven into the American self-image. It was Americans' destiny to push the frontier; a lifetime after it ceased to exist on a map, John F. Kennedy accepted the 1960 Democratic nomination for the presidency with a speech in which he described a "New Frontier," and Americans responded again. Kennedy's version wasn't an invitation to settle a continent but rather became a call for yet another frontier—a trip to the Moon, and a crusade to "bear the burden of a long twilight struggle . . . against the common enemies of man: tyranny, poverty, disease, and war itself." Its politicians may sing different lyrics, but the nation clearly still resembles those pioneer emigrants: idealistic, willful, and on the prowl for the next milestone.

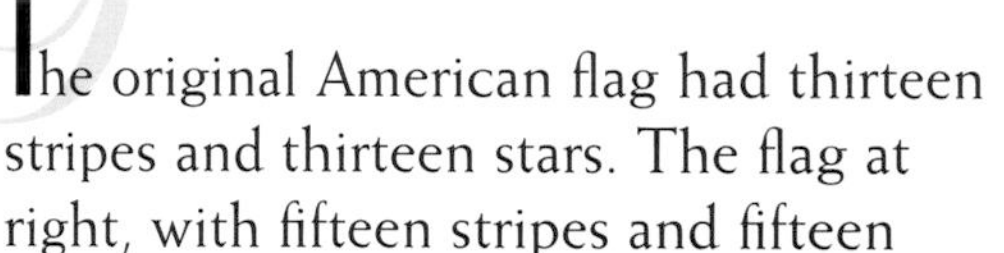

The original American flag had thirteen stripes and thirteen stars. The flag at right, with fifteen stripes and fifteen stars, was adopted in 1794 after Vermont and Kentucky joined the Union. Spain held claim to almost all land west of the Mississippi, although most of it was still "unexplored by Europeans, and most native people had never heard of a Spanish king.

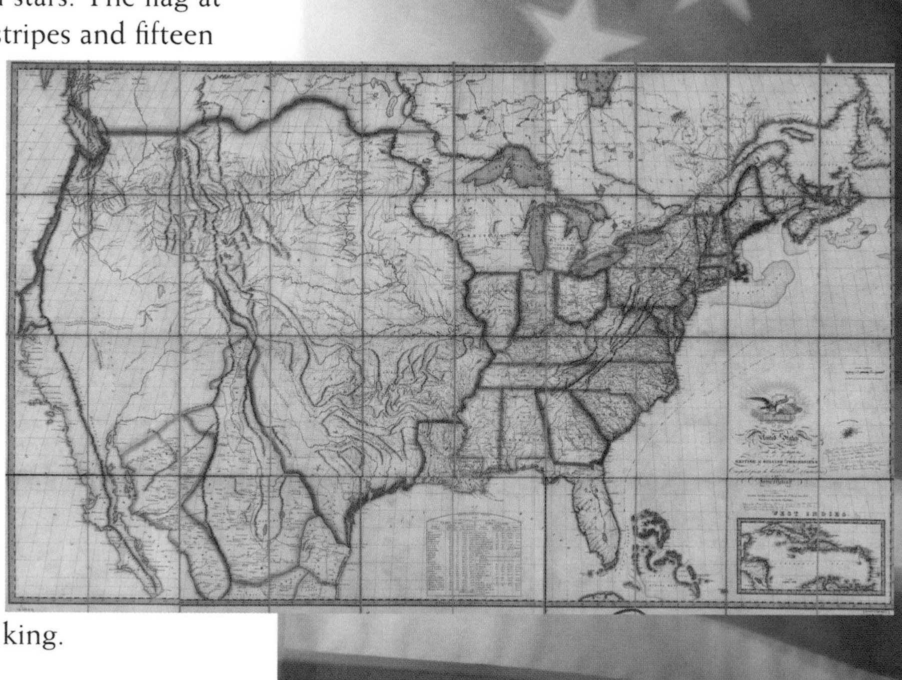

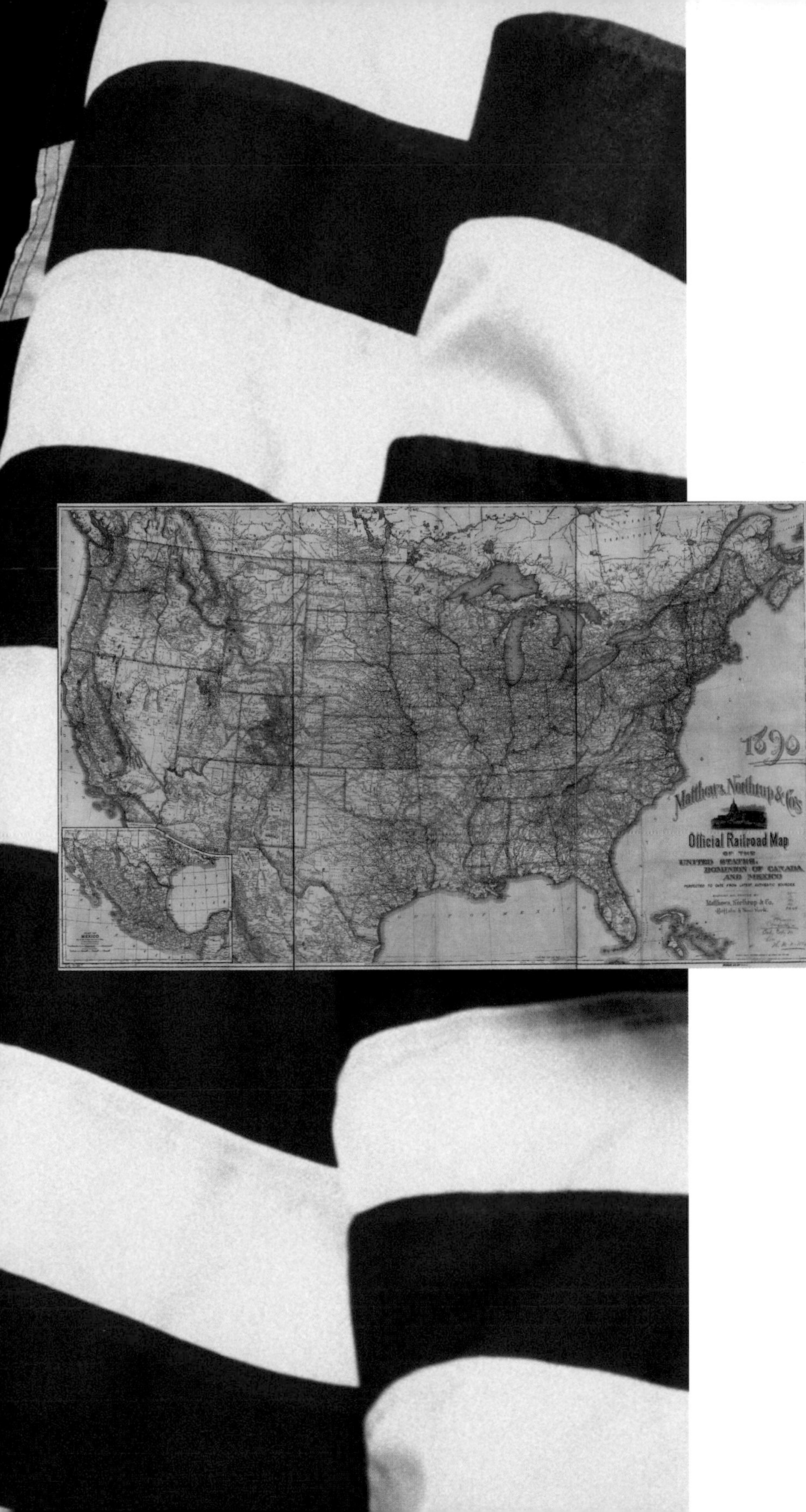

By 1853, the United States had acquired title to all the land of the "lower 48," although native residents still were not party to the deal. The turn of the twentieth century saw a much expanded flag with forty-five stars and thirteen stripes (the original number of stripes was restored in 1818). All states except Oklahoma, Arizona, New Mexico, Alaska, and Hawaii were in the Union.

Endnotes

Chapter 1: Surveying the West

1. Francis Parkman, *La Salle and the Discovery of the Great West* (New York: Modern Library Edition, 1999), 184–5.
2. Frank Bergon, ed., *The Journals of Lewis and Clark* (New York: Penguin Books, 1989), xxxiv.
3. Ibid, xxxvi.
4. Ingvard Henry Eide, *American Odyssey: The Journey of Lewis and Clark* (Chicago: Rand McNally, 1969), 4.
5. Ibid, xix–xx.
6. DeVoto, *The Journals of Lewis and Clark* (Boston: Houghton Mifflin, 1963), 4.
7. Bergon, 8.
8. DeVoto, 7.
9. Bergon, 42.
10. Bernard DeVoto, *The Course of Empire* (Boston: Houghton Mifflin, 1952), 463.
11. Ibid, 478.
12. DeVoto,*The Journals of Lewis and Clark,* 92.
13. Ibid, 104.
14. Ibid, 122.
15. Bergon, 171.
16. DeVoto, *The Journals of Lewis and Clark,* 188.

Chapter 2: Trappers and the Fur Trade

1. Washington Irving, *The Adventures of Captain Bonneville: Digested from His Journals* (Santa Barbara: The Narrative Press, 2001).
2. Hiram Martin Chittenden, *The American Fur Trade of the Far West* (Lincoln: University of Nebraska Press, 1986), 707.
3. Chittenden, 945.
4. Chittenden, 882–83.
5. Gregory M. Franzwa, *The Oregon Trail Revisited* (Tucson: Patrice Press, 1972), 3.
6. Alexander Ross, *The Fur Hunters of the Far West* (Norman: University of Oklahoma Press, 1956), 153.
7. George Frederick Ruxton, from *Adventures in Mexico and the Rocky Mountains,* reprinted in John A. Hawgood, America's Western Frontiers (New York: Knopf, 1967), 99–100.
8. Maurice Sullivan, *Jedediah Smith, Trader and Trail Breaker* (New York: Press of the Pioneers, 1936), 95.

Chapter 3: Clash of Destiny

1. Thomas Hart Benton speaking to U.S. Congress, *Congressional Globe* 29 Cong.,1st sess., 1846.
2. Walter Prescott Webb, *The Texas Rangers* (Austin: University of Texas Press, 1935), 8–9.
3. William Gilpin, *Mission of the North American People: Geographical, Social, and Political* (Philadelphia: J. P. Lippincott, 1873), 99.
4. Benton, 1846.
5. Texas State Library and Archives Commission, Austin Texas.
6. Gilpin, 99.
7. Wallace Stegner, *The Gathering of Zion* (New York: McGraw-Hill 1964), 24.
8. Ibid, 8.
9. Ibid, 9.
10. David Lavender, *California* (New York: W. W. Norton, 1976), 38.
11. Bernard DeVoto, *The Course of Empire,* 113.

Chapter 4: Native Resistance

1. Peter Nabokov, ed., *Native American Testimony* (New York: Thomas Crowell, 1978) 154–55.
2. Patricia Nelson Limerick, *The Legacy of Conquest: The Unbroken Past of the American West* (New York: W. W. Norton, 1987), 193.
3. James Wilson, *The Earth Shall Weep: A History of Native America* (New York: Grove Press, 2000), 166.
4. Nabokov, 149–50.
5. Ibid, 168.
6. Wilson, 229.
7. Ibid, 248.
8. Ibid d, 75.
9. Ibid, 274.
10. Nabokov, 230–31.

Chapter 5: A Shining Dream

1. Walter Colton, *Three Years in California* (New York: A. S. Barnes and Co., 1850), 246–47.
2. John Sutter, "The Discovery of Gold in California," *Hutchings' California Magazine,* vol. 2 (November 1857): 198.
3. Ric Burns, "The Donner Party Transcript" for *The American Experience.* David McCullough, host. (Boston, WGBA Television 1997).
4. John A. Hawgood, *America's Western Frontiers: The Exploration and Settlement of the Trans-Mississippi West* (New York: Alfred Knopf, 1967), 172.
5. Patricia Nelson Limerick, *The Legacy of Conquest: The Unbroken Past of the American West* (New York: W. W. Norton, 1987), 101.
6. Theodore Johnson, *Sights in the Gold Region, and Scenes by the Way* (New York: Baker and Scribner, 1849), 206.
7. Kevin Starr and Richard J. Orsi, eds., *Rooted in Barbarous Soil: People, Culture, and Community in Gold Rush California* (Berkeley: University of California Press, 2000), 4.
8. Author unknown, "The Pony Express," *Hutchings' California Magazine* July 1860: 3–4.
9. John Marshall, "The Discovery of Gold in California," *Hutchings' California Magazine* vol 2 (November 1857): 202.
10. Johnson, 207.
11. Demas Barnes, *From the Atlantic to the Pacific, Overland via the Overland Stage, 1865: A Series of Letters* (New York: D. Van Norstrand, 1866), letter of June 21, 1865.
12. James Sandoz, "Because He Is a Liar and a Thief," in *Rooted in Barbarous Soil: People, Culture, and Community in Gold Rush California* (Berkeley: University of California Press, 2000), 96.
13. Ibid, 95.
14. Hawgood, 199.
15. Stan Steiner, *Fusang: The Chinese Who Built America: The Chinese Railroad Men* (New York: Harper and Row, 1979), 130.

Chapter 6: The Open Range

1. E. C. "Teddy Blue" Abbott and Helena H.Smith, *We Pointed Them North* (Norman: University of Oklahoma Press, 1976), 6–8.
2. Walter Prescott Webb, *The Great Plains* (New York: Grosset & Dunlap, 1931), 155–56.
3. Ibid, 157.
4. Ibid, 488.
5. Richard Irving Dodge, *The Hunting Grounds of the Great West* (London: Chatto & Windus, 1877), 2.
6. Alan M. Hoyt, "Cowtown Marshalls 'Winged a Few,'" *Texas Longhorn Journal,* vol. 9, no.1 (January/February 1984): 128.
7. Dodge, 148.
8. Webb, 213.
9. Leonard J. Arrington, *Great Basin Kingdom: An Economic History of the Latter-day Saints* (Cambridge: Harvard University Press, 1958), 52–3.
10. Joseph McCoy, *Historic Sketches of the Cattle Trade of the West and Southwest* (Kansas City: Ramsey, Millet & Hudson, 1874), 40.
11. Ibid, 50.
12. Andy Adams, *The Log of the Cowboy: A Narrative of the Old Trail Days* (Lincoln: University of Nebraska Press, 1964), 191–92.
13. John A. Hawgood, *America's Western Frontiers* (New York: Alfred Knopf, 1967), 331.
14. Richard W. Slatta, *Cowboys of the Americas* (New Haven: Yale University Press, 1990), 80.
15. Ibid, 48.
16. Ray Allen Billington, *America's Frontier Culture: Three Essays* (College Station: Texas A&M University Press 1977), 685.
17. Webb, *The Great Plains,* 234.
18. Ibid, 236.
19. Slatta, 186.

Chapter 7: Land of Milk and Honey

1. Frederick R. Goddard, *Where to Emigrate and Why: Homes and Fortunes in the Boundless West and Sunny South, With a Complete History and Description of the Pacific Railroad.* (Philadelphia: The People's Publishing Co., 1869), 12.
2. Marc Reisner, *Cadillac Desert: The American West and Its Disappearing Water* (New York: Viking, 1986), 40.
3. Jonathan Raban, *Bad Land: An American Romance* (New York: Pantheon Books, 1999), 22.
4. Benjamin H. Hibbard, *A History of the Public Land Policies* (New York: Macmillan Co., 1924), 409.
5. Raban, 19.
6. Hamlin Garland, *Main-Travelled Roads* (New York: Macmillan Co., 1891)
7. Willa Cather, *My Antonia* (Boston: Houghton Mifflin, 1918), 7–8.
8. Raban, 62.
9. Patricia Nelson Limerick, *The Legacy of Conquest: The Unbroken Past of the American West* (New York: W. W. Norton, 1987), 126.
10. Leonard J. Arrington, *Great Basin Kingdom: An Economic History of the Latter-day Saints, 1830–1900* (Cambridge: Harvard University Press, 1958),
11. Ibid, 62–63.
12. Rose Wilder Lane, Autobiographical Sketch for *American Life Histories,* 1936–1940 (Washington D.C.: Library of Congress Manuscript Division, WPA Federal Writers' Project,1940).
13. Frederick Jackson Turner, *The Significance of the Frontier in American History,* ed. Harold Simonson (New York: Frederick Unger, 1963), 58.
14. James Wilson, *The Earth Shall Weep: A History of Native America* (New York: Grove Press, 1998), 285.

Selected Bibliography

Abbott, E. C., Smith, Helena H. *We Pointed Them North*. Norman: University of Oklahoma Press, 1976.

Adams, Andy. *The Log of the Cowboy: A Narrative of the Old Trail Days*. Lincoln: University of Nebraska Press, 1964.

Arrington, Leonard J. *Great Basin Kingdom: An Economic History of the Latter-day Saints, 1830-1900*. Cambridge: Harvard University Press, 1958.

Arrington, Leonard J. *Brigham Young: American Moses*, New York: Alfred Knopf, 1985.

Benton, Thomas Hart. *Congressional Globe*. 1846, 29:1.

Billington, Ray Allen. *America's Frontier Heritage*. New York: Holt, Rinehart and Winston, 1966.

Billington, Ray Allen. *Westward Expansion: A History of the American Frontier*. New York: Macmillan Co., 1967.

Billington, Ray Allen. *America's Frontier Culture: Three Essays*. College Station: Texas A&M University Press, 1977.

Cather, Willa. *My Antonia*. Boston: Houghton Mifflin, 1918.

Chittenden, Hiram Martin. *The American Fur Trade of the Far West*. Lincoln: University of Nebraska Press, Bison Edition, 1986.

Colton, Walter. *Three Years in California*. New York: A. S. Barnes and Co., 1850.

Dale, Edward Everett. *The Range Cattle Industry: Ranching on the Great Plains from 1865–1925*. Norman: University of Oklahoma Press, 1960.

DeVoto, Bernard. *The Year of Decision*, 1846. Boston: Little Brown, 1943.

DeVoto, Bernard. *Across the Wide Missouri*. Boston: Houghton Mifflin, 1947.

DeVoto, Bernard. *The Course of Empire*. Boston: Houghton Mifflin, 1952.

DeVoto, Bernard, ed. *The Journals of Lewis and Clark*. Boston: Houghton Mifflin, 1963.

Dodge, Richard Irving. *The Hunting Grounds of the Great West*. London: Chatto & Windus, 1877.

Eide, Ingvard Henry. *American Odyssey: The Journey of Lewis and Clark*. Chicago: Rand McNally, 1969.

Frazier, Ian. *Great Plains*. New York: Farrar, Straus, Giroux, 1989.

Franzwa, Gregory M. *The Oregon Trail Revisited*. Tucson: Patrice Press, 1972.

Garland, Hamlin. *Main-Travelled Roads*. New York: Macmillan Co., 1891.

Hawgood, John A. *America's Western Frontiers*. New York: Alfred Knopf, 1967.

Hibbard, Benjamin H. *A History of the Public Land Policies*. New York: Macmillan Co., 1924.

Hutchings' California Magazine.

Johnson, Theodore. *Sights in the Gold Region, and Scenes by the Way*. New York: Baker and Scribner, 1850.

Josephy, Alvin, Jr. *The Indian Heritage of America*. New York: Alfred Knopf, 1968.

Josephy, Alvin, Jr. *Now That the Buffalo's Gone: A Study of Today's American Indians*. New York: Alfred Knopf, 1982.

Lavender, David. *California*. New York: W.W. Norton, 1976.

Lavender, David. *Westward Vision: The Story of the Oregon Trail*. Lincoln: University of Nebraska Press, a Bison Book, 1985.

Lewis, Oscar. *The Big Four*. New York: Alfred Knopf, 1938.

Limerick, Patricia Nelson. *The Legacy of Conquest: The Unbroken Past of the American West*. New York: W.W. Norton, 1987.

Madson, John. *Where the Sky Began: Land of the Tallgrass Prairie*. Boston: Houghton Mifflin, 1982.

Manning, Richard. *Grassland*. New York: Viking Press, 1995.

McCoy, Joseph. *Historic Sketches of the Cattle Trade of the West and Southwest*. Kansas City: Ramsey, Millet & Hudson, 1874.

Milton, John R. *South Dakota*. New York: W. W. Norton, 1977.

Nabokov, Peter, ed. *Native American Testimony*. New York: Thomas Crowell, 1978.

Parkman, Francis. *La Salle and the Discovery of the Great West*. New York: Modern Library Edition, 1999.

Raban, Jonathan. *Bad Land: An American Romance*. New York: Pantheon Books, 1999.

Reisner, Marc. *Cadillac Desert: The American West and Its Disappearing Water*. New York: Viking, 1986.

Rodman, Paul. *Mining Frontiers of the Far West, 1848–1880*. New York: Holt, Rinehart and Winston, 1963.

Rolvaag, Ole Edvart. *Giants in the Earth: A Saga of the Prairie*. New York: HarperCollins, 1999.

Ross, Alexander. *The Fur Hunters of the Far West*. Norman: University of Oklahoma Press, 1956.

Ruxton, George Frederick. *Adventures in Mexico and the Rocky Mountains*. London: John Murray, 1847.

Ruxton, George Frederick. *Wild Life in the Rocky Mountains*. New York: MacMillan, 1916.

Sandoz, James. "Because He Is a Liar and a Thief." In *Rooted in Barbarous Soil*. Berkeley: University of California Press, 2000.

Slatta, Richard W. *Cowboys of the Americas*, New Haven: Yale University Press, 1990.

Smith, Alson J. *Men Against the Mountains: Jedediah Smith and the Great South West Expedition of 1826–29*. New York: John Day, 1965.

Smith, Henry Nash. *Virgin Land: The American West as Symbol and Myth*. Cambridge: Harvard University Press, 1950.

Starr, Kevin. *Americans and the California Dream, 1850-1915*. New York: Oxford University Press, 1973.

Starr, Kevin and Orsi, Richard J., eds. *Rooted in Barbarous Soil: People, Culture, and Community in Gold Rush California*. Berkeley: University of California Press, 2000.

Stegner, Wallace. *Beyond the Hundredth Meridian: John Wesley Powell and the Second Opening of the West*. Boston: Houghton Mifflin, 1954.

Stegner, Wallace. *Wolf Willow: A History, a Story, and a Memory of the Last Plains Frontier*. New York: Viking Press, 1962.

Stegner, Wallace. *The Gathering of Zion*. New York: McGraw-Hill, 1964.

Sullivan, Maurice. *Jedediah Smith, Trader and Trail Breaker*. New York: Press of the Pioneers, 1936.

Tatham's Characters Among the North American Indians. Annual of Biography and Obituary. London, 1820.

Turner, Frederick Jackson. *The Significance of the Frontier in American History*. Edited by Harold Simonson. New York: Frederick Ungar, 1963.

Twain, Mark. *Roughing It*. New York: New American Library, 1994.

Vestal, Stanley. *The Missouri*. Lincoln: University of Nebraska Press, a Bison Book, 1945.

Webb, Walter Prescott. *The Great Plains*. New York: Grosset & Dunlap, 1931.

Webb, Walter Prescott. *The Texas Rangers*. Austin: University of Texas Press, 1935.

Webb, Walter Prescott. *The Great Frontier*. Austin: University of Texas Press, 1964.

White, Richard. *It's Your Misfortune and None of My Own: A New History of the American West*. Norman: University of Oklahoma Press, 1991.

Wilson, James. *The Earth Shall Weep: A History of Native America*. New York: Grove Press, 1998.

WPA Federal Writers' Project. *American Life Histories, 1936–1940*. Washington D.C.: Library of Congress, 1940.

Index

page numbers in bold indicate images

Credits

Albert Bierstadt, "The Oregon Trail", 31"x49", The Butler Institute of American Art, Youngstown, Ohio: 120-121a

American Philosophical Society: 26-27, 29, 40a, 41b, 46-47a

Amon Carter Museum, Fort Worth, Texas: 210-211 (Charles M. Russell "The Medicine Man" ,1908, oil on canvas, 30 x 48 1/8 in.), 259 (Surviving Central Pacific Chinamen, Wong Fook, Lee Chao, Ging Cui, 1919, gelatin silver print, 1972.188.6), 283a (detail), 317 (Frederic S. Remington, "The Cowboy", 1902, Oil on canvas, 40 1/4 x 27 1/8 inches), 314-315 (Charles M. Russell "Smoke of a .45", 1908, oil on canvas, 24 x 36 1/4 in.), 328-329 (Charles M. Russell "A Desperate Stand", 1898, oil on canvas, 24 1/8 x 36 1/8 in.), 344-345a (Artist: John Ross Key, Harvesting near San Jose, California, 1874. Chromolithograph, 7 X 14 1/16 in., P1967.727)

Bettmann/CORBIS: 194a

Bruce Marshall: 123

Buffalo Bill Historical Center, Cody, WY: 10b (21.78), 18 (21.78), 19a (Gift of Olin Corporation, Winchester Arms; 1988.8.224), 68-69a (Gift of The Coe Foundation; 10.70), 72-73a (Gift of William B. Ruger, Sr. and Sturm, Ruger & Co.; 1997.4.8), 72c (Gift of The Coe Foundation; 36.64), 85 (Coat: 1.69.768; Rifle: Gift of Mr. and Mrs. Harry Schoss in Memory of Moses Kerngood, 1.69.2412), 94-95 (Gift of The Coe Foundation; 11.70), 99 (1988.8.3666), 290-291a (Gift of The Coe Foundation; 9.70), 308a (Gift of Lillian Burch Thomson; 1.69.2202)

California Historical Society: 249 (A-460, B-167), 330-331a (Gift of Mr. & Mrs. Reginald Walker; FN-16020)

California Section, California State Library, Sacramento: 256

Chadric Humphreys: 50-51, 82-83, 204-205, 254-255, 292-293, 376-377

Charles Gurche Photography: 17a, 22-23, 48-49b, 58b, 62-63, 63, 65d, 70, 72-73b, 108-109a, 283c, 318

Chicago Historical Society, ICHi-7069: 374-375a

Collection of the Hearst Art Gallery, Saint Mary's College of California: 252-253

©Collection of The New-York Historical Society: 53a (Captain Meriwether Lewis, Charles B. J. F. Saint-Mémin, c. 1807, watercolor on paper, neg. 51322), 244-245, 357

Columbia State Historic Park: 240

Copyright Smithsonian American Art Museum, Washington, DC/Art Resource, NY: 10a, 12-13, 200, 220-221, 225e, 272-273

Courtesy American Heritage Center, University of Wyoming: 360-361a

Courtesy, Colorado Historical Society: 65a (WPA-465 10026611, Chamberlain), 65e (F-15 10028472), 100 (WPA-465 10026611, Chamberlain), 103 (F-15 10028472)

Courtesy Frederic Remington Art Museum, Ogdensburg, New York: 67, 71

Courtesy Mercaldo Archives: 298a, 298b, 298c

Courtesy Museum of New Mexico, negative #7151: 158

Courtesy National Ranching Heritage Center, Lubbock, Texas: 356-357

Courtesy of Bancroft Library, University of California, Berkeley: 84-85 (1963.002:1427-B), 225d (brk00001 328_24a), 227a (1963.002:1427-B), 245 (brk00001 328_24a), 371 (HN000470a)

Courtesy of the Montana Historical Society, Gift of Col. Wallis Huidekoper: 11c (detail), 284-285 (detail)

Courtesy Prairie Edge, Rapid City, SD: 171a

Courtesy Texas State Library: 124b, 129a

David Cortner: 24, 37a

David R. Stoecklein Photography: 288a, 288b, 288c, 288d, 289a, 289b, 289c, 289d, 289e

Dennis Flaherty Photography: 9, 166-167, 167, 257, 265b, 276-277a, 276b, 278-279, 280-281, 281, 334-335

©Denver Art Museum: 80 ("Long Jakes; The Rocky Mountain Man,1844", Charles Deas Denver Art Museum Collection: Funds from Collector's Chouce 1999 and T. Edward and Tullah Hanley Collection by exchange, 1998.241), 102-103 (Wind River Country, 1860, Albert Bierstadt, Denver Art Museum Collection: The Charles H. Bayly Collection (Museum exchange with 1953.36), 1987.47)

Denver Public Library/Western History Department: 101, 115a, 120b, 184, 187b, 196b, 225c, 247, 251, 258, 262-263a, 323, 341a

Diplomatic Reception Rooms, United States Department of State, Thomas Moran: 76-77a

Ed Murphy, North Dakota Geological Survey: 27, 52

EMF Company, Inc.: 320a, 320d, 320e, 320g, 320h

Engraved by H.W. Smith from a photograph by Mathew Brady: 283d, 321

Engraved by Thomas B. Welch from a painting by S. S. Osgood: 129c

Frank Leslie's Illustrated Newspaper: 230 (March 29, 1884; Lagarde Measom), 290b (March 14, 1874; A. Lemon), 350-351a (July 28, 1888), 380b (May 1, 1889; from a photograph by C.E. DeGroff), 392 (May 8, 1869; based on a photograph by A.J. Russell)

From the Collection of Norm Flayderman, Ft. Lauderdale, FL: 81a

Getty Images: 90-91a, 115b, 115d, 118b, 127, 133, 134b, 137, 139, 140-141, 144-145, 145, 152-153a, 154-155, 156-157a, 156b, 160b, 169e, 181, 182b, 182c, 225a, 228-229a, 234-235a, 234b, 242, 246, 266-267a, 266b, 269, 273, 274b, 283b, 295, 302, 310, 311, 316a, 324-325a, 324b, 327, 339d, 344b, 345, 346-347, 347, 354-355a, 364-365a, 382-383

©Gilcrease Museum, Tulsa: 238-239a

Gregory Bertolini Photography: 388-389a, 390-391

Harper's Weekly: 13a (November 2, 1867; form a photograph by Savage and Ottinger of a painting by George Ottinger), 74-75 (September 9, 1876; W.M. Cary), 190-191 (August 22, 1874), 214 (August 5, 1873; W.M. Cary), 229 (October 12, 1878; I.P. Pranishnikoff), 237 (May 30, 1868), 260b (April 21, 1866; Theodore R. Davis), 264 (May 17, 1873), 271 (October 3, 1857), 331 (May 9, 1868; Theodore R. Davis), 339b (April 4, 1874; Frenzeny and Tavernier), 353 (March 28, 1868; Theodore R. Davis), 354b (December 23, 1871; A.R. Waud), 360b (April 4, 1874; Frenzeny and Tavernier), 372b (September 4, 1858; based on photography of Burr & Mogo), 377 (July 17, 1875; A.R. Waud), 379 (May 18, 1889), 383 (December 23, 1871; A.R. Waud), 395 (November 13, 1886; R.F. Zogbaum), 399 (December 24, 1887; R.F. Zogbaum), 400 (August 9, 1890; Frederic Remington)

Henry Howe; Historical Collections of the Great West, 1851: 262b

Illustrations by Brian Lemke: 88a, 88b, 88c, 89a, 89b, 89c

Independence National Historical Park Collection: 17c (Meriwether Lewis, Charles Willson Peale, c. 1807), 25a (William Clark, Charles Willson Peale, c. 1810), 25b (Meriwether Lewis, Charles Willson Peale, c. 1807)

©J.C. Leacock: 1, 6-7, 31c, 162b, 294, 355, 358-359a, 363, 387

Jackson Hole Historical Society and Museum, Jackson, Wyoming: 95

©Joan Myers 1982: 143

Joslyn Art Museum, Omaha, NE: 10c, 17b, 17d, 34b, 38-39b, 43a, 54-55, 66-67, 75, 92, 96-97a, 118-119a, 168-169, 169c, 172-173a, 172c, 174, 175, 176-177c, 176a, 176b, 177, 188c, 191, 192-193a, 192b, 197a, 199, 202-203a, 202b, 203, 206b, 212b, 216-217a, 216b, 218-219a, 222-223, 260-261a, 274-275a, 282-283, 296, 309, 322, 364b, 366-367, 372a

Kansas State Historical Society: 65c, 76b

Library of Congress: 42a, 42b, 105, 306-307 (Buckaroos in Paradise: Ranching Culture in Northern Nevada, 1945-1982, NV8-CF68-7)

Library of Congress, Geography and Map Division: 225b, 232, 368-369, 388b, 391

Library of Congress, Prints & Photographs: 11b (P&P LC-USZC4-668), 15a (SC-USZC4-683), 20b (LC-USZ62-117117 DLC), 68b (LC-USZ62-32333), 86b (LC-USZ62-8247), 226-227 (P&P LC-USZC4-668), 286-287a (GC, AP2.C65 & RBC)

Library of Congress, Rare Book and Special Collections Division: 233, 339a, 361, 362b, 370, 373

Manuscript Vertical File Collection. Baker Library, Harvard Business School: 386a

Missouri Bankers Association: 34-35a

Missouri Historical Society, St. Louis: 36-37a (Voorhis #2, Clark Papers), 36-37b (Objects 109, Clark Family), 40b (L/A 641, Clark Family Papers, Voorhis #1), 41a (L/A 646, Clark Family Papers, Voorhis #2), 96b (P.S. Srtickland), 152b (Enoch Long)

Museum of Nebraska Art. Kearney, Nebraska. Museum Purchase, made possible by Wayne and Virginia McKinney and The Platte Valley State Bank: 380-381a

National Archives, Brady Collection: 33

National Museum of American History, Smithsonian Institution: 20c

National Park Service: 106-107b

National Park Service, Harpers Ferry Center: 169b, 213

Nebraska State Historical Society: 362a (RG260-PH 0 1048), 384-385 (RG2608.1653)

Nevada Historical Society: 270

Northwestern University Library, Edward S. Curtis's "The North American Indian": the Photographic Images, 2001. http://hdl.loc.gov/loc.award/iencurt.cp03020: 172b

Oregon Historical Society, #OrHi58455: 56-57

Painting by Samuel A. Osgood. Courtesy New-York Historical Society: 228b

Panhandle-Plains Historical Museum Research Center, Canyon, Texas: 134-135a

peace pipe, photo by Hillel Burger, T599, Peabody Museum, Harvard University: 43b

"Photo: AKG, London", Verlag Clay & Co.: 11d, 340-341

Photo Courtesy of Paul F. Starrs, Professor of Geography, University of Nevada: 142

Private Collection: 23, 32-33, 37b, 38a, 38c, 41, 44, 45, 46b, 47, 48c, 53b, 57, 81b, 106c, 129b, 150b, 287, 299b, 304

Public Domain: 236-237

San Diego Museum of Man: 117 (John Oldenkamp), 155 (Ironmonger), 179, 182d (John Oldenkamp), 183 (John Oldenkamp), 188b, 195a (John Oldenkamp), 195b (John Oldenkamp), 196a, 197b, 198-199a, 206-207a (Addison Studio), 209a, 209b (Carpenter), 218b, 238b, 243 (Alfred Anderson)

©Shelburne Museum, Shelburne, Vermont: 79

Smithsonian Institution: 320b, 320c, 320f

Special Collections Department, University of Nevada, Reno Library: 231, 268

Steve Mohlenkamp Photography: 2-3, 112-113

Texas State Library and Archives Commission: 114, 122-123, 124-125a, 126, 128-129, 132-133

The Academy of Natural Sciences of Philadelphia, Ewell Sale Stewart Library: 30a, 30b, 31a, 31b

The Illustrated London News: 385 (May 1, 1858), 396 (December 13, 1890)

The San Jacinto Museum of History, Houston: 131

The Society of California Pioneers: 160-161a

The Walters Art Museum, Baltimore: 182-183a

Theodore Roosevelt: Ranch Life and the Hunting-Trail, 1888, Frederic Remington: 308b

©Tom Till: 4-5

Transcendental Graphics: 106a, 148, 149, 169d, 178b, 180-181, 185, 186, 187a, 188-189a, 194b, 195c, 198b, 201, 208, 212a, 215a, 215b, 223, 224, 265a, 285a, 286b, 297, 301, 303, 305, 312-313, 319, 326, 330b, 342-343a, 342b, 349, 350b, 352-353a, 352b, 374b, 378, 386b

University of Michigan Museum of Art: 10d (detail), 116-117 (Bequest of Henry C. Lewis 1895.80), 86-87a (Gift of Mrs. Edith Stanley Bayles and the late Mrs. Jane C. Stanley 1940.426),

University of Virginia: 20-21a

"Watching the Wagons" ©2002 Frank C. McCarthy, licensed courtesy of The Greenwich Workshop, Inc. www.greenwichworkshop.com: 11a, 170-171

Wayne Mumford: 48a (Maple leaf, Oregon), 60-61 (White Cliffs of the Missouri River, Montana)

Western History Collections, University of Oklahoma Libraries: 299a

Willard Clay Photography: 58-59a, 64-65, 65b, 78, 90b, 93, 104, 108b, 110-111, 113, 115c, 136, 150-151a, 159, 162-163a, 164-165, 300-301, 316b, 332-333a, 332b, 336-337, 337, 338, 339c, 348, 358b, 365

William Ranney, "Kit Carson", 1854 donated by Mrs. J. Maxwell Moran: 98

Winter Quarters By C.C.A. Christensen, Courtesy Brigham Young University Museum of Art. All Rights Reserved.: 146-147

Woolaroc Museum Bartlesville, Oklahoma: 169a, 178-179a

Yale Collection of Western American, Beinecke Rare Book and Manuscript Library, Yale University: 16, 28-29

Acknowledgments

The publisher would like to thank the following people for their generous help on this project:

Margaret Gordon and Laura Trounson, Assistants to the University Librarian, University of California, Santa Cruz; Alan Ritch, Associate University Librarian and Director of Collections, University of California, Berkeley Libraries; Erica Nordimeier, Photographic Duplication Coordinator, Bancroft Library, University of California, Berkeley; Linda Fisk, Registrar, San Diego Museum of Man; Coi Drummond-Gehrig, Photo Sales Clerk, Denver Public Library; John Anderson, Preservation Officer, Photo Archives, Texas State Library; and Candy Judd at candyscorral.com.